THE NEW MODERNS
FROM LATE TO NEO-MODERNISM

PETER EISENMAN, *Wexner Center for the Visual Arts*, Ohio State University,
Columbus, Ohio, 1985-9, aerial view

FOSTER ASSOCIATES, *Renault Distribution Centre*, Swindon, England, 1982-3

HELMUT JAHN, *O'Hare Airport Extension*, Chicago, 1984-8

REM KOOLHAAS – OMA, *The Netherlands Dance Theatre*, The Hague, 1985-8, entrance foyer

CHARLES JENCKS

THE NEW MODERNS
FROM LATE TO NEO-MODERNISM

ITSUKO HASEGAWA, *Bizan Hall*, Shizuoka, Shizuoka Prefecture, Japan, 1982-4

RIZZOLI
NEW YORK

ALSO BY CHARLES JENCKS

Meaning in Architecture, (with George Baird), 1969
Architecture 2000, Predictions and Methods, 1971
Adhocism (with Nathan Silver) 1972
Modern Movements in Architecture, 1973
Le Corbusier and the Tragic View of Architecture, 1974
The Language of Post-Modern Architecture, 1977, Fifth Edition 1987
The Daydream Houses of Los Angeles, 1978
Bizarre Architecture, 1979
Late-Modern Architecture, 1980
Signs, Symbols and Architecture, (with Richard Bunt & Geoffrey Broadbent), 1980
Post-Modern Classicism, 1980
Free-Style Classicism, 1982
Architecture Today, 1982 (*Current Architecture*), Second Edition, 1988
Abstract Representation, 1983
Kings of Infinite Space, 1983
Towards A Symbolic Architecture, 1985
What is Post-Modernism?, 1986, Third Edition, 1989
Post-Modernism, The New Classicism in Art and Architecture, 1987
The Prince, The Architects and New Wave Monarchy, 1988

Jacket front: PETER EISENMAN, *Wexner Center for the Visual Arts*, Ohio State University, Columbus, Ohio, 1985-9 (photo: Jeff Goldberg). *Jacket back*: ZAHA HADID, *Kurfurstendamm 70, Berlin*, 1985, rotational perspective. *Front flap*: FOSTER ASSOCIATES, *B3 building, Stockley Park*, England, 1987-9, detail of elevation.

First published in the United States of America in 1990 by
RIZZOLI INTERNATIONAL PUBLICATIONS INC.
300, Park Avenue South, New York, NY 10010

Published in Great Britain in 1990 by
ACADEMY EDITIONS
an imprint of the Academy Group Ltd, 7 Holland Street, London W8 4NA

ISBN 0-8478-1212-X
LC 89-64021

Printed and bound in Hong Kong

CONTENTS

INTRODUCTION

The New Moderns? Another phrase, another movement – do we really need this redundant one, with its double emphasis on the new New? As the reader will discover, I'm not entirely convinced. Our age suffers semantic inflation and there is no need to multiply labels in excess of the movements they purport to describe. But there *has* been a partial shift in the mood and practice of the dominant mode in architecture – Late-Modernism. This tradition, still the reigning professional approach, has given birth to an offshoot. And, to continue this biological metaphor, the new branch has not yet grown into a whole trunk, but it has affected the rest of the tree.

The New or Neo-Modern is closely related to what has been called 'Deconstructivism' - in an exhibition organised by Philip Johnson and others at the Museum of Modern Art in 1988. There's more to it than this fashionable borrowing from philosophy, but still the 'New' in the label, insofar as it is unique, relates to the shift in Modernist doctrine brought about by Derrida and Deconstruction. This started in France in the late sixties and reached the architectural world, and Peter Eisenman and Bernard Tschumi, ten years later. It fundamentally changed the social ideology of Modernism towards a non-humanism, and the formal ordering of architecture towards decentring, chance and frenzied opposition. The shift was at once ideological, stylistic and typological, and when changes occur on all three levels we may speak of a 'new' movement.

Nevertheless, in the articles and dialogues that follow, the partiality of this transformation will become clear. There is still so much overlap between Late- and Neo-Modernism that I, and the architects interviewed, slip ambiguously from one-term to the other. Slipperiness, it happens, is a favourite concept of Deconstructivism, but I hope it is not used here evasively. In engaging in what is now appropriately called 'dialogic' – with Peter Eisenman, Richard Meier and Philip Johnson – the existing ambiguity of this changing tradition is shown. It oscillates back and forth between a Late-Modernist emphasis on function, technology and pragmatism and all those 'de's' and 'dis's' emphasised by Deconstruction.

Another theme of these essays, which I can't claim to have entirely discovered, is that Modernism in many of its varieties is essentially bourgeois. To be more precise it is the style and psychological expression of the bourgeoisie coming to terms with (or suppressing) its historical role; in particular its incredibly creative and destructive role. This idea, first enunciated by Karl Marx in *The Communist Manifesto,* has recently found new twists in the writings of Tom Wolfe and Marshall Berman – twists which I tie up into a different kind of knot in the first essay. But throughout one will find echoes of this strange phenomenon: that the Modernist is the typical middle-class professional denying his past and present place in social and economic life. This denial leads directly to abstraction, contradiction and quite a bit of unintended humour.

RICHARD MEIER, *Museum for the Decorative Arts,* Frankfurt, 1979-85

My own attitude towards this is ambivalent, as it is to Late- and Neo-Modernism in general. As a critic and historian I will always be committed to following anything that is creative and architecturally important, even if it leads in directions I don't always find beneficent. In terms of constructed buildings the 1980s remain a Late-Modern decade dominated by an approach formulated in the 1960s. The plurality of other schools is still, in the West, overshadowed by this professional orthodoxy. Obviously my sympathies and philosophy are with Post-Modernism – the very movement all the New Moderns purport to dislike. Luckily, however, as a pluralist, I, unlike them, don't have to choose one approach exclusively. There is a place, even if limited, for the deconstructive, mechanistic and disorienting structures they de-structure. To make a parallel they would surely reject, the New Modernism is at once like the Comic and Rococo traditions: it's full of sophisticated play and laughter, sometimes hidden to its creators.

So, reader, *hypocrite lecteur, mon semblable, mon frère,* smile as you peruse these disjointed structures with their cocktail sticks and frenzied warps and think of Modernism performing yet another pirouette in its two-hundred-year dance. The performance isn't over and I give it another fifty or sixty years of life until the world, with its grand ecological contradictions, is reluctantly forced to accept the Post-Modern world view. Until then the dynamic underlying Modernism, of disjunctive and luxurious growth, has a limited future.

Finally, the justification of this work is its daring invention, beauty and technical skill – all values celebrated by Modernism, although not exclusive to it. The driving force of Modernism remains 'make it new' and this, coupled with aesthetic play, remains to legitimise the movement. For many people such justifications are not enough, but they do reflect a technological culture in a direct way and fulfill its own limited canons of art.

*   *   *

A few of the essays here, written over the last fifteen years, were previously collected in *Late-Modern Architecture,* 1980. Some of them were given as conference papers, others were in response to a book, building or exhibition. Some of them are entirely new, written for this collection. But all of them are concerned with the slide from Late- to Neo-Modern architecture and in this sense, form a unified perspective on a vast field.

SECTION I
LATE AND NEW MODERNISM

THE NEW MODERNS

'Nothing is so dangerous as being too modern, one is apt to grow old-fashioned quite suddenly.'

Oscar Wilde

Nothing will more effectively reinvigorate Modernism than killing it off. Like a voracious phoenix Modernism not only rises from its ashes but positively feeds off them. It has died many times since its mythical 1820s birth with the notion of the avant-garde in France. A particularly fertile period of Modernism in Europe, from 1870 to 1900, led to such boredom with the 'old-fashioned new' that it was declared dead in Samuel Lublinski's *Der Ausgang der Moderne (The Exit of the Modern,* Dresden 1909).[1] But then the next year Virginia Woolf saw it rise anew: 'On or about December 1910 human nature changed . . . All human relations shifted – those between masters and servants, husbands and wives, parents and children. And when human relations change there is at the same time a change in religion, conduct, politics and literature'.[2]

1910, the year of the first Post-Impressionist Exhibition and the death of King Edward VII, was an *annus mirabilis* for Modernism in literature and the arts, but for architecture the end of the First World War marks the re-rise of the movements, when all competing 'isms' claimed the birth of a new era: Purism, Dadaism, Expressionism, Constructivism, Neo-Plasticism – to name but a few of the contenders for the new New.

There's nothing like the end of a world war to signal a shift in culture and establish a conceptual *tabula rasa. L'Esprit Nouveau,* Le Corbusier and Ozenfant's journal, summarised some of this born-again 'new spirit' – a phrase that already had quite a venerable history in the nineteenth century. Fiercely polemical, this new *Zeitgeist* was set in opposition to academicism and the reigning Ecole des Beaux-Arts , reminding us (after the idea of its murder/rebirth) of the second great truth of Modernism: not only must it feed off the corpse of its predecessor and thrive on the *tabula rasa,* but it must be against the reigning culture – the *arrière-garde,* whether this is real or fictitious. To be new Modernism must characterise any opposition as staid, nostalgic and uncreative, or else it fails to re-establish credentials as the avant-garde. From this it follows as night the day that Modernism and (for want of a better word) Traditionalism have a vested interest in keeping each other in place. For logical and political reasons, the health of the former depends on the existence of the latter.

What about the 'New Moderns' today? This slightly ridiculous and certainly redundant label once again proves the truths of our little theorem. It has probably popped up in all the arts as a reaction against a renewed traditionalism. And in architecture it has emerged fully born from the ruins of the International Style (and cognate modes) and in opposition to what it now characterises as old-hat: Post-

BERNARD TSCHUMI, *Folie,* Paris, 1986-7. Neo-Constructivist aesthetic but Deconstructivist ideology of a decentring, parafunctional architecture.

Modernism. In fact this last movement almost deserves the credit for galvanising the New Mods into action: like a loathed political party which has been in power too long it has helped crystallise a unified opposition.

The birth of the New Mods (and a phoenix should always have a precise moment of ascension) was in Spring 1977 when Peter Eisenman published his editorial 'Post-Functionalism', in the pages of his significantly named magazine *Oppositions*.[3] Reacting to two exhibitions *Architettura Razionale*, 1973, and 'Ecole des Beaux-Arts', at the Museum of Modern Art (a Vatican of the New), 1975, Eisenman characterised both exhibitions as Post-Modern and, what was even worse, well within the five hundred year-old tradition of humanism. To this decrepit dinosaur he opposed, inevitably, a Modernism that was anti-humanist. Basically it summarised the currents of nineteenth- and twentieth-century art that were abstract, atonal and atemporal. The tactic of being a-anything was as typical as being non- or dis- other things. Modernism proceeds by negations, like the phoenix.

Using Michel Foucault's idea of a new *épistémè* which breaks with humanism, Eisenman postulates a new modern architecture that displaces 'man away from the centre of his world', negates the idea of authorship and functionalism and puts in their place an 'atemporal, decompositional mode', a method of design with form 'understood as a series of fragments – signs without meaning'. If this sounds familiar it's because Deconstruction had already by then invaded the most prestigious departments of literature in the Ivy League, and has now become an orthodoxy. As often happens, a literary event preceded an architectural one: the written and spoken word led a change in the more dependent sign systems, the visual arts and architecture.

The phrase 'neo-modern' started to be mentioned in New York circles about 1982 and it's probably no accident that the *Zeitgeist* picked this city to re-launch its hardy bird. Here the debate with Post-Modernists was most acute, while Philip Johnson's AT&T building had just been finished – a monumental classical slab which seemed to represent nothing so much as the gravestone of Modernism and a change of heart for one of its former protagonists.

I can't remember where I first heard or read the term 'neo-modern', but I believe it was Ada Louise Huxtable referring to the work of Richard Meier. In any case by 1983 many New York critics had started to adopt it as a polemical counterpoint to Post-Modernism, and it appears in a *Newsweek* article by Douglas Davis to describe a new mood and style: 'Elegant New Geometry'.[4] Davis gives several key examples of the kind of architecture I had termed Late-Modern: the Hong Kong Bank, Richard Rogers' Inmos Factory, a Gwathmey-Siegel house and their revivals of Modern furniture – the Neo-Hoffman and Neo-Mackintosh chairs on which Meier and others were ringing the changes. Were these really 'Neo' or rather really 'Late'? – and does it matter?

For a movement to be adequately 'neo' there must be a sufficient period of death, mourning and reconsideration before a revival. After all the phoenix waits five or six centuries in the desert before arising and Neo-Classicism – the model for all true 'Neo's' – waited fifteen centuries before reviving Roman dress and other customs. Without a sufficient period for both forgetting and reconsidering the past, one has 'survivals' not 'revivals'. This is one reason I would dispute Davis' hasty application of the term to Norman Foster, Richard Rogers and a host of other architects. They

PETER EISENMAN, *House 11 A*, 1978-80. The house without a centre which is 'excavated' into the ground, as if into the past and unconscious, is based on a series of fragmented forms – L-shapes – which symbolise instability, the unfinished.

JEFF KOONS, PETER HALLEY, *New York Art Now* at the Saatchi Gallery, 1987. New Modern art is a continuation of Late-Modernism, Minimalism and what's been termed Unexpressionism. The constant search for 'otherness' and the new New leads to the unspeakable – silence. (Saatchi Gallery)

consider themselves a *continuation* not a re-invention of Modernism. But he and those critics, such as Paul Goldberger, who started using 'neo-modern' would argue that although there is an unbroken continuity of the Modern tradition, there is also a fundamental change in attitude.

The New-Moderns they say are no longer utopians who wish to change society but rather aesthetes who play with Modernist forms: their essential message is not ethical but stylistic, a new baroque elaboration of the language synthesised in the twenties. Goldberger claims that the ultimate neo-modern buildings are Bernard Tschumi's *folies* at the Parc de la Villette because they are Mannerist fantasies with no social or ideological intentions.[5] This assertion is both right and wrong: right because Tschumi's fire-engine-red pavilions are an elaborate play with Constructivist forms arising from Chernikhov, and wrong because Mannerism is also characteristic of Late- and Post-Modern architecture, and Tschumi intends these *folies* to illustrate the theories of Deconstruction.

It is this ideology, akin to Eisenman's, which really defines the New Modernism: it is indeed new to architecture. Anti-humanism, decentring, the 'displacement of man away from the centre of his world', in Eisenman's words, may have existed in Modern literature and philosophy, but these disruptions did not happen in architecture. The reason is obvious. Architects, until recently, had to justify their buildings functionally and positively as furthering the goals of society. Now the New Moderns no longer believe in this humanism; rather they present their work as a self-justifying play with metaphysical ideas. The key architects who follow this agenda are Eisenman, Tschumi, Libeskind, Fujii, Gehry, Koolhaas, Hadid, Morphosis and Hejduk, but not Foster, Rogers, Hopkins, Maki and Pei. The former are Neo-Modernists and Deconstructionists, the latter are Late-Modernists who continue the Modern Movement in an elaborate and complex form.

The Power and Weakness of Labels

But do these distinctions matter? There are some architects, such as Richard Meier, who consider themselves neo-modern and use the term polemically as a stick to beat Post-Modernists. There are others, such as Coop Himmelblau, Philip Johnson and Peter Cook, who might find themselves cutting back and forth between all styles and ideologies. And most architects, like most people, are bored by labels, finding them reductive and constricting, like ill-fitting suits.

There is much to be said for the view that all labels – stylistic, ideological, historical – distort the perception of architecture and reduce it to verbal categories. This contamination by language cannot be denied: architecture is created and perceived through non-linguistic codes which have their own integrity, and words can just get in the way. At the same time, however, words and classifications cannot be avoided in creation and perception. As semiologists have shown, our universe is fatally immersed in the linguistic sign, the most dominant sign system of all. It follows that the only escape from a bad label is a better one; or rather a complex set of classifiers which does justice to the rich diversity of intentions in a building.

E H Gombrich has shown the ambivalence of all labels in his essay 'Norm and Form' which includes a section labelled very poignantly 'Classification and its Discontents'.[6]

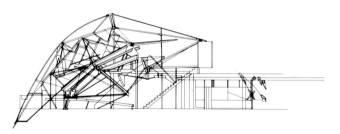

COOP HIMMELBLAU, *Rooftop Conversion*, Vienna, 1986-8. The Deconstructivist aesthetic of explosive space, frenzied cacophony, skews, cocktail sticks, warps and distortions.

CHARLES GWATHMEY, *De Menil House*, Long Island, 1984. All the visual hallmarks of Modernism are taken to an extreme and used as retrospective icons of a former movement thus producing a Late- not Neo-Modernism.

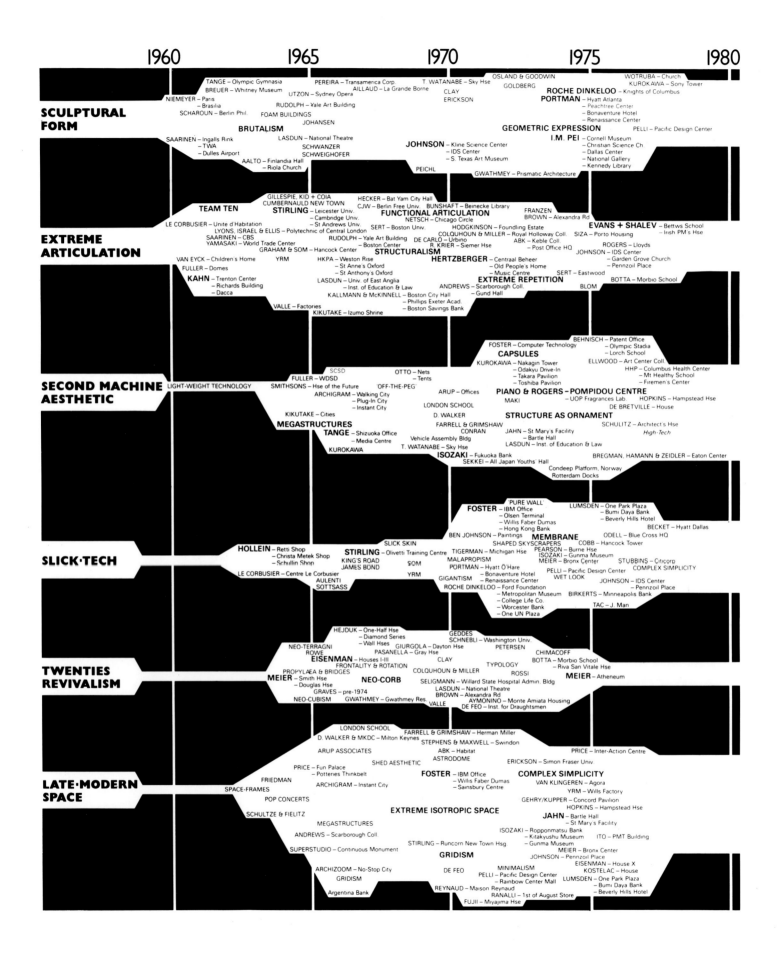

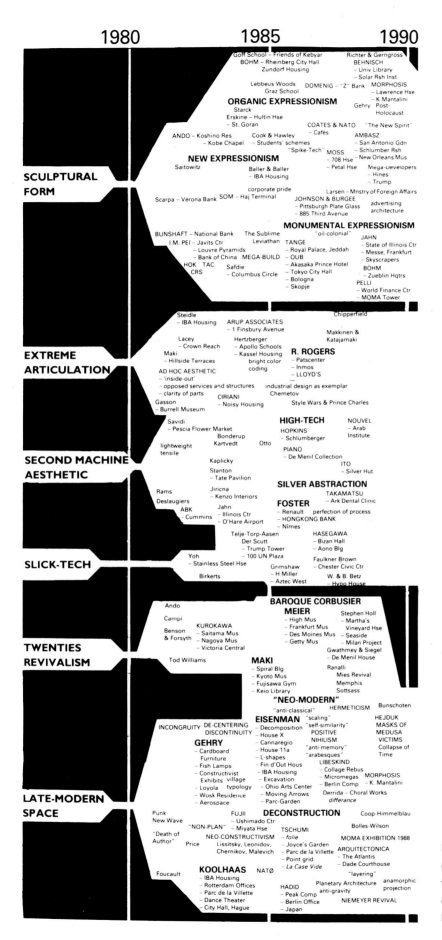

1980   1985   1990

SCULPTURAL FORM

Goff School – Friends of Kebyar
BÖHM – Rheinberg City Hall
Zundorf Housing

Richter & Gerngross
BEHNISCH
– Univ Library
– Solar Rsh Inst

Lebbeus Woods
Graz School

DOMENIG – "Z" Bank

MORPHOSIS
– Lawrence Hse
– K Mantalini

ORGANIC EXPRESSIONISM
Starck
Erskine – Hultin Hse
– St. Goran

Gehry   Post-
Holocaust

COATES & NATO
– Cafés

"The New Spirit"

ANDO – Koshino Res
– Kobe Chapel

Cook & Hawley
– Students' schemes
"Spike-Tech" MOSS

AMBASZ
– San Antonio Gdn
– Schlumber Rsh
– New Orleans Mus

NEW EXPRESSIONISM
Saitowitz

Baller & Baller
– IBA Housing

– 708 Hse
– Petal Hse

Mega-Developers
– Hines
– Trump

corporate pride

Scarpa – Verona Bank

SOM – Haj Terminal

Larsen – Mnstry of Foreign Affairs
JOHNSON & BURGEE
– Pittsburgh Plate Glass
– 885 Third Avenue

advertising
architecture

MONUMENTAL EXPRESSIONISM

BUNSHAFT – National Bank
I.M. PEI – Javits Ctr
– Louvre Pyramids
– Bank of China MEGA-BUILD
HOK   TAC   Safdie
CRS   – Columbus Circle

The Sublime
Leviathan

"oil-colonial"
TANGE
– Royal Palace, Jeddah
– OUB
– Akasaka Prince Hotel
– Tokyo City Hall
– Bologna
– Skopje

JAHN
– State of Illinois Ctr
– Messe, Frankfurt
– Skyscrapers
BÖHM
– Zueblin Hqtrs
PELLI
– World Finance Ctr
– MOMA Tower

EXTREME ARTICULATION

Steidle
– IBA Housing

ARUP ASSOCIATES
– 1 Finsbury Avenue

Chipperfield

Makkinen &
Katajamaki

Lacey
– Crown Reach
Maki
– Hillside Terraces

Hertzberger
– Apollo Schools
– Kassel Housing
bright color
coding

R. ROGERS
– Patscenter
– Inmos
– LLOYD'S

AD HOC AESTHETIC
– 'inside-out'
– opposed services and structures
– clarity of parts
Gasson   CIRIANI
– Burrell Museum   – Noisy Housing

industrial design as exemplar
Chemetov

Style Wars & Prince Charles

SECOND MACHINE AESTHETIC

Savidi
– Pescia Flower Market
Bonderup
lightweight   Kartvedt   Otto
tensile

HIGH-TECH
HOPKINS
– Schlumberger

NOUVEL
– Arab
Institute

Kaplicky
Stanton
– Tate Pavilion

PIANO
– De Menil Collection

ITO
– Silver Hut

Rams
Deslaugiers
    ABK
– Cummins

Jiricna
– Kenzo Interiors
Jahn
– Illinois Ctr
– O'Hare Airport

SILVER ABSTRACTION
TAKAMATSU
– Ark Dental Clinic
FOSTER
– Renault   perfection of process
– HONGKONG BANK
– Nimes

HASEGAWA
– Bizan Hall
– Aono Blg

SLICK-TECH

Telje-Torp-Aasen
Der Scutt
– Trump Tower
Yoh   – 100 UN Plaza
– Stainless Steel Hse
Birkerts

Grimshaw
– H Miller
– Aztec West

Faulkner Brown
– Chester Civic Ctr

W. & B. Betz
– Hypo House

TWENTIES REVIVALISM

Ando
Campi
Benson
& Forsyth
KUROKAWA
– Saitama Mus
– Nagoya Mus
– Victoria Central
Tod Williams

BAROQUE CORBUSIER
MEIER
– High Mus
– Frankfurt Mus
– Des Moines Mus
– Getty Mus

Stephen Holl
– Martha's
Vineyard Hse
– Seaside
– Milan Project
Gwathmey & Siegel
– De Menil House

MAKI
– Spiral Blg
– Kyoto Mus
– Fujisawa Gym
– Keio Library

Ranalli
Mies Revival
Memphis
Sottsass

LATE-MODERN SPACE

"NEO-MODERN"
"anti-classical"
INCONGRUITY DE-CENTERING
DISCONTINUITY
EISENMAN
– Decomposition
– House X
GEHRY
– Cardboard
Furniture
– Fish Lamps
– Constructivist
Exhibits   village
– Loyola   typology
– Wosk Residence
– Aerospace

– Cannaregio
– House 11a
– L-shapes
– Fin d'Out Hous
– IBA Housing
– Excavation
– Ohio Arts Center
– Moving Arrows
– Parc-Garden

HERMETICISM
"scaling"
"self-similarity"
POSITIVE
NIHILISM
"anti-memory"
"arabesques"
LIBESKIND
– Collage Rebus
– Micromegas
– Berlin Comp
Derrida – Choral Works
    difference

Bunschoten
HEJDUK
MASKS OF
MEDUSA
VICTIMS
Collapse of
Time

MORPHOSIS
– K. Mantalini

Punk
New Wave

"Death of
Author"

Foucault

FUJII
– Ushimado Ctr
"NON-PLAN" – Miyata Hse
Price   NEO-CONSTRUCTIVISM
Lissitsky, Leonidov,
Chernikov, Malevich

KOOLHAAS   NATØ
– IBA Housing
– Rotterdam Offices
– Parc de la Villette
– Dance Theater
– City Hall, Hague

DECONSTRUCTION

TSCHUMI
– folie
– Joyce's Garden
– Parc de la Villette
– Point grid
– La Case Vide

HADID
– Peak Comp
– Berlin Office
– Japan

Coop-Himmelblau

Bolles-Wilson

MOMA EXHIBITION 1988
ARQUITECTONICA
– The Atlantis
– Dade Courthouse
"layering"

Planetary Architecture   anamorphic
anti-gravity   projection
NIEMEYER REVIVAL

LATE-MODERN ARCHITECTURE with the Neo-Modern developing in the early 1980s within two of the six traditions. Architectural species wax and wane, sometimes merge, but the meaning of each tradition is partly created in opposition to others including Post-Modern ones (not shown).

There is no lover of art, he says, who is not impatient with the academic historian and his concern with pigeonholes. Any work of art is unique, ineffable and demands a fresh experience on its own terms — a suspension of disbelief and the habitual categories of classification. And yet, as he also points out, any experience of art is made through concepts which also have their own pre-existence and autonomy. If all art perception has this double aspect — demanding both the suspension and re-fashioning of concepts — so too does the experience of architecture. Hence when we confront a new development, or marginal variation of tradition, we must invent a new terminology that catches these nuances.

In the last twenty years of writing on architecture I have developed a dense thicket of terms and their branching relations which together become 'evolutionary trees' — undulating and pulsating diagrams which show the dynamic development of schools, ideas and architects. The basis for this classification is admittedly eclectic, partly the result of following structuralist theories of Claude Lévi-Strauss, and ordinary evolutionary diagrams familiar in biology. Also I have made use of George Kubler's idea of 'fibrous bundles' developed in his book *The Shape of Time*,[7] and the idea of Anthony Blunt that any movement consists of many definers, many more than the usual four or five given in textbooks on art. Finally, my undulating diagrams, with their many terms, come from the observation that architecture today is characterised by fragmentation, pluralism and mutual opposition. All of this has led to my classification of current architecture into two basic traditions: Late- and Post-Modernism. This classification has its discontents but it has also been partially accepted by many historians and architects.

The most controversial aspects of this division, I suppose, are the relative value given to Post-Modernism and the question of whether Late-Modernists aren't really just 'Modernists' as many architects still call themselves. I have argued at length that they differ in style and intention from the 'High Modernists' — Le Corbusier, Gropius, Mies and others who established the paradigm in the twenties — and so demand another prefix to mark this distinction, but I can understand their reluctance to use such an unwieldly and slightly negative term as 'Late'; it sounds like they are at the end of a dying tradition. My belief is that indeed the paradigm is ending, but it will probably go on — as did Late-Gothic, Late-Renaissance and Late-Baroque — for another hundred years. In the final analysis Modernism is the ideology and style of modernisation and both will last until the Second and Third Worlds are fully industralised and the problems of modernisation are so acute everywhere that a Post-Modern paradigm is adopted by the whole world. At that point ecology and semiology, not economy and materialism, will be the leading modes of thought — obviously not something that is going to happen tomorrow.

Thus 'Late-Modern' can be a relatively neutral descriptive term which has a positive future. Indeed Late-Modern architects often now out-perform their traditional and Post-Modern competitors, just as the cross-bow out-performed the rifle for fifty years, when it was threatened by obsolescence. The challenge of Post-Modernism, I would argue, has made both Neo- and Late-Modernism flourish, an ironic situation for all concerned. Indeed when I came to write on architecture of the 1980s, in *Architecture Today*, I devoted almost twice as much space to Late- as to Post-Modern developments — not obviously because I prefer this tradition, but rather because it has been more productive and in some senses more 'creative'.

In any case the point I want to stress is that these terms are relational and refer to a network of classifiers. As Anthony Blunt points out in *Some Uses and Misuses of the terms Baroque and Rococo as applied to Architecture*,[8] one needs at least ten or more definers to capture anything as complex and statistical as a whole period. I have given thirty variables in the charts that follow, definers that vary from ideology to style to design ideas – any one of which (such as Robert Venturi's 'complexity and contradiction') could be the subject of a whole book and mini-movement.

Given this heterogeneity, which is almost bewildering in its profusion, three points should be made. The classification of any architect within one tradition rather than another will be a matter of degree – a question of counting and weighing many variables, not just one or two; traditions resemble complex, multiform, organic entities which are fuzzy like neural networks rather than precise like military manoeuvres; and the critic must elucidate the rich profusion of species and genera while still distinguishing the few main phyla: Neo-, Late- and Post-Modern architecture as well as traditional building. Obviously unlike an animal an architect can, and often does, jump from one species to another while by and large remaining faithful to an overall approach. It is this relative consistency which makes classification possible, if fuzzy at points.

Rethinking Modernism – 'Modern-Next'

In addition to the writings and buildings of Eisenman and some other Deconstructionists, the architect who, through his work and theory, has most clearly defined the New Modern is the Japanese architect Kazuo Shinohara. In a key text of 1988 called 'Chaos and Machine' he gives it the strange appellation 'Modern-Next'.[9] It is worth quoting from this text extensively as well as illustrating his Tokyo Institute of Technology Centennial Hall, for together they convey the new paradigm most clearly.

Shinohara, born in 1925, is part of the generation of architects who formed the Metabolist Movement in the 1960s, although slightly older. Like them he has explored many attitudes towards mechanical imagery, primitivism and tradition, but in his most recent 'fourth style' these concerns reach maturity. A key point was reached in 1987 when he finally became convinced of an earlier thesis, the idea that the new, information-oriented city, Tokyo, naturally expressed 'chaos', or as he also termed it 'The Beauty of Progressive Anarchy':

> Chaos is a basic condition of the city . . . Modernism, which had come via the United States, was becoming Japanised. Optimistic, technologically-oriented urban projects with huge concrete structures were popular among young architects. The architects dreamed of Japanese versions of Le Corbusier's 'La Ville Radieuse' . . . However, I believed that it was impossible to create a city through a unified system . . . In the last one or two years, people have shown increasing interest in Tokyo. Many people use as a working principle the idea that a confused, disorderly city is attractive. Various people have begun to talk about the attractiveness, that is the 'beauty' of Tokyo, including those that only a few years ago were calling Tokyo nothing but a giant village.[10]

KAZUO SHINOHARA, *Centennial Hall*, view of the west end with the 'flying beam', flying stairway, perforated aluminium wall and sliced forms.

Although Shinohara alludes here to the economic and social theories of Jane Jacobs – which are of course foundation ideas of Post-Modernism – he does not directly connect this chaotic, anarchistic beauty to the growth of small businesses and the economy. Nevertheless the connection exists and Shinohara intuitively understands that urban vitality and economic dynamism must mean visual anarchy and, as he calls it, 'the collection of an infinite number of urban functions' (instead of the Modernist reduction to four or five purified functions – work, habitation, circulation, recreation). Again following Jane Jacobs, he sees these 'infinite functions' as subsuming mixed uses and overlapping cultures, but adds to these notions the ideas of Chaos science, and the current interest in fractals and fluctuating systems which characterise all life.

> Tokyo, the backward 'giant village' ... had never committed itself to the modernist vision of an industrial society but had instead leapfrogged that stage and had begun to demonstrate its unique qualities with the emergence of an information-oriented society. Chaos is not the result of poverty in Japanese cities today. Economic and social prosperity is evident in the commercial and entertainment centres of Tokyo. However, in terms of the visual environment composed of forms, colours, and materials, Tokyo is probably one of the most chaotic cities in the world. One can see, nevertheless, that in each individual building or urban facility, effort has been expended to provide order by one means or another.[11]

Shinohara goes on to point out the mixture of order and chaos in building regulations and high technology, where geometry and control at a micro level are balanced by randomness and 'noise' on a macro scale; it is precisely this mixture he calls 'progressive anarchy' and seeks to represent in his architecture. He grants at once that those who hold to classical and modern canons of beauty will not find this chaos, or Tokyo, beautiful because they lack the unity and memory which are essential in virtually all aesthetic systems; but these absences are, for him, an essential part of the 'Modern-Next'.

Another part is the way that organisms, and higher level machines like computers have a built-in flexibility that can deal with randomness and fluctuation:

> The study of chaotic phenomena is a new area of mathematics and physics. It is concerned with 'disorder, instability, variety, heterogeneity, and temporality'. Every system (of life) possesses a subsystem that 'fluctuates', to use Prigogines' expression . . . It is impossible to predict whether the system will disintegrate into 'chaos' or become a 'dissipative structure' on a more differentiated and advanced level of organisation. This is because more energy is required to maintain the structure than the previous, simpler structure.[12]

Shinohara then reiterates that he is not interested in 'unlimited chaos', but rather the kind of fluctuating, geometrical chaos that is evident in such advanced technology as the lunar spacecraft, and the most sophisticated fighter plane – the F14A Tomcat – both of which have awkward-looking movable parts. His Centennial Hall is meant to recall such flying machines, especially the stainless steel half cylinder that smashes through the abstract volumes and hovers in the air like the truncated wing of a 747. This is one type of 'geometrical form that fluctuates'.

Another type is the implicit 'lines of reference in plan', the axes set up within primary volumes – 90, 45, 30 degrees – and the slight deviation from these. Together both sets of axes form a new 'bundle of relationships between function and form that

KAZUO SHINOHARA, *Tokyo Institute of Technology Centennial Hall*, Tokyo 1987-8, view from the south. The 'flying beam' bends in the middle visually uniting the train station to the right with the centre of campus to the left.

KAZUO SHINOHARA, *Centennial Hall*, view from the train station with train, car, telephone wires and chaotic urban environment – a 'borrowed landscape' which is represented in the dissonant metallic architecture.

characterise organic and high-technological mechanisms ... these elements are juxtaposed so that a new bundle of relationships including fluctuation and randomness is generated among them'.[13]

Shinohara concludes his text by pointing out how this new approach adds to Modernism the ideas of chaos, random noise, information exchange and a complex 'bundle of relationships' that is getting 'more and more difficult to see'. Although we may not be able to perceive his implicit geometric orders, we can easily see their complex 'difficulty' and also the emphasis on Modernist technology and the machine – both of which lead him to his goal, the 'Modern-Next'. In visual terms the results are very close to the work of Frank Gehry and the Deconstructionists.

The Centennial Hall is a perfect illustration of Shinohara's theories. The juxtaposition of fragmented pure geometrics – the square, trapezoid, half-cylinder – generate the random noise which reflects the train station and urban chaos to the east, the messy jumble of telephone and electrical cables, the anarchic street signage, the random coming and going of grey aluminium trains and shining automobiles, all that urban reality condemned by Modernists in the pages of the *Architectural Review* as 'The Mess That is Man Made America', or the Modernist Peter Blake as *God's Own Junkyard*. This representation of mess is indeed the antithesis of the urban harmony which Le Corbusier and mega-structural designers of the 1960s had been promoting, but it is brought to a poetic intensity not found in the undesigned street environment where collisions just happen. Interestingly enough these juxtapositions and the inverted half-cylinder vaguely recall Le Corbusier's Ronchamp with its upturned and sagging roof. In its way the building has a comparable memorialising function to this church although here it is the progress of technology, not religion, which is being celebrated.

Formally and structurally the half-cylinder is a typical word of the Neo-Mods. Like the 'anti-gravitational architecture' of Zaha Hadid this form is a conceptual 'flying beam' that hovers out over space. Shinohara has conceived it as the symbol of 'a machine floating in the air', an airplane wing or fuselage, but it is equally illustrative of the 'suspended satellites' and 'explosive cantilevers' of Deconstructionist aesthetics. Like most Decon work it is bent – here in the middle, in plan, to connect visually the train station and chaotic city to the heart of the campus. And its cylindrical purity is further distorted and violated by a dissonantly curved window and 'flying' escape stairway. Here and elsewhere is the 'violated perfection', the rhetorical figure which at one time was the title of the first Deconstructivist Exhibition at the Museum of Modern Art.[14]

On the inside this 'flying beam' is the long tube-like corridor one finds at airports with walls that slope away from one and an underbelly that presses down into conference and conversation rooms below. One might feel slightly giddy in these warped and compressive spaces were it not for the muted pallette of greys and thick pile carpet. It's not unlike a fun-house at the circus, except the floors are flat and the sustained mood is austere. Deconstructionist architects, such as Eisenman, would no doubt have tilted the ground plane but also kept to the high-minded spectrum of silvers, greys, blacks and whites. In this sense the Neo-Mods remain Still-Modernists – intellectuals who contemplate the frenzy of street life rather than vulgarians who descend into it.

The characteristic hallmarks of the neo-modernist style are everywhere evident.

KAZUO SHINOHARA, *Centennial Hall,* view from the conversation area to conference room with the 'flying beam' bent overhead. The juxtapositions are calmed down by the greys, whites and neutral tones.

Perforated aluminium panels, a favourite material, are gridded and then sectioned at an angle. Other rectangular panels jump up in steps or get sliced at sixty degrees. All pure volumes fly into each other with an awkward dissonance that suggests a rather impressive collision between two 747s. This explosive quality is as anti-classical as can be, since parts are attached in 'an impromptu manner' and are intended not to make up a whole image. It sounds violent and uncontrolled, the architectural equivalent of a sixties Happening, but this violence is also mediated by a pervasive austerity and abstraction. Indeed Kazuo Shinohara is not the wilful romantic one might expect from reading this description, but a modest, retiring professor as unassuming in manner as he is scrupulous in thought. Because he has really thought through the implications of Modernism and recent developments in Chaos science, urban reality and biology, his Centennial Hall stands out as the most convincing example of Neo-Modernism. This is not to say it doesn't have the problems of this approach – an over-emphasis on abstraction, chaos and hard surfaces – but rather that these faults are marginalised by such a perfectly controlled explosion.

The New-Modern Corpus

How do we judge such work? Eisenman and Tschumi have, from time to time, followed a certain Deconstructionist argument which holds that good and bad, like all standards, are relative to a culture and ultimately meaningless. This position, which as good Deconstructionists they also contradict, would make discrimination virtually impossible. Yet judgement continues, and Shinohara continues to speak of 'beauty' as if it were meaningful not as harmony, but as a fuzzy sort of notion ('fuzzy theory' is as important as Chaos theory). In conversation he mentioned the beauty of fractals and difference, two notions which Eisenman also supports under the labels of 'self-similarity' and 'otherness'. There is indeed a growing neo-modern metalanguage that justifies and directs this architecture, a constellation of related terms which allows the designer to discriminate between permissible and wrong moves (although the idea of a 'mistake' is left very fuzzy). When, on separate occasions, I asked both Shinohara and Eisenman how they would discriminate good from bad architecture, the answers were very ambiguous – not to say evasive. I presume, however, they make distinctions all the time and that these relate to the overall neo-modern corpus, summarised here in a diagram of thirty variables to relate to the other forms of Modernism.

This lexicon of stylistic terms, design ideas and norms is drawn from a wide variety of sources – notably Deconstructionist theory and the writings of Eisenman, Shinohara, Koolhaas, Hadid, Tschumi and Libeskind. It is representative rather than complete, but it gives a fair composite picture of what the new architect is up to – an ideal type Neo-Modernist rather than any real one. What kind of generalised portrait emerges?

The ideal type Neo-Mod will, ideologically speaking, displace the question of what style he or she is using as silly or reductive, and only admit to operating between styles (term 1 in the diagram). The reason for this, following the allusive arguments of Derrida, is that all categories are slippery and subject to contradictions and it is the job of the architect to 'deconstruct from within' the assumptions and styles which exist (4), to 'reinscribe' values and operate with the antinomy 'deconstruction/reconstruction',

	NEO-MODERN (1976-)
	IDEOLOGICAL
1	hermetic coding, between styles
2	*différance*, 'otherness'
3	asemantic form
4	deconstruction from within, reinscribing
5	autonomous artist
6	mandarin works for 'vanquished'
7	fragmented, destructive/constructive
8	architect as metaphysician
	STYLISTIC
9	self-contradictory, weaving
10	disjunctive complexity, awkward dissonance
11	explosive space with tilted floors, cocktail sticks, warps, distortions, anamorphism
12	extreme abstraction, alien
13	frenzied cacophony, 'violated perfection', 'random noise'
14	dissociation between form and content
15	Degree Zero Aesthetic, emptiness, 'machine eroticism'
16	thematised ornament: fractals, scaling, self-similarity, catachresis, apocalypse
17	represents private code
18	pro-restricted metaphors: planetary arch, flying beams, knife blades, fish, bananas
19	traces of memory – ghosts, excavations
20	comic destructive, *non sequitur*
21	private symbolic
	DESIGN IDEAS
22	non-place sprawl, point grids, chaos theory
23	indeterminant functions, flux
24	ahistorical and 'Neo-Constructivist'
25	rhetorically redundant, sublime
26	space and mass interpenetrated – 'chora'
27	discontinuous sculptural object
28	fractures, 'space of accidents'
29	de-composition, de-centring
30	dis-harmony, 'random noise', layering of discontinuous systems

NEW MODERN ARCHITECTURE CLASSIFIED ACCORDING TO THIRTY VARIABLES. The categories here are parallel with the list that appears later in this book and are drawn from the architects' own words or are implicit in their architecture. The meaning of this architecture is related to Modern, Late- and Post-Modern work either by extension or opposition.

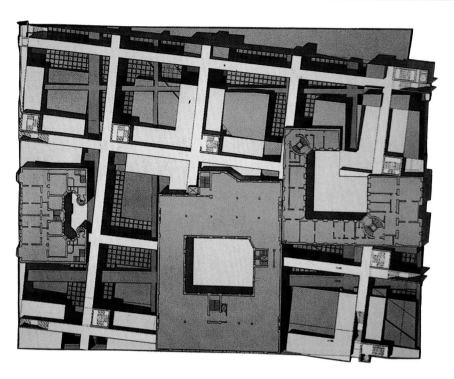

as Tschumi puts it (7). This makes their architecture ambiguous, like Post-Modernist work, but not in accord with the tastes and values of the local inhabitants.

Indeed, New Modern architecture is usually based on hermetic or private codes (1). A good example of this hermeticism is Peter Eisenman's social housing in Berlin which represents all sorts of interesting things such as the eighteenth-century past, the Berlin Wall, the adjacent buildings and their mutual collision. The only problem is that no one could decode these meanings unless they had an Eisenman text in hand. It is true the 3.3 metre base now has written on it the words 'Checkpoint Charlie' referring to the traumatic transition point just in back, but this was added by a sign artist intent on making Eisenman's architecture communicative. He, instead, just varies the size of abstract grids ('self-similarity') (16), sets them at an angle to each other, and then colours them light green, white, grey and red. In his hermetic code the green grid represents the adjacent nineteenth-century building and the angled white, red and grey grid represents the Berlin Wall and Mercator grid of the world, but no one would know this unless they were told. In fact many Berliners to whom I have talked misread the building as a jolly example of Post-Modern decoration – an interpretation which must be extremely painful to Eisenman who dislikes this tradition.

The ideal-type Neo-Modernist characteristically uses an asemantic form (3) where there is a dissociation between form and content (14) – the Berlin Wall represented by the incongruously cheerful grid of staggered windows. Also this type of architect will base his autonomous creations (5) on metaphysical suppositions (8) concerned with the 'end of architecture', an apocalyptic metaphysics which stems from the Holocaust, the Atom bomb, and the destructive aspects of modernisation and Modernism – that is, the harnessing of instrumental reason not to the project of the Enlightenment but to the forces of darkness.

This strong anti-modern streak in the New Modernism is best illustrated by the cryptic writings and projects of Daniel Libeskind. They are, he says, 'not theories' and 'not architecture'. Like Leon Krier, who has exerted a tremendous influence through not building his visions, Libeskind has had a profound influence with pure projects that are not contaminated by realisation. His models and drawings take much of the neo-modern aesthetic to an extreme as a frenzied cacophony of 'cocktail sticks', 'flying beams', 'excavations', 'tilted floors and walls', and 'self-contradictory inscriptions'. All of this is put to an apocalyptic end. It represents a new style of building 'not for the victors who have dominated architecture for five thousand years, but the vanquished – an architecture for losers'. Virtually all of the New Moderns have been haunted by Libeskind's uncompromising and incomprehensible 'otherness'.

The feeling of an alien landscape is inherent in the Modernist drive towards the unknown, the new and the 'next' and much Neo-Modernism shows this same attitude of estrangement. Like High-Tech architecture it insists on using products which have never been seen before. Even where Late-Modernists use a familiar glass and steel combination, they will stretch the slenderness ratios to new limits and produce unfamiliar proportions. Norman Foster's use of fuzzy glass with white dots to produce a gradation of light and visibility is a typical case. The familiar proportions of solid to void, spandrel to window, are melted into each other to create a curtain wall that seems to glow with a radioactive halo of shimmering particles.

NORMAN FOSTER, *B3 Building at Stockley Park*, 1987-9. The relentless search for the new has resulted in this strange glowing curtain wall made from tiny white dots embedded in the glass like atomic particles attracted to the bottom and top of each floor. Functionally this serves to give maximum light in the centre of each floor, but the motive is as much stylistic as utilitarian.

PETER EISENMAN, *Social Housing and Museum*, plan, IBA, 1982. The key to the hermetic code is only cryptically present in this plan which was never fully carried out. The existing nineteenth-century building is at the bottom, centre.

PETER EISENMAN, *Social Housing*, IBA, Berlin, 1982-7. The green and white grid represents the existing nineteenth-century buildings, the angled white, red and grey grid represents the Mercator grid of the world and the 3.3 metre base represents the Berlin Wall just in back of the building – representations which are hermetically coded.

Jean Nouvel, when he isn't being semantic and Post-Modern, will also use High-Tech in an abnormal way which recalls the proportions of Japanese architecture, very small buildings and even furniture. Both Foster and Nouvel, like the Neo-Modernists, enjoy the extreme repetition of prefabricated elements perhaps as much for their mesmerising otherness as for the cost. When a pure form is repeated *ad nauseum* it is not only monotonous but sublime, especially if it is beautifully detailed. In their insistence on the alien, the Late- and Neo-Modernists clearly share a common norm.

One important difference, however, is the value given to humour. A New Modernist, such as Frank Gehry, will abjure the old commitment to consistency and high-seriousness as he combines one technology with another in a way that defies logic. The *non sequitur*, the odd conjunction of 'fish and snake' shapes, the comic destruction of customary shapes (20), are made even odder and funnier by their warp and distortion (11). Peter Eisenman has introduced the same tactic with his 'banana' concept – the gratuitous form which results from intersecting two systems and representing this positively. Clearly the Neo-Mods have responded to the Post-Modern critique and also brought humour back to architecture.

This all too brief portrait of the ideal type New Modern illustrates only a few of the thirty variables shown in the diagram, but it suggests the key ideas. The typical architect will take a few elements from all the previous traditions including the rejected one, Post-Modernism. He or she will not really deal with the post-modern critique of urban anomie, destruction or deracination – except by intensifying it.

Bernard Tschumi's Parc de la Villette is characteristic in this respect since it is built of three discontinuous systems ('point grids', 'cinematic promenades' and 'surfaces') which are meant to reflect the non-place sprawl of suburbia, the de-regulation of free enterprise, the de-composition and de-centring of a society in flux. Not for him utopia, these *folies* are everyday reality turned into fire-engine-red machines that relate to nothing – except themselves and Neo-Constructivism. The hedonism and gratuity of this gesture is breath-taking, especially since the Parc already has one really expensive folly – a sixty million dollar meat market that never opened, but instead has been turned into a Museum of Science and Technology. Tschumi's pavilions declare their uselessness and atemporality with a panache that Modernists and functionalists would have found shocking. This is one more reason why, as opposed to many architects, I would never call these architects 'Modern'. They have fundamentally extended and distorted the paradigm of the 1920s.

Modernism as the Style and Religion of the Bourgeoisie

Let us step back from the argument so far and take a wider look at the way Modernism has developed through all its changes over the last 150 years and yet retained certain assumptions and a general direction. In this broader perspective I'll make use of some ideas developed in the 1980s while New Modernism was in the process of formation, above all the most important reconsideration of Modernism by Marshall Berman, *All That is Solid Melts into Air*, subtitled 'The Experience of Modernity' and first published in 1982. No thorough discussion of modernity can take place today without being informed by this book, although its implications may be misunderstood even by the author himself.[15]

JEAN NOUVEL, *Institut du Monde Arab*, Paris 1984-7. The silver high-tech aesthetic used at a very small scale to break down the huge volume and increase the repetition of horizontal elements. Two Modernist tropes combine – 'the Strange' and 'the Sublime'.

DANIEL LIBESKIND, *City Edge Competition*, IBA, Berlin 1987. A 'flying beam' to be held up by cocktail sticks' would connect a reference to Albert Speer, at one end, to Mies van der Rohe, at the other. This extraordinary scheme was a project for social housing!

PETER EISENMAN, *Carnegie Mellon Institute*, Pittsburgh, 1988, perspective. The intersection of two geometries at an oblique angle produces an overlap which Eisenman turns into a non-functional volume he calls a 'banana' – to show its gratuity. Although such bananas don't have a purpose the clients, scientists, didn't want him to take them out. Mies, in the perspective, wonders what's going on with this New (non-functional) Modernism.

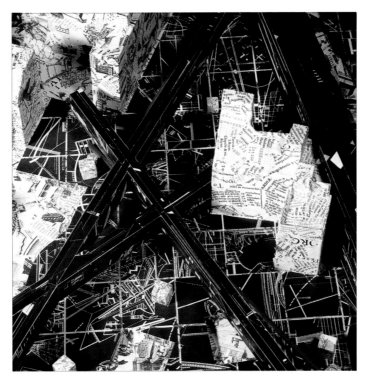

Berman develops the argument of his title that Modernity is essentially involved with evanescence, continual change, rapid obsolescence, constant revolution – and this title comes from Karl Marx's *The Communist Manifesto*:

> Constant revolutionising of production, uninterrupted disturbance of all social relations, everlasting uncertainty and agitating, distinguish the bourgeois epoch from all earlier times. All fixed, fast-frozen relationships, with their train of venerable ideas and opinions, are swept away, all new-formed ones become obsolete before they can ossify. All that is solid melts into air, all that is holy is profaned, and men at last are forced to face with sober senses the real conditions of their lives and their relations with their fellow men.[16]

The inventive reading Berman gives to this, and Marx in general, is to turn *The Communist Manifesto* of 1848 into 'the first great modernist work of art' and, as if that weren't a radical enough notion, show that Marx actually celebrated the destructive change brought about by capitalism and the bourgeoisie. Secondly, and just as importantly, Berman connects up modernisation with Modernism. This may seem an obvious pairing, and every textbook on Modern architecture makes it in a general way, but Berman brings out its dark side, the continual destruction necessitated by industrial innovation and relentless change, the nihilism inherent in wiping away neighbourhoods and the past. Previously, apologists for Modernism – and Berman turns out to be one – had underplayed the Faustian bargain struck by developers and Modernists between destruction and creation and only accentuated the progressive side. With Faust and Marx as his main characters, however, Berman makes clear that over a two hundred year period modernisation and its ideology of Modernism are tragically implicated in the annihilation of ethnic domain, roots or anything that stands in the way of the bourgeoisie. The Faustian power of capitalism 'melts all that is solid into air' and Modernism is *the* style and religion of this incandescent force.

With this fundamental insight in mind we can begin to understand the schizophrenia and pathology of Modernists, who celebrate continual revolution but have a guilty conscience about the inevitable destruction entailed – even of themselves. The bourgeoisie, Berman points out, have to hide this guilt:

> Their secret – a secret they have managed to keep even from themselves – is that, behind their facades, they are the most violently destructive ruling class in history. All the anarchic, measureless, explosive drives that a later generation will baptise by the name of 'nihilism' – drives that Nietzsche and his followers will ascribe to such cosmic traumas as the Death of God – are located by Marx in the seemingly banal everyday working of the market economy. He unveils the modern bourgeois as consummate nihilists on a far vaster scale than modern intellectuals can conceive.[17]

This secret of the Modernist and bourgeois alike helps explain the self-destructive streak which runs through modern movements over two hundred years, the constant return to the blank canvas, ground zero, the *tabula rasa;* it helps explain why these various movements last barely ten years in the nineteenth century, and a mere two years today. The quick substitution of 'isms' – all the fashions which become 'wasms' – shows the dark secret which Modernists can never admit to themselves – their art movements *are* fashions, their class identity is bourgeois. This last secret is the most

FRANK GEHRY, *Edgemar Farm Conversion,* Santa Monica, 1987-9. Gehry juxtaposes geometries and materials in an impromptu manner. The strange anamorphic distortions of the stairs are increased by this wide-angle photo.

BERNARD TSCHUMI, *Folie,* Form follows fiction and friction not function in this scenario where design and use are fixed independently. Many of the Deconstructionist aesthetic tropes, such as tilts and fragments, are carried through with exemplary autonomy.

disturbing of all and must be denied at all costs behind a succession of anti-bourgeois slogans (*épater les bourgeois*) and anti-middle-class styles.

Nietzsche faces this ambivalent truth as clearly as Marx and in the famous lines from *Thus Spake Zarathustra,* he sings the praises of the new superman, the destructive creator:

> He who must be a creator in good and evil – verily, he must first be a destroyer, and break values into pieces. Thus the highest evil is part of the highest goodness. But that is creative goodness. Let us speak thereon, ye wisest men, however bad it be. To be silent is worse; all unuttered truths become poisonous. And whatever will break on our truths, let it break! Many a house hath yet to be built. Thus spake Zarathustra.[18]

Le Corbusier was the architect most affected by these cruel truths which he read as a young man in Paris in 1908. He might have noticed the phrase 'many a house hath yet to be built', but in any case he later proposed the destruction of Paris' historic centre and its creative replacement by glass and steel towers dedicated to the new supermen – businessmen, 'captains of industry' as he kept calling them, the new leaders of the bourgeoisie. In a letter of 1908 to his teacher and guru Charles l'Eplattenier, he adopts the Nietzschean rhetoric – 'burn what you love, love what you burn' – and then for the rest of his ceaselessly creative life carries out this destructive creation, firing his architectural office every seven years or so, changing styles and approach every ten years; even in the 1920s changing his name several times.[19]

There is no doubt that Le Corbusier saw himself as the Nietzschean future man dedicating himself to 'transvaluing all values', overcoming the mediocrity of mass culture, and turning himself into a kind of creative superhero – painting in the morning, city planning and architecting in the afternoon, writing at night. Through will-power and hard work he, like Picasso and Duchamp and other Modernists, became the ultimate bourgeois – the self-developed over-achiever, the widely-balanced hero of Marx's Communist utopia, the man who could do everything. Had jogging been fashionable, he would have run marathons.

The culture of Modernism, with its litany of super-saints and creative giants, its roll-call of new orthodoxies and schisms, has no doubt become a religion – or perhaps pseudo-religion is the better word since it is also applied to Marxism, nationalism, the cult of self-development and other secular creeds. The way Modernism has become an ideology and faith since Nietzsche proclaimed the Death of God has been noted before, but I'm not sure whether the stylistic and iconographic implications of this shift have been observed. Adolf Loos, in the early part of this century, formulates a reason for the chaste international style which will be without ornament. In his polemic *Architecture,* 1910, he laments the fact that the architect 'possesses no culture', unlike the peasant or Papuan rooted in a tradition, and therefore will draw whimsical ornament and adopt false, fashionable styles. The architect is the quintessential bourgeois: 'Like almost every town dweller,' Loos writes, 'the architect possesses no culture. He does not have the security of the peasant to whom the culture is innate. The town dweller is an upstart.'[20] The cure for this, Loos makes clear in his writings and buildings, is an abstract, white, geometric style which is based on functions and understated in appearance – like the proverbial silent butler in British theatre.

ADOLF LOOS, *Goldman and Salaatsh Building,* Vienna 1909-11. The new style was to be white, chaste, austere, understated – anti-bourgeois, anti-eclectic, anti-historical. Loos formulated this twentieth-century code, Le Corbusier and Gropius perfected it, and variants have recurred with each new Modernism ever since – the degree-zero style.

CESAR PELLI, *World Financial Center Towers and Battery Park City* (by others), 1982-7. Except for several details the housing and offices are abstract, geometric, functional, timeless and huge – perfect containers for Modern Man and Woman.

Overall he gives a powerful, cumulative argument that the new bourgeoisie, as opposed to the aristocracy and peasantry, has no valuative system and thus, like Nietzsche's superman, has to invent one *ex nihilo* based on utility, strength through competition and higher-order abstract perception – like listening to Beethoven's symphonies. With hindsight it is easier to say that this cultural Modernism has become *the* style of the bourgeoisie and that among its many formal variants Loos' stripped functionalism, the zero-degree abstraction, has become the leading mode. This white abstract style represents, at once, good taste, the healthy life that appealed to Loos, Le Corbusier, Voysey and Lethaby – that is skiing, tennis, aerobics, holidays in the mountains and by the sea – and the liberation from the past, the aristocracy, eclecticism and, most importantly, the guilt of continual destruction. All of these historical overtones are purged and the new city is prepared as a clean white slate ready for redevelopment. This *tabula rasa* is of course to be controlled by the new class – that is, the combination of bureaucrats, government officials and corporate leaders who have dominated city life from London to New York, from the Docklands to Battery Park City.

To an extent which would have pleased Adolf Loos these upstarts and yuppies have thrown off most of the knick-knacks and superficial historicism of their nineteenth-century forbears and embraced an abstract, timeless, utilitarian style – although like most other classes today they still decorate their houses with traditional elements. Confident and unsentimental about roots, willing to sacrifice almost anything for economic and technological progress, they have created huge, abstract monuments which are so typical of today's commerce – the shopping centre, or, even more, the gigantic convention centre which might have up to six major exhibition spaces. As Peter Eisenman predicts, the convention centre is set to become the building type of the nineties, a replacement for that of the eighties, the museum.

That Modernists evolved a chaste style which rejected their bourgeois roots is a thesis argued with force and irony by Tom Wolfe in *From Bauhaus to Our House,*[21] 1981. Noting the way the Bauhaus and the glass and steel blocks of the Avenue of the Americas in New York resemble ideal socialist schemes, he draws the following conclusions:

> First the new architecture was being created for the workers. The holiest of all goals: perfect worker housing. Second, the new architecture was to reject all things bourgeois. Since just about everyone involved, the architects as well as the Social Democrat bureaucrats, was himself bourgeois in the literal, social sense of the word, 'bourgeois' became an epithet that meant whatever you didn't like in the lives of people above the level of hod carrier. The main thing was not to be caught designing something someone could point to and say of, with a devastating sneer: 'How very bourgeois'.[22]

As Wolfe notes, with further irony, the working class has nearly always disliked the white abstractions made in their name and preferred to live in something more poly-chromatic and exuberant.

Putting together Marx, Loos, Wolfe and Berman we may summarise an argument: all periods of history have a unique style or set of modes, and the new, bourgeois class has a distinctive style based on the antinomy 'destruction/creation'. Because this class

I M PEI, *Jacob K Javits Center*, New York, 1979-86. Perhaps the building type of the nineties with six convention centres, fifty loading docks and 1.8 million square feet enclosed under one roof. Megabuilding for megacrowds doing megabusiness – 'all that is solid melts into glass'.

is without strong roots and culture, it develops an abstract geometric style where, if there is any ornament, it will consist in such utilitarian things as structure. This timeless mode rejects not only history but its social genesis, the bourgeoisie itself, as it embraces the vision of a utopian working class – a proletariat that has never existed, but one which will be miraculously without self-interest, difference, bad taste, and individuality.

But why should the bourgeoisie be so relentlessly anti-bourgeois? Why should the Modernist do everything to deny his social background? (There are far fewer female Modernists than male.) Is it that he can't face the destruction inherent in development, the deracination and cultural annihilation which Marx and Nietzsche expose? The fact that all new Modernisms, for two hundred years, must deny their predecessors, throw their ancestors on the 'scrap-heap of history' as the Futurists proposed for each generation, and suppress their own identity, their own tradition? The fact that Modernism is, culturally speaking, suicidal?

Something like this must explain the constant reappearance of destructive imagery, of Brutalist and minimalist styles which recur in a new guise – as Classicism used to do – every twenty years. In this sense Modernism is nothing else than the bourgeois denying his own existence, a destruction turned tragically inwards. We find many echoes of this from Le Corbusier's constant invocation to 'start again from zero', to Roland Barthes' anti-bourgeois degree-zero style; from the constant death and rebirth of the avant-garde to the metaphor of the phoenix, from the attacks on consumerism, ornament and representation, to the advocacy of a counter-style which is supposedly unconsumable – too difficult for the middle-class to swallow.

The New Moderns continually make this last opposition as they insist on their purity and anti-populism, their avoidance of contamination by commerce. Kenneth Frampton's defense of Tadao Ando's architecture – which is itself firmly based on Le Corbusier's degree-zero style – is the archetype.

> . . . Ando's architecture is critical in the sense that it resists being absorbed into the ever-escalating consumerism of the modern city . . . Ando has stoically refused the nostalgic ethos which such vernacular elements display . . . Ando values the 'silence' of modern form for its resistance to consumption . . . when it comes to the evaluation of functional forms, Ando remains opposed to both bourgeois comfort and the ideals of ergonomic convenience, since for him such criteria are contaminated by consumerism.[23]

This renunciation sounds plausible at first, and Frampton drives home his message by calling Ando's work 'subversive'; but then one notes the conventional nature of this purgation and stoic silence, the way it follows the customary modernist pattern of renunciation, and it only takes another second of reflection to realise that Ando, like Le Corbusier before him, has become the focus for new wave fashion – indeed fashion photographers – and even more well-known internationally than those architects who are more accessible, representational or nostalgic. Ché Guevara's revolutionary purity was turned into a consumerist product, and the Modernist pure of heart suffers this success too. The really bourgeois styles today are always anti-bourgeois.

*   *   *

TADAO ANDO, *Chapel on Mount Rokko*, Kobe, Japan, 1985-6. 'The "silence" of modern form'.

This detour to a form of psycho-history brings us back to patterns that still remain in the New Modernism, the most constant of which is the New seen as something alien or 'other'. 'Make it strange' is a constant romantic injunction of two hundred years, a command which necessitates the constant paradoxical destruction of the 'Tradition of the New'. Forgetfulness is an important mental skill to cultivate and it is no surprise that our quintessential New Mod, Peter Eisenman, has made an acrostic from his name – 'amnesia'. Always churning out new figures of speech and visual tropes from his rhetoric machine, he constantly moves ground that covers familiar ground, from 'anti-memory' to 'dissimulation', 'catachresis', 'arabesques' and so on through thirty or more terms. Each one extends his architecture in small ways giving it life, keeping it free from cliché and repetition, and yet each one recalls the constant return of the Modern to abstraction, the 'other' and destruction/construction.

The creative transformation of old/new Modernism is no small matter in an era when so much architecture, produced by large firms, has become predictable. 'The Life of Forms in Art', Henri Focillon's phrase, is to be respected just as the goal of the Modernists – self-development – has its point.

If there is an obvious problem to the New Modernism it is its extreme hermeticism, the lack of a social basis and wide appeal, the inability to be understood except by a small coterie. Also the architecture over-emphasises chaos, as if every event in the universe were a thunderstorm rather than more predictable weather. In the 1960s a 'real' Modern architect, Mies van der Rohe, decreed that – 'you can't make a new architecture every Monday morning'. The New Moderns, being true to the demonic strain in their tradition, have replied – 'Oh, but you can, and *that* is the point of Modernism. There's not much else for a Modernist to be.'

LEON KRIER, *Portrait of Peter Eisenman as Homo Americanus:* the flying, fragmenting hero of the New – exploding, walking over glass, and surrounded by abstract shards of decomposed architecture.

PETER EISENMAN, *Wexner Center for the Visual Arts,* Columbus, Ohio, 1983-9. The rhetoric machine of Eisenman at work here producing 'self-similarity', 'dissimulation', 'anti-memory' and other tropes in a new/old modern style.

LATE-MODERNISM
AND POST-MODERNISM

The Modern Movement, capitalised like all world religions, had its Heroic Period in the twenties and its Classy Period, its dissemination and commercialisation, in the fifties. By the late sixties, it had lost much of its ideological power and, with the death of Le Corbusier in 1965, it had lost much of its moral and spiritual direction. As a utopian movement, or at minimum an avant-garde attempt to influence society, it always had a normative role, a role which has recently diminished if not disappeared altogether. Recently heretical groups within Modernism have flourished that have revived one or another of the founding faiths – Futurism revived by Archigram, Neo-Constructivism by some Italians – there has even been Archizoom's Neo-Dadaism. But the essence of the Modern Movement became somewhat hollow at its core – in the academies and schools of architecture where it continued a prolonged existence under the heading of 'Late Mies', 'Late Kahn', or even the baroque appellation applied to Richard Meier's work – 'Post Johnson-Corb'. All these trends grew out of the International Style, but were as different from it as Late Gothic architecture was from High Gothic. As we shall show, they have enough in common to be grouped together as a school of Late-Modernism, and distinguished from the other main, current approach of Post-Modernism. No doubt these labels are unwieldy, but they make the basic point which is often obscured today that the high period of the Modern Movement is definitely over and that current approaches have evolved out of it. Here we'll define the essential ways Modernism has transformed itself into something still recognisably Modern with aspects that are exaggerated, or 'Late'.[1]

Late-Modernism

To illustrate the overlapping of present architects into the two major tendencies, we can recall how they have responded to the general disenchantment with Modernism. The environmental 'crisis', the unpopularity of Modern housing estates, the boredom with Modern aesthetics are too well known to need recounting, but it is to these pressures that both Late-Modernists and Post-Modernists have reacted.

The Late Modernists have, for the most part, taken the theories and style of their precursors to an extreme and in so doing produced an elaborated or mannered Modernism. By contrast Post-Modernists have modified the previous style, while building upon it, but in addition also rejected the theories almost completely. Brief illustrations of both new schools will bring out their similarities and differences.

The work of Arata Isozaki and Herman Hertzberger is some of the most convincing Late-Modernism around. It responds to the anonymity of Modernism with extreme articulation and in the case of Hertzberger with extreme cellular multiplication, in an attempt to provide identity. Where Modernists emphasised mass, volume and linear

RICHARD MEIER, *The Atheneum*, New Harmony, Indiana 1975-9, West Entrance front. White architecture with ribbon windows, piano curves and exaggeration of circulation – called among other things 'Post Johnson-Corb'.

43

circulation spines, Hertzberger emphasises sub-centres, various routes, and individual constructional elements. Where the International Style was purist and closed as a unified aesthetic, the Hertzberger aesthetic is impure and open to addition, modification and, to a degree, personalisation. His Beheer office building is claimed to be a 'monument to democracy'; an open, anti-authoritarian building because it breaks down the centralised bureaucracy into a lot of little so-called 'work islands' and then invites these small centres to be used, decorated and modified at the request of the users. And yet on an architectural level one can see that Hertzberger hasn't in fact changed the basic style and ideologies of Modernism. There is still the fundamental idea that architecture can shape social behaviour, especially mass behaviour and that of large corporations, and the basic abstract style of concrete block, glass brick and constructional expression. A Post-Modernist, by contrast, might have used styles, spaces and social imagery more local to the area, or stemming from the Dutch tradition. When I interviewed several people there in 1977 I found that, although most of the young people liked the scheme and personalised it in various ways, the non-average employee was excluded by, or dubious of, its machine aesthetic. An older woman who commuted from Amsterdam would have preferred more soft wooden surfaces in a different ambience. I'm not suggesting that architecture *must* follow traditional taste cultures here, but rather that Late-Modernists do still have a commitment to a unified and exclusive aesthetic even when they talk of democracy and participation.

The same can be said of Norman Foster's and Richard Rogers' work, which, while trying to get closer to popular imagery than Modernism, still remains essentially wrapped in its thrall of technological fantasy. Indeed the so-called London School – Foster, Rogers, Farrell and Grimshaw, Derek Walker *et al* – is all Late-Modernist precisely because it takes technological imagery to an extreme that the Modern Movement never reached. Partly this is due to the presence of this technology on a massive and efficient scale: something that the Pioneers never enjoyed. When glass, steel and ventilating technology allow one to do away with all the conventional elements of doors, walls, parapets and rooms, then it's likely that leading architects will make an expressive virtue of these absent parts, for expression is always partly dependent on a distortion of the accepted code. What gives Foster's and Rogers' work its peculiar, exhilarating quality however is the exaggeration of the distortion. Some is so stripped of familiar elements that, conceptually, the entire building is a wall, with no roof and bottom, with no joints and entry, rather like a magical box. Mies may have adumbrated this Mannerism, but his buildings always retained some scaling elements, many of them Classical.

Why is the Pompidou Centre Late-Modern and not Modern? Because, like a work of Art Nouveau, the expression of joints and structure is so obsessive and poetic that it dominates other concerns. The muscular *gerberettes* and their accentuated curving sections have all the overtones of an Art Nouveau insect, such as Adler's *Bat*, and the way pin joints are celebrated is reminiscent of Horta's *Maison du Peuple*. This 'structuralism' would have been condemned in the twenties as structural acrobatics, but quite clearly here the architects are trying to be popular, not Modern, and take advantage of the widespread love of the meccano-set image which is now deep in our

HERMAN HERTZBERGER, *Centraal Beheer* offices, Apeldoorn, 1968-74. Interior street with its planting, omnipresent concrete block and overhead duct-work. If one accepts that aesthetic celebration of movement and technology then one has to applaud the intricate beauty of these parts – concrete block versus glass block versus silver light fixture and ducts. A Chinese puzzle of grey tones against which more colourful patterns are placed by the users. A deeper pluralism is however absent, traditionalists are excluded.

Centraal Beheer offices. An office for a thousand workers some of whom commute from Amsterdam. Hertzberger has broken up the Modernist slab office building into roughly fifty-six cubes or 'work islands' which are organised in a grid of interior 'streets' and coffee bars. The attempt to break down the image and function of hierarchical bureaucracy is party successful. None the less old Modernist problems remain: the repetitive machine aesthetic, unclear communication (the entry had to be marked 'ingang' and unintended metaphors ('rabbit warren' etc).

society. They have succeeded because, as with all fantasy, they haven't compromised the basic image.

Thus if we read the service facade in depth we find five distinct layers of technology accentuated by different colours. The first layer of circulation is a black cage; then some green pipes to either side are followed by cross-bracing painted silver (the exoskeleton of this rectilinear insect) followed in turn by heavy blue ducts that taper downward – a veritable colonnade of paired columns reminiscent of Perrault's Louvre nearby. This, the strongest visual layer, is followed by a layer of orange metallic cabinets, and then finally a grey wall.

Although compositional rules appear to have played no part, there is an interesting Classical-Baroque air about this facade: a 'rusticated' basement level of extract units and heavy blue horizontals, then two storeys of building which graduate in openings like a *palazzo*, and at the top not a cornice line but instead an implied roof line – the continuation of the blue ducts. To complete the comparison with a Baroque *palazzo* there is the overall division of the facade into bays, a near symmetry and two stressed side verticals – all like Bernini's Palazzo Chigi-Odescalchi in 1664. The bay rhythm (A, A, BCB, A, A, A, A', BCB', A', D) bears comparison with the way this *palazzo* was altered (to 3,1,7,1, 3 bays).

This historical parallel may seem absurd at first, especially since it is Post-Modernists and not Late-Modernists who refer to historical models. And yet there is an unmistakable *palazzo* feeling to the overall horizontal facade which is so strong that it won't disappear, especially since the Pompidou Centre is surrounded by a similar type, the Parisian *hôtel*. But, and this is typical of Late-Modernism, the coding is apparently unintended, the comparison, or metaphor, inadvertent. Piano and Rogers don't intend their building to be read symbolically much beyond its literal messages or celebration of technology. As opposed to a Post-Modern version of the same building, there is no real interest in making a comment on the language and context of Paris. True the building holds street lines and tries to be low, but there is no acceptance of a street-side entry, no conversation with the ground floor, indeed not even much use of this all-important level. The street floor, as in so much Modernism on stilts, is a grand desolation.

But if these are its faults as seen from a Post-Modern position, what are its Late-Modern virtues? Aside from the technological fantasy already mentioned, it has an extreme logic (repetitive sandwich slabs of warehouse space), extreme circulatory emphasis, extreme flexibility (which may not be used) and the extreme pragmatism of Modernism. One can find parallels with the Berlin Free University, the ultra-logic of Eisenman and the decorative structures of Paolo Portoghesi. Basically this is a decorated toy box of technical tricks which the French executive fancies as much as Monsieur Hulot. It is an oversize meccano set painted in French blues and reds sitting in the heart of limestone Paris.

As a completely unlikely occurrence it is probably appropriate for its role as a culture centre, and as a supermarket of culture it is no doubt very successful – as popular as the Eiffel Tower (the standard comparison). The problem is however that one can't support such supermarkets very far – one, for Paris, is enough.

MATHIAS UNGERS, *Messe Skyscraper*, Frankfurt-Am-Main, 1983-5. While the gridded geometry is very Modernist, the scale, form, and references to the red-coloured stones of the local masonry are historicist.

G BERNINI, *Palazzo Chigi-Odescalchi*, Rome, 1664, extended by N Salvi, 1745, so that it had sixteen pilasters instead of eight. The typical Baroque *palazzo* had a rusticated base, giant order of pilasters, side entrances, complex rhythm of bays and a pronounced cornice. Note the window 'ears', a metaphor comparable to the Pompidou *gerberettes*, or 'arms'.

RICHARD ROGERS and RENZO PIANO, *Pompidou Centre*, Paris, 1971-7. Architecture about construction, technology and movement – the three canonic subjects of Modernism are here given a Mannerist emphasis. The Classical code of Perrault's Louvre, and other *palazzi* is implicit, but unintended? (Compare with Bernini's Palazzo Chigi-Odescalchi).

KEVIN ROCHE, *One UN Plaza*, New York 1974-6 (above), AN-THONY LUMSDEN AND DMJM, *Bumi Daya Bank Project*, Jakarta, Indonesia, 1972-6, model (below), and *Manufacurer's Bank*, Los Angeles, 1974 (opposite). Late-Modernist fragmentation of the slab. Kevin Roche's tower opposite the United Nations slides back three times and also decreases the scale by a small horizontal grid. Anthony Lumsden undulates the wall on the Manufacturer's Bank, or gives it a bevelled base on the Bumi Daya Bank Project. For this bank and its petro-dollars he also provides an oil-slick surface. There is enough in common between these schemes to character-ise a shared approach to the skyscraper: an emphasis on the stretched skin, the ambiguities of reflection and scale distortion, and the exaggeration of single themes perceivable in an instant.

Difficult cases

We can now summarise the qualities of Late-Modernism and contrast them with Post-Modernism: basically the Late-Modernist approach is pragmatic rather than idealist, and also *ultra*-modern in its exaggeration of several modern aspects – extreme logic, extreme circulatory and mechanical emphasis, a mannered and decorative use of tech-nology, a complication of the International Style (Richard Meier for example) and an abstract rather than a conventional language of form. To these essentially Mannerist qualities ought to be added the most ultra-modern and mannered one of all: the tendency to shock by discontinuity, by newness, by being a self-sufficient, avant-garde statement cut off from traditional architecture. Norman Foster's buildings have those qualities as much as Peter Eisenman's. Other architects who should be added to this list are John Hejduk, Denys Lasdun, Cesar Pelli, Helmut Schulitz, Fumihiko Maki and most of the Metabolists, Gordon Bunshaft, Kevin Roche and many corporate practitioners, Piet Blom and Riema Pietilä, John Andrews and a host of architects who are pushing the mainstream tradition hard in an attempt to deal with the failures of Modernism. Of the eight qualities or definers mentioned above these architects each have five or six – enough to group them together in spite of varying styles.

In like manner Post-Modernism must be defined as a loose overlap of qualities, although opposite to the previous ones: an interest in popular and local codes of communication (Portmeirion for example), in historical memory, urban context, ornament, representation, metaphor, participation, the public realm, pluralism and eclecticism.

Thus, to simplify, we may say that if six of the ten possible attributes are present in a work that is sufficient to define it as Post-Modern. Unmentioned is perhaps the most obvious definer and one that is shared by both groups – the evolution out of Modernism and therefore the continued presence of the International Style, in some form. This aspect is most clear to a traditional architect, and is why he continues to censor both Late- and Post-Modernism without making distinctions. For us, however, it is crucial to make the distinctions between these two schools because of the significant philosophical differences. Briefly they may be described as differences over an intention to communicate: Post-Modernists, in an attempt to reach the various users of their buildings, *doubly-code the architecture* and use a wide spectrum of communicational means whereas Late-Modernists remain within the restricted and hermeneutic language of Modernism.

Having drawn these distinctions in terms of number and degree however, it is not surprising that several architects fall between schools, or sometimes, as in the case of Philip Johnson and Mathias Ungers, go back and forth. This vacillation is not surprising given both the philosophical confusion of the moment and the opposite demands on the architect – that he should design both conventional glass and steel skyscrapers and contextual buildings. In fact if we were looking for stylistic definers alone, as historians usually do, we would only be partly successful in classifying schools. Thus we might speak of the Late-Modern 'slick-tech' look, the faceted glass polyhedron which develops the stretched skin surface beyond Modernism. Here the work of Pelli and DMJM shares a lot with John Portman, Norman Foster, Philip Johnson, Arata Isozaki and so many commercial developers who use mirror plate.

Generally speaking the surface of these buildings is isotropic and endless, a grid of repeated shapes which might be extended infinitely, but which has, in volume, many subtle variations. Johnson's Minneapolis tower staggers the corner so many times that it becomes a faceted wall; his Houston towers set triangular shapes in counterpoint to rectangular planes; Kevin Roche's recent skyscrapers in New York also play these tricks in scale and massing in a way which might be called 'Picturesque-Modern'. Isozaki and others have developed the 'smash joint', that is a non-joint joint where two homogeneous surfaces going different directions are 'smashed' together without a change in articulation, without space, mouldings or the typical sculptural modulations of Modernism. The ambiguities are as interesting as the break with tradition. The visual hallucinations caused by repeated reflections and layered transparency add an interest lacking in Modernist skyscrapers, but clearly they are Late-Modern rather than a complete break with the previous style.

It is instructive to look at several architects whose work appears to be going Post-Modern without, however, having the majority of P M definers. The recent work (1977) of Michael Graves and Paolo Portoghesi fits partly into both schools; it has historical roots, without the references being easily understood; it uses elements decoratively without wishing to use them conventionally. In short, it partly establishes a communication with the users as Post-Modernists do more thoroughly and it partly treats architecture as esoteric sculpture, as do the Late-Modernists.

The Casa Papanice in Rome starts, as many of Portoghesi's buildings do, from where Borromini left the Baroque: as an enjoyable game of walls sliding in and out to accent the doors and windows, the erotic zones of architecture. The Baroque slight curve *is* clearly recognisable, no one could miss it, and since Rome is largely a Baroque city one can find many contextual reasons for this revival including a response to the site, a curving in to frame a tree, or to catch light, etc. Portoghesi has drawn an explanatory plan analysis which shows the three basic generators of curves (poles of access, light and function) and how they are organised on a grid set diagonally to the 'front' of the building.

The light-catching curves create a pool of lightness, emphasised by concentric curves above the windows. The explicitness of the metaphor here is Post-Modern, the desire to communicate on the literal level so that the viewer becomes sensitised to certain themes which he then seeks to find in more subtle instances. The metaphor of defining 'pools of place' is just as explicit above the twin 'hearts' of the house – the hearth and dining alcove which also receive their telescoping curves. It is a very convincing attempt to give back to the house those traditional centres which were overlooked by Modernists. But, as with Frank Lloyd Wright, who also accentuated these centres, they are dramatised with unconventional ornament and esoteric symbols: not mouldings but stepped 'saucers', not dados but horizontal stripes painted green (for children) and blue (for adults). Who would understand this symbolism and the fact that Portoghesi used it partly to keep the client from covering the wall with his questionable paintings (a very Modernist stance to battle the taste of the client).[2] Furthermore the popular images latent within these forms call up metaphors which tend to undercut the seriousness of the work; the flying saucers look like an Art Deco restaurant lounge, the stripes like Christmas packaging.

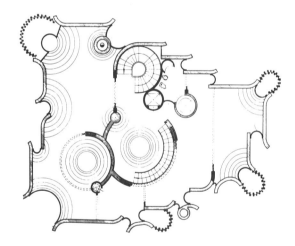

PAOLO PORTOGHESI, *Casa Papanice*, Rome, 1970. Reflected ceiling plan showing graduated circles and the restricted gamut of inflected walls .'Pools' of space with their ceiling 'ripples', organised on a grid set diagonally to the basic axes, so that the eye is continuously moving to the corner views.

Casa Papanice. Bedroom balconies, 'striped candy-cane' and stepping stone 'coins' carry out the kitsch metaphors which are underscored by the glazed tiling in glistening stripes of green from the ground, blue from the sky and gold from the owner. The Rococo lightness to the overall building comes partly from the white background and delicate verticals.

Of course Portoghesi, like Charles Moore and others, intends these whimsical meanings and enjoys a flirtation with kitsch, especially in a building which asks for it. Here the client wanted his house to be featured in films — and it already has been a backdrop for three, including a science fiction film and melodrama with Monica Vitti. So a sophisticated acknowledgement of opposed taste-cultures is being made: Borromini for the classes and Rockefeller Center for the masses. But it is arguable that the presence of these images — the 'organ-pipes' on the roof, the 'money-pavement' on the ground and the 'sugar-cane' balconies — distracts us from deeper meanings. We are inclined to dismiss this work because of some superficial facility and aberrant readings. That is, when we see the roof cylinders rising up and down in easy staccato rhythms, like organ-pipes in so many shlocky music halls, we doubt the presence of richer meanings. The glistening exterior tiles, in candy stripes of blue, green, brown and gold, also look trite.

Yet these surface images should not trick us into dismissing Portoghesi any more than Rococo embellishments should make us disregard Balthasar Neumann. Architects and intellectuals are as likely to be taken in by superficiality as the general public, although in opposite ways, and both the Baroque and Rococo have been underrated by them until quite recently. For similar reasons I think Portoghesi's lightness and good humour have been underrated.[3] They are like the froth and cheerfulness of a German Rococo church, something that reveals *and* conceals a basic seriousness and creativity.

We have mentioned the ripples of circular motifs which define pools of space, and the way light is modulated on these curves. If we look closer at the curved window areas of the living-dining spaces we see how controlled is the quality of spatial differentiation. There is the general diagonal pull towards exterior views (marked V in plan) which keeps the eye moving laterally away from the dining and fire places to focus on exterior events. As in Baroque buildings the eye is further pulled across surfaces by the horizontal bands which, like a Borromini cornice, continue across interruptions. These swirling lines are then played in a different key in the ceiling, light fixtures and mirrors (which reflect views of the ground, thus establishing yet another relation to nature). But the connection of inside and outside space isn't complete as in so much Modern space. The window articulation (what Portoghesi has called 'the dialectic window' to distinguish various types of treatment) varies the view in significant ways. The inflected walls curve back to back (D in plan) for major views, or alternate curved and flat surfaces for more hidden and mysterious views (E). Thus exterior space is implied rather than seen at these points and an element of expectation and surprise is introduced. The graduation in light intensity further intensifies both in the curved wall and graduated steps of the saucers. Such refinements both inside and out make this a subtle use of kitsch motifs for very non-kitsch ends.

If Portoghesi's work does not quite use conventional ornament to communicate directly neither does Michael Graves'. Rather they both use complex transformations of historical imagery which have to be analysed, sometimes laboriously, to be perceived. Since about 1976 Graves has introduced recognisable mouldings, split pediments, keystones, lattice-work, Cretan columns — in short historicist recollections — into his work. Previously it had been restricted more or less to the vocabulary of the twenties and Juan Gris.[4]

PAOLO PORTOGHESI, *Casa Papanice*, dining area is marked by concentric curves as are the fireplace and various lighting conditions, natural and artificial.

Casa Papanice, schematic spatial analysis of public area with zones of A-access, B-light, C-functions: dining, sitting, fireplace. In addition, different lighting and edge conditions can be seen when a wall curves out, D, or exposes an edge and turns in E. V signifies important corner views.

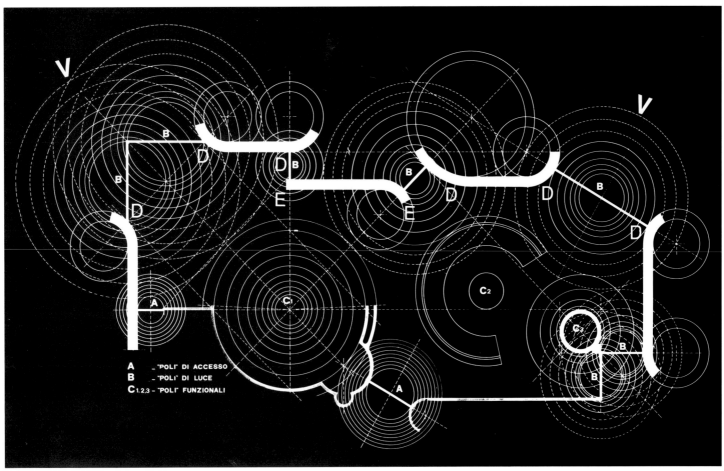

A _ 'POLI' DI ACCESSO
B _ 'POLI' DI LUCE
C₁.₂.₃ - 'POLI' FUNZIONALI

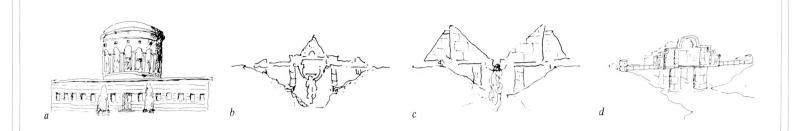

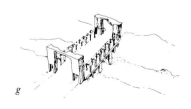

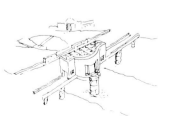

His Cultural Bridge project – to unite the two towns Fargo and Moorhead with a cultural centre – consists of symbolic images of unity and division which relate to historic forms. First of all the bridge itself is, as Graves pointed out to me in conversation, a heavy Palladian gesture rather than the thin shells of Modernism and Maillart.[5] It has the overtones of many existing bridges including those with buildings such as the Ponte Vecchio. The placement of a heavy form over water, on the middle of two arms, is quite naturally a very strong symbol of unification, of binding two halves, in this case two competitive communities, together.

Graves has shown the etymology of meanings in his exquisite thumb-nail sketches which we can follow in detail. First the rotunda of Ledoux, a massive cylinder surmounting a horizontal, bridge-like base (a), then a pyramidal form from Castle Howard is placed over another Ledoux theme of water spilling through a half cylinder (b). Next the pediment is broken in its centre so that the void, rather than solid, symbolises unity (c). This created a problem with respect to the sky since Graves wanted to keep the tripartite organisation of bridges – basement, *piano nobile* and attic. So he went to a new formal and historical solution, proposing a profile stepped up and relating to the *Serliana* (d) (a motif which can be seen in the final project, now quite thick and covered with an abstract grid).

The next step consists of simplifying this arch, thickening it and stepping up walls (e) rather than the profile (in the final project they've become overscale glazed elements – giant windows, 'eyes'). Then, the last sketch shows an early synthesis of the central block: the dropped keystone out of which water pours (f) (or like Ledoux's Chaux, a sculptural mass of symbolic water frozen into rock); the 'legs', 'eyes' and strong anthropomorphic imagery which will become even stronger with the addition of a 'nose'; finally the thick vaults of unification.

In the adjoining sketches the evolution of the bridge may be seen, with its emphasis on the edges, and disunity, as well as the framed exedra of the centre. The distinctive step here is the addition of two end 'triumphal arches' with their jagged inside edges, what Graves calls his 'English-Muffin-fork-split' (g). Twin pergolas, later to become a heavy raised cornice of building, emphasise the duality once again. The inspiration for this was, apparently, the dual-centre projects of Asplund as well as a painting of an arch at Kew by Richard Wilson, 1762. Finally, the inverted pyramid of glazing in the centre was partly inspired by the lantern of Borromini's San Carlo alle Quattro Fontane and its perspective effect of diminishment.

To all these explicit references should be added the bridge column capitals which relate to many Modern concrete constructions, the handling of the broken pediment related to Mannerist architecture and the blue, red and orange colouring present in Cubist painting. The references are thus quite specific and numerous. Two general points might be made concerning their efficacy and relation to the architecture we are discussing; as a precise set of meanings their significance would be totally lost to the citizens of Fargo and Moorhead. The codes are too esoteric, the meanings too private to Graves and architectural scholars, to communicate the depth of reference intended. For those willing to go through the above analysis the bridge is, no doubt, a multivalent work sending out a criss-cross of elaborated meanings quite marvellously complicated in their inter-relations. But for the uninformed beholder there are not enough explicit

MICHAEL GRAVES, *Fargo/Moorhead Cultural Center Bridge*, 1977, above and below: referential sketches showing historical transformations from Ledoux etc (see text). Centre: rendered elevation, 1978. The basic theme of two communities unified by an arch, yet still separate – its break and twin in the background – comes through even if the specific references remain hidden.

HANS HOLLEIN, *Rolls Royce Grill on Wall Street*, 1966, predicts the recurrence of this temple image. The associations of business propriety with the Parthenon are not fortuitous as historians have shown.

PHILIP JOHNSON and JOHN BURGEE, *AT & T Building*, New York City, 1978 – 84, re-establishes the conventional New York skyscraper code of an articulated masonry frame culminating in a pitched roof of Classical provenance. Various historical codes underlie this form including the column (ie base, shaft, capital, entablature), the Pazzi Chapel (base), the Chippendale highboy (top) and the Rolls Royce radiator.

cues for this rich interpretative process to take place; in this way the scheme is characteristic of the private language games of Late-Modernism. Secondly however, and in contradiction to this privacy of meaning, there is a general penumbra of historic meaning which would, I believe, be perceived.[6] It is a question of suggested metaphor, implicit rather than explicit coding, and here Graves' work has a breadth and particularity of reference which is quite apt.

In gross terms most people would probably perceive the dominant images of unification and division. The 'arms' of the two arches reach out to meet each other, but don't yet touch, implicit metaphors of striving for civic unification. This theme of 'unified-duality' is repeated often enough – the broken arches are offset in plan – to be readily perceivable. Furthermore the repeated symmetries, like those of the human, are echoed forcefully throughout and we all know, because it is a fact of our bodies, that this symmetry of two things constitutes a single whole. As mentioned, the eyes, nose, mouth and legs are implicity coded and they underline this basic body metaphor. For these reasons the Fargo/Moorhead Bridge is a very appropriate symbol of cultural unification, and Post-Modern in the clarity with which it expresses this symbol. Like all of Graves' work it is also very convincing as a sensual and sculptural composition.

Post-Modernism

Post-Modernists, to turn now to the other major school, double-code their buildings so that they communicate with their users as well as other architects, and it is this attempt which ties them to previous traditions – the Classical language, Queen Anne Revival and Art Nouveau, to name three.[7]

As an example of double-coding let me illustrate Philip Johnson's recent design for the AT & T building in New York, which has been called by Paul Goldberger 'Post Modernism's major monument'.[8] As pointed out by Goldberger the top of this skyscraper looks very much like a Chippendale highboy or an eighteenth-century grandfather clock. Furthermore it will function as an eighteenth-century fantasy scheme of Ledoux or Boullée if, as intended, smoke from the heating system pours out of the hole in the broken pediment. The bottom continues the historical allusions including, within, a 'forest of columns' and, without, a very Renaissance motif, the *Serliana*, or according to Johnson, the front of Brunelleschi's Pazzi Chapel.

The ambiguity of formal reading here is shared by the main shaft of the elevation which, at thirty miles an hour (the speed of a New York taxi driver) might look like a modern, granite sheathed skyscraper: or, more slowly and carefully, like a work of Louis Sullivan, that is, 'Pre-Modernist'. The divisions and syncopations come directly from the classical skyscraper tradition – the Auditorium Building in Chicago of Adler and Sullivan. But behind this, in fairly strong contrast is a traditional modern skyscraper trying to get out, or rather stay in.

These codes are fairly explicit and some of them are shared by both the man in the taxi and the architect. Depending on how the granite and ornament are handled, I think further meanings will become equally clear.

If the reticence of the side elevation is anything to go by then the building will start to approach the Gucci Look, or better the Lanvin Mode. It will be perceived as in the Fifth Avenue or Bond Street Style, signifying fastidiousness and boredom, that combination of good taste and uncreativity which has made prestige commissions so remorselessly funereal. If the detailing follows the front elevation then there is more hope for the scheme; it will take the cosmetic associations and tie them with the more local sustaining meanings I have mentioned. This amalgam could be witty and even appropriate. The skyscraper as elongated grandfather clock, as gigantic Lanvin perfume bottle, as Renaissance chapel, as Neo-Fascist colonnade, as imprisoned Lever Building, or Rolls Royce radiator. The New Yorker may be well pleased to see these meanings come into his skyscraper, and delighted by the elegance with which the thirty-foot pediment lifts up its ears, gently, at the ends. 'Chippendale indeed, we can put that grandfather clock right opposite the front door'. The skyscraper has been given a diminutive model, a perfume bottle, or furniture case.

So the building makes use of quite contradictory codes in an entertaining way; it's not the most creative synthesis of double-coding and it will probably be heavily criticised for that (eg for being a conventional glass and steel building inside a conventional Louis Sullivan). But a degree of credit should go to Johnson, I feel, for the sensitivity with which he has combined local, New York codes. Although it is not as confident as the Chrysler Building and other historicist skyscrapers of the twenties and thirties it is still the first New York skyscraper for a long time to go beyond the flat-top look.

Probably younger designers working on smaller commissions have greater scope for developing historicist imagery than those trained in the International Style. Particularly those trained by the historicists at Yale (Venturi, Moore and Scully) have a freedom of expression denied to their teachers, who had to struggle against Modernism. James Righter and Peter Rose, who worked under Charles Moore, have developed his flat, wood-sheath aesthetic to the point where it can make quite straightforward allusions to a monumental architecture of the past, to Palladianism and the nineteenth century. Their justifications for these images appear convincing because they are tied very closely to the local context or the symbolic function of the building. For instance the ski-lodge, Pavillon Soixante-Dix, is given its steep roofs because of heavy snows, and the omnipresence of this vernacular form in the area. The cut-out arch motif relates to local buildings *and* acts as a symbolic gate welcoming the skiers. The sun-deck, a semi-circular Palladian exedra influenced by the Villa Trissina, also has a symbolic role of welcoming, as well as a practical function of sunbathing, and viewing the skiers' approach. The architects have underlined these symbolic considerations: 'The intention of the building is to affirm the importance of skiing as a social event, to give every participant a sense of the romance of being in the North, outside, with friends. To do this, the building itself must have a presence, a feeling of monumentality, even if that monumentality is derived from familiar images.'[9]

If the exedra, symmetry, chimneys and entrance all remind us of monumental buildings, then other clues remind us of Modernism: the flattening of the arch at its top, the flat, skin surface and the absence of ornament, except for a thin strip of neon light, under the arch. This is another kind of double-coding, half Modern, half something else, which is characteristic of Post-Modernism. One Post-Modern architect in Japan, Yasufumi Kijima, is really trying to resurrect significant ornament, even if he isn't altogether succeeding. Several of his houses use pan-tile and sliding screens in a

HANS HOLLEIN, *Austrian Travel Bureau,* Vienna, 1978. Placed under a Secessionist gridded barrel vault, are various conventional signs of foreign travel: a Lutyens dome for India, Moroccan palm tress and a ruined Greek column encasing a chrome support. The cashier's till is marked by reticent Rolls Royce grills, another ironic use of a conventional sign. Hollein, an admirer of Johnson, has also recently moved towards a Post-Modern use of historical reference.

applied ornament, the mouldings and repeated patterns are etiolated and brittle. Indeed one might characterise Post-Modern ornament in general this way and try to see this thinness as a positive quality. Since the nineteenth century, machine-made ornament has been over-precise as compared with the hand-crafted variety. Although this and other factors led to its rejection by Modernists, I think the precision has its own virtue – a linear, elegant sleekness attacked by traditionalists. In a sense this is precisely the virtue of the Miesian aesthetic; and Kijima's Matsuo Shrine looks rather as if Mies had decided to detail coffered tunnel vaults and Japanese Doric rather than I-beams. The result is quite surreal. His conceptual drawing, made after the building was complete, as is his practice, reminds one of Escher's transformations of one thing into another. Here an upside-down Corinthian column and its fluting transform themselves into a colonnade, while the dome of the Pantheon transmutes into the coffering of the barrel vault. These two Western images are then attached to Eastern motifs, the lily pond and Japanese shrine. The contrast is just kept from becoming kitsch by the elegant smallness and detailing of the scheme. Here precise ornament is a help. Each pre-cast detail, each capital and entablature, fulfils its role like the part of a well-built machine. The copper shingles are stretched taut around the cylindrical roof like steel plates on the hull of a ship. The pristine entrance arch curves in an exact arc like a polished gear wheel. What could be more twentieth-century *and* traditional than this image of the extruded temple? 'Kijima, as one would guess, discusses his use of hybrid ornament with a certain irony: Each part of a building should have its own innate life. Substantiating the boundaries among these various parts is architectural design . . . one of the major points in style is the ability of ornament within a style to communicate a definite mood. But this does not mean that a style is consequently fixed or that there is a fixed relation between ornament and style. Ingenuity and an original solution to the problems at hand must always play a part in architectural design. I employ beautiful decorative elements of both the East and West to ornament my buildings. People who cannot understand the essentials of what I am doing despise such work as mere imitation. I have no desire to refute their assertions. Each person has his own level of ability.'[10]

Clearly Kijima's work is not imitative, whatever else it is. One is tempted to call it hallucinatory, a delirious combination of opposites, East and West, traditional ornament and machine aesthetic. The double-coding is there with a vengeance. What adds to the feeling of a reverie is the fact that symbolic forms, which had a precise historical role, are now being quite resemanticised *in their totality*. Whereas Michael Graves uses historical fragments, he keeps them implicit enough so that the previous meanings don't entirely communicate. My own view of Kijima's building is that in this particular context, as a shrine gateway, the hallucinatory meanings are plausible and almost appropriate. The comment of the machine metaphor on religious persuasion is also plausible today in the age of mass-cults, even if it is not a pleasant thought.

Certain problems of Kijima's shrine face all Post-Modernists and if these problems are not entirely solved at least here they are faced. First of course is the question of a plural culture and the corresponding double-coding – two traditions in Japan, or many sub-cultures in the West – a pluralism which Kijima tries to acknowledge rather than disregard like Late-Modernists. Second are the questions of ornament and

J V RIGHTER, P ROSE AND P LANKIN, *Pavillon Soixante-Dix*, St Sauveur, Canada, 1976-8. The skiers aim towards the embracing arms of the exedra, the social area and sun deck on which skiers always lounge about waiting for things to happen. The false front, reminiscent of local buildings, also reminds one of a cathedral porch with its two towers.

YASUFUMI KIJIMA, *drawing of Matsuo Shrine*. As in one of M C Escher's drawings elements transform themselves both in space and in content. Here a Corinthian column becomes the colonnade, while the coffers of the Pantheon become the barrel vault. The mirror of the water perhaps prompted these reflections.

than disregard like Late-Modernists. Second are the questions of ornament and beauty; concepts, indeed words, on which there has been a fifty year moratorium. Lastly there is the question of explicit versus implicit reference and the difficulties of going from one level of communication to the other in a free and intelligent way. No Post-Modernist has mastered these problems as, the Baroque architect did, yet one, Thomas Gordon Smith, who has studied Baroque, is beginning to find a way.

Smith studied painting and sculpture at Berkeley before he went on to study architecture there and the visual confidence of an artist can be felt behind his drawings. Indeed, some of them have a free-flowing ease which makes them appear much more facile and instantaneous than they are: in reality many studies occur which use xerox, model building, photography and sketch in alternation before the design is resolved and the free-hand perspective is made. The results show a resolution of parts, curve answering curve, asymmetrical volume balancing a column rhythm, that is quite remarkable in an architect so young. (Smith, born in 1948, started producing his eclectic projects in 1975 at the age of twenty-seven, which is old for a Renaissance artist/architect, but young for one trained today in the university system).

The Richard and Sheila Long House, is a subtle abstraction of historical quotes. As the aeriel perspective shows, the house picks up the curves of the landscape, rather the way the Rococo church *Die Wies* picks up the undulations of the surrounding mountains. Two terrace views, two ovals, organise north and south elevations, while a third curve, that of the entrance driveway, determines the west front. Thus three curves determine a pinwheel or modified Y plan, which rotates around the family dining-room.

Approaching through the west entry, an egg-shape shifted axis, one reaches the foyer/stairs, another oval which forces movement in a counter direction. Then one is turned again toward the south terrace.

> From mid-point in the foyer the vista through the serpentine hall reveals half building, half landscape. I hope that one's vision, while walking through the hall, will be like a pan-in [during a] film. At one point the door frame will be revealed, then [the view] will pan-out to only landscape. I began the bedroom plan as a simplified version of Dientzenhofer's St Xavier. The phallic allusion became apparent later, and in this case appropriate to exploit? My objection to Tigerman's Daisy House is that it expresses a single idea – it seems obsessive.[11]

Personally, I find Tigerman's symbolism only explicit in plan, but the importance of this quote is that it shows Smith's interest in merging historical allusions with other things – the landscape, a filmic procession and the context of the bedroom. This is an accomplished eclecticism and one which uses previous solutions as a method of creativity. Like Graves' use of historical fragments they provide a test, or question, for the new function. Here, for instance, Kilian Ignaz Dientzenhofer's church plan, a dumb-bell shape which mediates between a centralised and longitudinal plan, places entrance and study area on the axes which previously were given to narthex and altar. There is no question of sacrilege here because the allusion is implicit, as is that of the phallic symbol. And the treatment of the ceiling, rather than merging grandiloquent vaults, is a modest, even gentle, rise and fall.

It is one of Smith's great strengths that he can design beautiful curves without falling

THOMAS GORDON SMITH, *Matthews Street House*, coloured perspective, 1978. A formal Classical front and an informal, green stucco behind, staggered in plan to the right. The public area is picked out in pinks, reds, blues and golds, reminiscent of Greek colourings, while the flat green shades recall the pastel colours of the surrounding houses. Significant points are highlighted in red.

Matthews Street House, Michelangelo and Dientzenhofer motifs combined with the San Francisco painted-house vernacular.

into the twin dangers of bathos and cliché. So much Post-Modernism is calculatedly ugly and ill-proportioned: Robert Venturi enjoys a dislocation in scales and Robert Stern gets a similar pleasure by distorting his mouldings, placing windows in disproportion to the cornice etc. Thomas Gordon Smith, who obviously has learned from these architects, nevertheless strives after a unification and resolution in his work. This, inevitably, is like the Baroque response to Mannerist distortion and disunity. The south view of the Long House shows a gentle swell of curves up to the end of the semi-enclosed terrace; then they cascade down in easy sweeps. An S-curve is answered by three U-curves; the bedroom door is answered by the gable window; the split Michelangelesque pediments are also in counterpoint. The beauty of this antiphony recalls that of the best Picturesque or Neo-Queen Anne design.

Actually many of Smith's design ideas spring from San Francisco architects, and the more general Bay Area tradition: in particular the emphasis on cheap, decorative construction and the superimposition of aedicular entrances. It is not surprising then to find in his Matthews Street House a mixture of the bungalow and Maybeck portico, of the explicit symbol of a Classical entrance *and* the cheap stucco box. These contradictions are a very deep part of the Bay Area tradition.

The plan, on a tight street lot of 130 x 30 feet, shows a sophisticated use of layered space, layered at right angles to the central axis. Since one side of the lot borders the adjoining house, Smith closes off this view and orients the secondary axis to one side, the south. This asymmetrical symmetry then is felt in other places. It pushes the major axis slightly to the left of centre of the lot, which then allows other spaces, or rooms on the right side. In elevation this produces the staggered rhythm A/A' characteristic of the bungalow, but also an asymmetrical wall-plus-column set against two columns. A walk through this shifted symmetry is a varied experience. First the outdoor round terrace with its bed of strongly coloured foxgloves, then the Doric portico set at right angles to movement, then four more slots of space at right angles to the axial approach, the largest of which, a demi-oval, is the sitting area of the living room. Beyond this are three more spaces, shifted now slightly to the right and centre of the lot – the kitchen space below the private bedrooms. The cut-away aerial perspective shows the resolution of these spaces and the complex geometrical patterns, which include an eclectic mixture of diagonal floor tiles, Solomonic columns, sash windows staggered up the wall and Japanese figural shapes.

All in all the eclecticism is quite masterful, even if overpowering. As the coloured perspective shows there is a basic division between the grand public space and the modest private realm behind. Each realm receives its appropriate symbolism, and the irony of the shifted symmetry is indicated by the displaced Corinthian column banished way out in the garden, where ruins are conventionally placed. One may object to the exaggeration of historical references, but as mentioned there are reasons for this including the local context of exaggerated bungalow design.

*   *   *

In conclusion, one should reiterate that there are real philosophical and social points which divide Late-Modernists and Post-Modernists, and they focus on the basic issue

THOMAS GORDON SMITH, *Richard and Sheila Long House,* Carson City, Nevada, 1977, project. The broken curve, the semiform, the elliptical usage (in both senses of the word) relate this to Baroque architecture, but the materials are local and informal.

Matthews Street House, aerial perspective showing the resolution of various sources – Maybeck, Bay Area, Michelangelo, Baroque and Japenese. Note the tiny scale, seemingly large because of the historical references.

Matthews Street House, plan. A central axis shifted slightly to north of the lot, allows a spatial development and orientation to the south. Basically the eye is led westward in a sequence of several spaces opening south. The shifted axis is common to eighteenth-century French *hôtels,* Lutyens and now Post-Modernists.

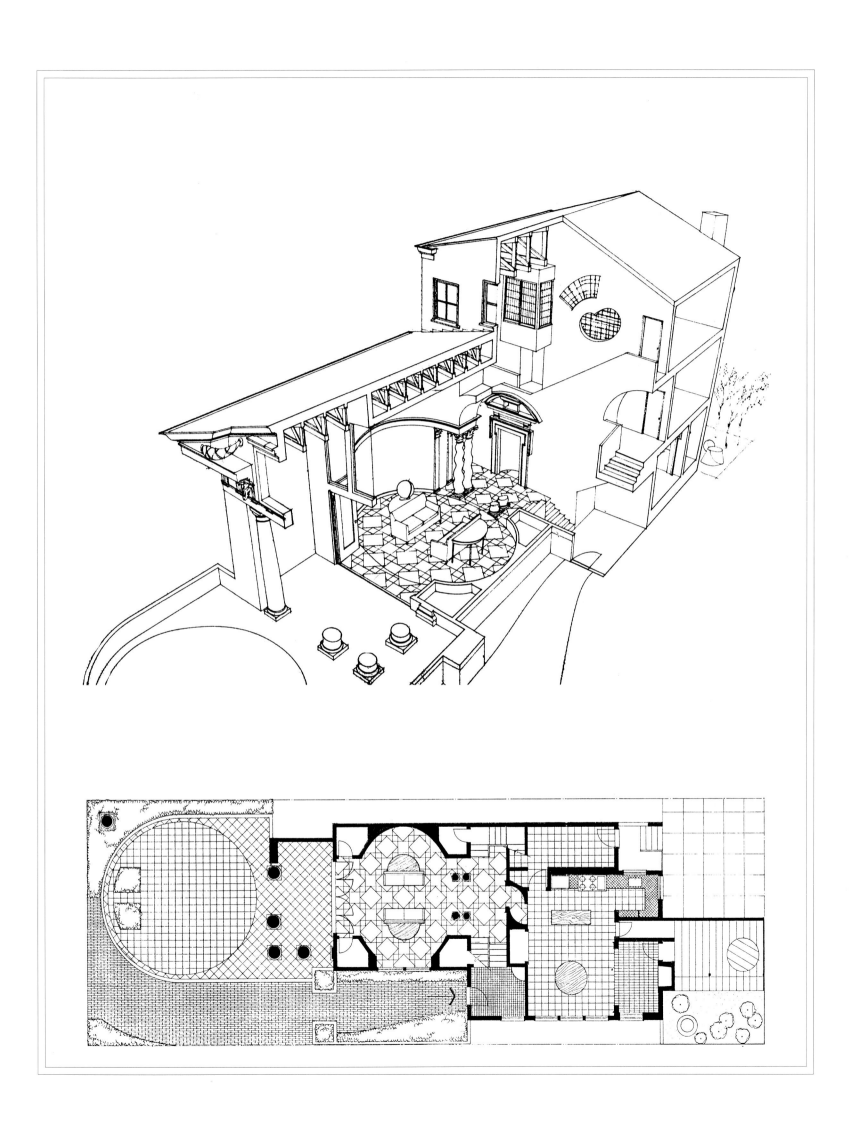

of architecture as communication. Late-Modernists stress the aesthetic aspect of the architectural language, whereas Post-Modernists, in an attempt to say more and say it coherently, stress the conventional aspects. Each school has a certain validity and acts as a challenge to the other. The perennial truth of Late-Modernists, that beauty can result from technical perfection and that the means of architecture are also, partly, its ends, remains a challenge to Post-Modernists whose handling of new technologies tends to be rudimentary. Their counter-claim that architecture is a social art which communicates in a conventional code has, however, wider validity because it encompasses the technical and aesthetic codes within its framework. For such reasons I suspect that a future architecture will evolve out of Post-Modernism, but probably long after this name has been forgotten and a new label has been found. It is also likely that Late-Modernism and Post-Modernism will evolve towards each other, as they continue to compete, and approach some amalgam that might be termed 'Baroque Modern' (or is it 'Modern Baroque'?). But enough of labels.

This essay, published in Architectural Design, 1978 *was a first attempt to distinguish Late-Modernists from the group they were confused with, both popularly and in the press. As can be seen from the list of definers it was not as complete or systematic a definition of each movement as I later arrived at. There are only ten of some thirty classifiers; Hitchcock and Johnson, when defining the International Style, made it somewhat easier with only four major categories, but many would say they oversimplified the complexity of the Style not to mention the Modern Movement. Since this essay was written Michael Graves and Paolo Portoghesi have become quite explicitly Post-Modern.*

RICARDO BOFILL and OFFICE, *Les Echelles du Baroque*, Paris, 1984-7. Modernist curtain wall and concrete and Baroque plan, rhythms and ornament.

THE RHETORIC
OF LATE-MODERNISM
A Pictorial Essay

The following pictorial essay is an attempt to illustrate some rhetorical figures that are the basis for classifying Late-Modern architecture, below. Every architectural language has its own peculiar rhetoric which the historian and critic must define. To do this he might borrow terms from many sources not only from music, art and literary criticism. Here semiotics and classical rhetoric have been added to this heterogeneous list. The use of an architectural language has as much to do with counterpoint as perspective, synecdoche as proportion and thus any extensive appreciation of a building will naturally make use of these various terms.

HANS HOLLEIN, *Retti Candle Shop,* Vienna, 1965.

MODERN (1920-60)	LATE-MODERN (1960-)	POST-MODERN (1960-)
IDEOLOGICAL		
1 one international style, or 'no style'	unconscious style	double-coding of style
2 utopian and idealist	pragmatic	'popular' and pluralist
3 deterministic form, functional	loose fit	semiotic form
4 *Zeitgeist*	Late-Capitalist	traditions and choice
5 artist as prophet/healer	suppressed artist	artist/client
6 elitist/for 'everyman'	elitist professional	elitist and participative
7 holistic, comprehensive redevelopment	holistic	piecemeal
8 architect as saviour/doctor	architect provides service	architect as representative and activist
STYLISTIC		
9 'straightforwardness'	Supersensualism/Slick-Tech/High-Tech	hybrid expression
10 simplicity	complex simplicity-oxymoron, abiguous reference	complexity
11 isotropic space (Chicago frame, Domino)	extreme isotropic space (open office planning, 'shed space') redundancy and flatness	variable space with surprises
12 abstract form	sculptural form, hyperbole, enigmatic form	conventional and abstract form
13 purist	extreme repetition and purist	eclectic
14 inarticulate 'dumb box'	extreme articulation	semiotic articulation
15 Machine Aesthetic, straightforward logic, circulation, mechanical, technology and structure	2nd Machine Aesthetic, extreme logic, circulation, mechanical, technology and structure	variable mixed aesthetic depending on context; expression of content and semantic appropriateness towards function
16 anti-ornament	structure and construction as ornament	pro-organic and applied ornament
17 anti-representational	represent logic, circulation, mechanical technology and structure, frozen movement	pro-representation
18 anti-metaphor	anti-metaphor	pro-metaphor
19 anti-historical memory	anti-historical	pro-historical reference
20 anti-humour	unintended humour, malapropism	pro-humour
21 anti-symbolic	unintended symbolic	pro-symbolic
DESIGN IDEAS		
22 city in park	'monuments' in park	contextual urbanism and rehabilitation
23 functional separation	functions within a 'shed'	functional mixing
24 'skin and bones'	slick skin with Op effects, wet look distortion, sfumato	'Mannerist and Baroque'
25 *Gesamtkunstwerk*	reductive, elliptical gridism, 'irrational grid'	all rhetorical means
26 'volume not mass'	enclosed skin volumes, mass denied; 'all-over form' – synecdoche	skew space and extensions
27 slab, point block	extruded building, linearity	street building
28 transparency	literal transparency	ambiguity
29 asymmetry and 'regularity'	tends to symmetry and formal rotation, mirroring and series	tends to asymmetrical symmetry (Queen Anne Revival)
30 harmonious integration	packaged harmony, forced harmonisation	collage/collision

Classifying Movements According to Thirty Variables

Architectural historians usually classify movements according to a few stylistic categories, but here a more extended list of variables is used to bring out the complexity of the situation: the overlap, contradictions and differences among movements. Each variable may need a gloss to be fully understood. For instance the term 'utopian and idealist' in regard to architectural form, contains the notions that the Modern architect claimed to think out each design problem 'afresh' with regard to 'human needs' which generated a 'programme' of 'functions' which was 'socially responsible'. Each notion, indicated by inverted commas, may have been assumed by a Modern architect, and many were enunciated by the theorists and propagandists. If one tried to list all of these notions the list would become impossibly large – in fact a book. So the chart is, like any diagram, reductive.

The pictorial essay concentrates on *style* and *design ideas* since it would be vain to group visually according to *ideological* categories; but ideology is nonetheless important for understanding these movements. The order of the essay does not follow the order of the list and leaves out many categories, again for visual convenience and logic.

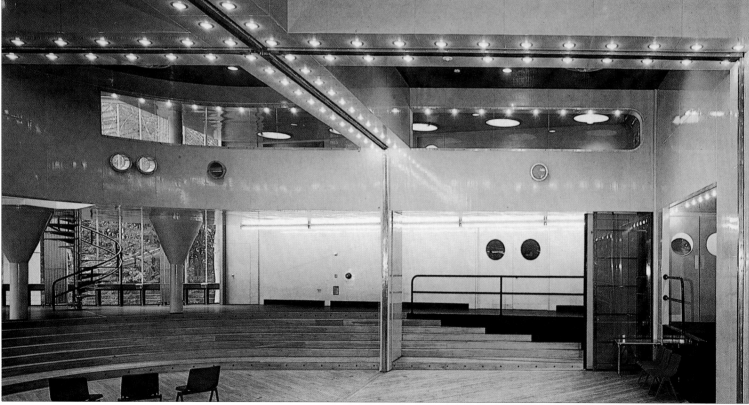

Wet-look Distortion, Synecdoche

The fantasy inherent in Slick-Tech revolves around the notion of effortless mechanical control – which is well-illustrated by James Stirling's giant executive toy produced for Olivetti. Like their sleekly wrapped domestic equipment with its continuity of plastic over all parts, the auditorium undulates in all-over GRP. This rhetorical device, synecdoche, a substitution of part for the whole or one element for others, is coupled with a distortion of syntax (no usual joint, or gutter, between wall and roof) and a dissonance of colour (cream clashing mushroom). Thus an odd but interesting building. Note the gentle curved S-panels and their resemblance to the 'soft-touch Divisumma eighteen portable electric printing calculator' as well as the classical cyma. On the inside panels placed between Hollywood lighting fixtures can be raised or lowered to create one of four possible conditions. This 'Yellow Submarine', with its Master Control Room under the portholes, uses other explicit metaphors and this places it on the road to Post-Modernism; whereas the Hyatt Regency in Dallas seems to be unconscious in its imagery (the animalistic head and tail, the Art Deco set-backs would seem to be fortuitous). Both buildings emphasise the slippery wet-look and the distortions caused by a reflective surface that is not entirely flat. This produces highlights and again a sfumato which is not displeasing. The Supersensualist fascination with gloss and reflection is most apparent in the hotel – 'the largest glass sculpture in the world' as one Texan put it. Other images – 'a glittering Xanadu', 'a pile of silver' – also focus on the silver glass which, incidentally, blinds rush-hour traffic when the sun shines. Typically James Bondian fantasies are also served by this grand hotel: the 200 foot atrium highlights the space-capsule elevators; the revolving restaurant, on its 560-foot tower, is surrounded by a network of krypton bulbs (they last eleven years) which can give Dallas, on occasion, two full moons at night.

WELTON BECKETT ASSOCIATES, *Hyatt Regency Hotel*, Dallas, 1976-9.

JAMES STIRLING, *Olivetti Training School*, Haslemere, 1969-73

Hyperbole of the Second Machine Aesthetic

The syncopation of a rhythmical beat both horizontally and vertically, in the Sky Building and Pompidou Centre, ends in a striking rhetorical figure: a giant ship or sexual shape, or three exclamation points, and mechanical ducts. Rhythm contrasts with figure, a steady beat with a theme, and this binary opposition, as always, provides some drama. Without it the syncopations have no climax. Indeed the Pompidou Centre gains its power through contrast, as the glimpse between masonry Paris shows. Place it in suburbia, or repeat it, and its point would be lost (as in the countless 'Eiffel Towers').

Graves, Schulitz and Gehry exaggerate their 'figures' to the point of architectural hyperbole. A balcony cantilevers way out over pine trees; a window rotates away from the wall, cantilevers, and drops its glass; a box tumbles through the wall and roof and knocks a 'chicken coop' (chain link) askew. Colour, in these cases, just underscores the hyperbole. The yellow sun sails accentuate the depth of the balcony; the red, green and white of the window set the forms in rotation; and the grey corrugation, red wood and silver pipe outline a trapezoid seen spiralling backwards.

In some of this play, or 'architecture about architecture', we have the autonomy that critics such as Manfredo Tafuri and Peter Eisenman see as typifying recent work. Such gratuitous expression has, however, characterised architecture of every period. Decorative flourishes, redundant structures, walls with no ostensible purpose have always been used as part of the expressive repertoire. What perhaps makes these expressive elements Late-Modern is their insistence on uselessness.

MICHAEL GRAVES, *Alexander House*, Princeton, 1971.

HELMUT SCHULITZ, *Architect's House*, Los Angeles, 1976-7

YOJI WATANABE, *Sky Building 3*, Tokyo, 1967-9.

FRANK GEHRY, *Architect's House*, Santa Monica, 1978.

RENZO PIANO & RICHARD ROGERS, *Pompidou Centre*, Paris, 1971-7.

Extreme Articulation, Syncopation, Contrast

Following on directly from the last work of Le Corbusier at La Tourette and Chandigarh was a style of architecture much more articulate than the International Style. For the white, planar skin volumes of the twenties, it substituted the three-dimensional facade, the *brise soleil,* the 'push-pull' of precast concrete elements, the expression of shuttering work in concrete, indeed the expression of all possible functions. This extreme articulation could, on occasion, enunciate more than one might want to know. The Boston City Hall expresses its council chamber, mayor's office, stairway, entrance, 'dentil frieze' of offices, brick podium, heating ducts, pour joints, shuttering marks, and 'problem of the corner' (or rather *'solution'*). The Clark University Library expresses even more. This 'action architecture' was, however, a welcome change from the 'dumb box', the blank office block which had the temerity to express just its vacuous self.

A primary means of articulation was the precast constructional unit and its repetition between dark voids. By varying the size of the unit and the rhythm of voids quite a syncopated melody could be played as in the Boston City Hall. Here we find a steady beat of top windows (a,b,a,b, etc) amplified below in larger windows (A,B,A,B, etc) while it both continues (on two levels) and is interrupted (on one). This interrupted rhythm and fugal counterpoint were inspired by Stravinsky's music, among other sources. The clash of opposing themes, in all its sculptural weight, is reminiscent of Michelangelo. There are even Mannerist inversions at certain points: a stair hangs out over space instead of resting on supports, and a concrete fascia makes two right-angled turns to end up as an oversized balcony.

Extreme articulation is obviously an enjoyable exercise with its suspensions and counterpoint, staccato and trills and it shows Late-Modernism moving towards a Baroque *complexity* and nineteenth-century *contradiction* – these two keywords of a poetics not confined to Post-Modernism. One can even see it operating on the planning level in a project by Denys Lasdun which sets zig-zag themes against saw-tooth themes, each being a transformation of the other. Even the details pick up the staccato.

KALLMANN, McKINNELL & KNOWLES, *Boston City Hall,* Massachusetts, 1964-9.

DENYS LASDUN & PARTNERS, *University of East Anglia,* Norwich, 1964.

JOHN JOHANSEN, *Clark University Library,* Worcester, Massachusetts, 1966-89.

Structure/Construction as Ornament

Modern architecture expressed structure 'honestly'; Late-Modern architecture expresses it 'vehemently', and the same is true of construction. As a result both necessities approach the condition of ornament, although often on a gigantic scale. Stirling's work will set two basic constructional themes at forty-five degrees to each other, or at some division of this number, producing as a result dissonant angles of twelve and a quarter degrees. The Leicester building uses a constructional diagonal to finish off the top (avoiding direct light) and to produce a giant 'dentil frieze'. Lasdun repeats structural and constructional windows at such length that they induce the hypnotic effects of Op Art and Islamic ornament. Against this endless rhythm are set regular counterbeats, above and below, which indicate circulation and other functions.

John Portman's horizontal ornaments (the tiers of walkways) have become a cliché of Hyatt Hotels. They are made mildly interesting by set-backs which would have been still more interesting if the geometry wasn't entirely predictable. Not surprisingly the greatest structural ornamentalists come from the Miesian School in Chicago. Helmut Jahn uses steel I-beams and triangular roof trusses with a precision and virtuosity that the master would have admired (while perhaps keeping reservations about the strong red, white and blue colouring). Very simple logical parts are taken to a Late-Modern extreme, repeated at length and given a separate colour to accentuate their difference (*the* truss, *the* curved glass panel, *the* translucent fibreglass panel, *the* white I-beam etc).

JOHN PORTMAN, *Hyatt Regency Hotel,* San Francisco, 1970-2.

HELMUT JAHN with C F MURPHY ASSOCIATES, *Saint Mary's Athletic Facility,* Notre Dame, Indiana, 1976-7.

DENYS LASDUN, *Institute of Education and Law Building,* London, 1965 and 1973-8.

JAMES STIRLING, *Leicester University Engineering Building,* 1964 (with JAMES GOWAN).

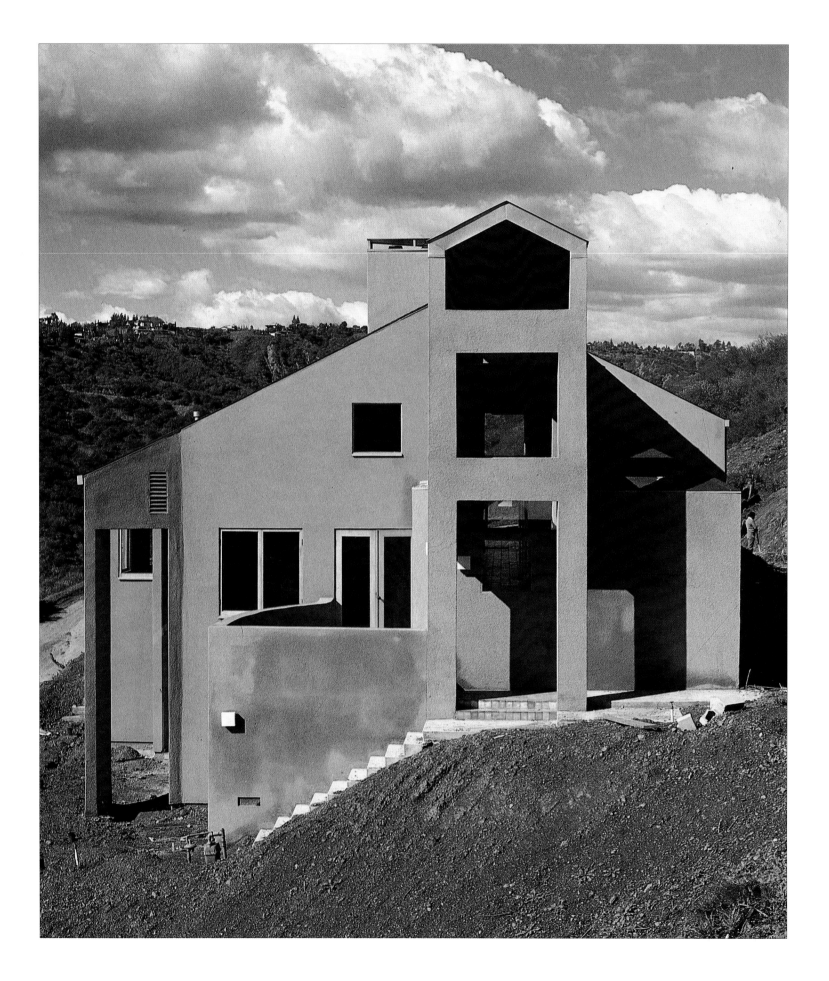

Complex Simplicity – Oxymoron

If Modern architecture tended to a distilled simplicity where many requirements were purified towards simple, regular shapes, then Late-Modernism, keeping this overall simplicity, allows it to become irregular and complex. The mixture 'complex simplicity' is itself a form of oxymoron, a slightly paradoxical juncture of opposed qualities. These may be, as in the buildings illustrated here, complicated plans unified by the simplicity of one or two materials, or perhaps a picturesque outline made up from regular, primary solids; or a simple monolithic image made complicated in its details. All of these latent contradictions exist to give interest to the work. They also keep it comprehensible.

For instance Roland Coate's and Eugene Kupper's houses have such complicated plans and volumetric shapes that they need a simple material to unify the variety. Coate uses grey concrete on almost every surface thus equating opposites (wall and roof, stair and bedroom), another oxymoronic trick. It produces a building that is an interpreter's delight (cave/house, German bunker/Aztec altar). The three concrete cylinders that press up, enigmatically, into nothing; are they totems, columns in search of a roof, fortified pillboxes or a place where a ritualised Californian sacrifice is performed?

The Nilsson House develops a complicated Post-Modern spatial sequence but pulls this together with a repetitive structural spine and constant use of painted stucco. The forms are basically simple (pitched roof, flat wall, void in shadow) but the composition is asymmetrical and relates to the slope of the hill. The complex space is layered at right angles to this slope, but as a series of simple parallel walls. The variety of window size is great, but the voids have a similar shape. Complex simplicity is a series of 'yes, but' statements.

ROLAND COATE, *Alexander House*, Montecito, 1972-4.

EUGENE KUPPER, *Nilsson House*, Los Angeles, 1976-9.

Reductive, Elliptical Gridism

The reduction of architecture to a few concerns obviously has a rhetorical power, the power of an unambiguous slogan. If this truism found expression in Mies' slogan 'less is more', then certain Late-Modernists have exaggerated this idea even further to 'less than less is more than more is nearly nothing'. Some Late-Modern buildings of Norman Foster simply try to disappear while others seek to reflect the environment. The power of these statements is not only what they say boldly, but also what they leave out. Slogan alternates with ellipsis, an overpowering, single image with an absence of signs, a silence. The duality – slogan/silence – is often built with the most neutral of forms, the grid.

Philip Johnson's twin towers in Houston illustrate these rhetorical figures: two trapezoidal, minimalist black wedges are placed ten feet apart on edge. A tension is inevitably created between the two sharp angles pointing, aggravatingly, towards each other (and ten feet apart for three hundred feet!). From some angles of view the diagonal chamfers of the roofs line up to produce a 'double-whole', one building out of two. This paradox is further heightened by another. The space between the two forms is itself a mirror image of the two wedges – a third building that isn't there. So the ellipsis suggests a positive presence, the silence another slogan (to Pennzoil). Add to these visual illusions the grey-bronze reflective glass and the way the surface changes with the changing light and one feels an aesthetic vertigo that is opposite to the stability of Miesian skyscrapers. Where they were harmonious, Johnson's are dissonant; where they repeated a visual element to create order, Johnson multiplies the repetitions (between towers and space frame) to create optical vibrations. Although the Pennzoil is a simple building (or two) like Modern skyscrapers it is a complex simplicity, responding to the boring box with distortions, exaggerations and ellipses. Kurokawa responds to the boring box with the Big (boring) Box, an extreme example of reductivism. Here a scaleless, blank white structure hides the most extraordinary *mélange* of functions within, including a place to shoot ducks by laser gun. However, the promise of these functions is revealed by the rotating facade images and the single view in, which, because it is the only void in the building, has an undeniable pull.

PHILIP JOHNSON & JOHN BURGEE, *Pennzoil Place*, Houston, 1974-6.

KISHO KUROKAWA, *Big Box*, Tokyo, 1974.

Extreme Isotropic Space – Redundancy and Simplicity

A consequence of Le Corbusier's Domino system and the Chicago frame, the neutral grid of caged space, is the 'free plan' of Modernism. Exterior and interior walls are freed of their load-bearing role and thus movable partitions can articulate the interior without constraint. As structural spans become wider (over 100 metres of column-free space are now spanned in auditoria) and the structural supports are placed on the outside, a complete isotropic, sandwich space developed – the same in every direction. The mammoth American department store, with its endlessly disappearing perspectives, became an ironic harbinger of an egalitarian society to come. Mies' endless, 'universal' space was becoming a reality, where ephemeral functions could come and go without messing up the absolute architecture above and below. The complete disjunction between pure architecture and pure commerce was thus achievable, with each realm given its complete autonomy.

When one sees the stunning results of Norman Foster all these wishes and ideas seem to have come true. Ethereal open space flows between a green ground (with its electrical outlets) and a baffled ceiling (with its mechanical and lighting grid). Open space shoots to the blue-tinged wall and beyond out into the view of the townscape, around pure white columns, across yellow bands of spotlit toilets, down the side of heating and cooling ducts to arrive at infinity. The wall disappears (or at least only thin glass fins remain as structure). The feeling of freedom and openness, like riding the freeways of Los Angeles, is conveyed. The space has an awesome grandeur, at once relaxing and sublime, comforting and endless, a modern equivalent to the wide-open prairie or the *parterres* of Versailles.

And yet one's enthusiasm for isotropic space is tempered by the fact that, on occasion, it can be excruciatingly boring, known at a glance, and the knowledge that it results quite logically from the most rapacious exploitation of real estate. The maximum coverage for the minimum expense is a dull sandwich. Perhaps this knowledge doesn't altogether kill our enjoyment of isotropic space, any more than the knowledge of Louis XIV's totalitarianism ruins our experience of Versailles; but it certainly dampens the enthusiasm. Extreme isotropic space thus comes as a *double-entendre*: the sign of the sublime and the rapacious. It also gains power through an effective use of two rhetorical devices – redundancy and simplicity.

The Wills Tobacco Factory, the largest column-free space in Europe when built (180 by 90 metres), shows the functional advantages of isotropic space: even light distribution, easy to clean, and complete flexibility to move machines and production lines around when the technology changes. Helmut Jahn's Bartle Hall gives 60,000 square metres of column-free exhibition and meeting space (two city blocks). Again services occur on the sides and above in the triangular truss and below in the floor. The seats and trusses augment the feeling of infinity. The Pompidou Centre with a clear span of forty-eight metres also features the giant truss, but this time as an elegantly polished silver zig-zag with padded elbows. The conventions of Late-Modern space are thus established: gridded, endless and isotropic, with perimeter supports and services top and bottom. In this space is a collage of changing activity.

HELMUT JAHN with C F MURPHY, *Bartle Exhibition Hall*, Kansas City, Missouri, 1977.

YRM with SOM (Chicago), *Wills Tobacco Factory*, Bristol, 1969-74.

NORMAN FOSTER, *Willis Faber Head Office*, Ipswich, 1972-6.

RENZO PIANO & RICHARD ROGERS, *Pompidou Centre*, Paris, 1971-7.

Extreme Repetition

Repetition is itself a rhetorical category which in language might result in alliteration and assonance. Architecturally analogous recurrences also occur which correspond to the repetition of an initial consonant (a marked structural member for instance) and the resemblance of proximal vowel sounds (the similar voids or 'back-ground' between structural members). *Extreme* repetition is then just another Late-Modern exaggeration of an existing rhetorical device. Modern architecture justified repetition as a productive device, whereas now that it is exaggerated we can more clearly appreciate its persuasive power. The effect of extreme repetition may be monotony or a hypnotic trance: positively it can elicit feelings of the sublime and the inevitable because it so incessantly returns to the same theme. A musical figure repeated at length, such as that in *Bolero,* acts not just as a form of mental torture but as a pacifier. Repetitive architecture can put you to sleep. Both Mussolini and Hitler used it as a form of thought control knowing that before people can be coerced they first have to be hypnotised and then bored. Too many curtain walls in New York seen in succession can cause the same kind of sickness that too many Bridget Rileys in London seen in succession have caused.

Philip Johnson's IDS Center staggers steel set-backs in ziggurat profiles. This central court is covered by a veritable orgy of ice-cube holders buzzing away in perspective overhead and reflecting, in part, off the staggered sides. The three sky-scrapers repeat their exterior structures at length. The World Trade Center shoots a stainless steel filigree of Gothic arched mullions 110 storeys, and it contains 10,000,000 square feet of rentable office space. *That* is late-Capitalist extreme repetition (the Empire State Building had a mere seventh of the capacity). The CBS Building gives a sublime zoom of dark granite canon shots into the sky, looking much larger than its thirty-eight storeys. The reason is that this 'structural wall' is made from sharp-angled members which catch the light, create chiaroscuro, and thus accentuate the speed of ascent. The John Hancock Center is another external load-bearing building, a 'trussed tube' which accentuates the speed and distance by perspective diminishment.

MINORU YAMASAKI, *World Trade Center,* New York, 1962-7.

EERO SAARINEN & ASSOCIATES, *CBS Building,* New York, 1965.

BRUCE GRAHAM & SOM (Chicago), *John Hancock Center,* Chicago, 1967-9.

PHILIP JOHNSON & JOHN BURGEE, *IDS Center,* Minneapolis, 1972-5.

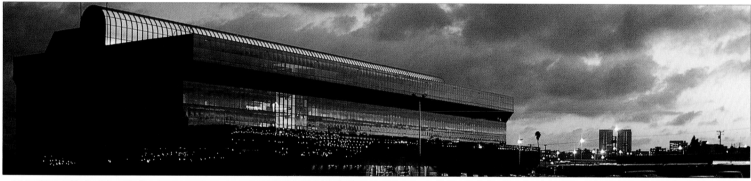

Slick Skin/Op Effects

As the curtain wall continues to evolve towards 'less and less' (mullion) it approaches the ideal condition of a membrane, a surface that can flow easily around corners and over rooftops as if it were skin, or at least inflatable plastic. This diminishes the role of the four facades and the frontality inherent in most buildings. It tends to isolate the building as a free-standing sculpture and do away with all scaling devices – even the mullion disappears in the pure glass skin building. Furthermore it decreases the mass and weight while enhancing the volume and contour – the difference between a brick and a balloon. All these aesthetic effects are made possible by developments in stronger glass walls, thinner gaskets and various new means of assembly including small clips and glass structural fins. They lead to a Late-Modern curtain wall, the slick skin membrane which is quite different from the Modern one with its strong vertical divisions, its 'skin and *bones*'.

In England Norman Foster has pushed the technology furthest with his 'Big Black Piano' in Ipswich. The partially reflective black glass moves around the existing site-lines with a kidney or piano shape. From some angles the building reflects the environment, from others it is transparent and, depending on the light, opaque and translucent. Thus four visual conditions are provided with the same material with the added quality of sfumato – the gentle merging of one condition into the next. In Los Angeles the 'Silver' architects Anthony Lumsden and Cesar Pelli have developed the same four conditions of the slick skin, playing on the resulting ambiguities sometimes for their semantic meanings.

Anthony Lumsden, for instance, has designed a bank which alludes to the silver standard and an area of investment where this bank's money is possibly headed. The oil-slick surface, the strong phallic rise of the shaft from a heavier base, and the ripples of one side suggest a series of meanings without naming them, like the symbolic poetry of the nineteenth century. Pelli's 'Blue Whale' is equally wide in its metaphorical overtones, some of which may be a fortuitous outcome of purely slick skin decisions. For Pelli's primary concern is with developing the inherent aesthetic characteristics of the membrane; above all its ambiguity and paradox.

The 'Blue Whale' is actually, with its metaphors and Mannerism, half a Post-Modern building. The Mannerism consists in setting up a series of expectancies in order to break them. For instance a linear, extruded shape would indicate the circulation takes place frontally and on an axis down the spine – but it actually occurs on the diagonal (see plan). The semi-cylinder protruding from one side and its circular platform would indicate a vertical circulation ramp. But actually vertical circulation is by escalator at right angles to these circles. This view also shows the typical mixture of transparency, relection (and therefore a doubling of the cylinder), opacity and semi-transparency; in other words aesthetic, Mannerist ambiguities which support the semantic ones. It would be wrong to assert that Post-Modernism alone is Mannerist: indeed Late-Modernism is by its very definition an exaggeration of Modernism, and almost all the thirty definers mentioned at the outset have a Mannerist component. The night view of the 'Blue Whale' shows how Mannerist the slick skin can be under varying conditions as it turns, chameleon-like, an orange-black and yellow.

ANTHONY LUMSDEN, *Branch Bank Project*, Bumi Daya, 1976.

CESAR PELLI & GRUEN ASSOCIATES, *Pacific Design Center*, Los Angeles, 1975-6.

NORMAN FOSTER, *Willis Faber Head Office*, Ipswich, 1972.

Enclosed Skin Volumes

The slick skin membrane allows, as we've seen, a greater scope for volumetric articulation than the previous curtain wall, an aspect which these skyscrapers share. Breaking down the apparent mass, density, weight of a fifty-storey building is part of the motive. One way this is done is by destroying the four-square morphology, by adding extra facades, by making a facade of the corner and a broken one as Philip Johnson has done; or by fragmenting the facades vertically or on both planes. The latter building by Kevin Roche treats aluminium and green-tinted glass as if it were a light material, by folding it in and out and cantilevering large chunks of it. This is probably the most distorted 'skyscraper' to date and it represents a genre that should be given another metaphor ('skyholder'?). At the base the entrance flares out to welcome the user with its 'stiff upper lip'. (Late-Modernists are just beginning to articulate these traditional symbolic centres and the results are somewhat rigid). A distortion of scale is also created by the horizontal treatment of aluminium frame. The familiar floor to floor module is reduced to one-third its usual size, thus making the building both bigger in appearance and smaller in grain.

The 'skywedge' in Boston also uses the all-over slick skin module to break down the scale and weight. Its designer, Henry Cobb, describes a motive behind using reflective glass which is shared by all these architects. 'The reflective glass is very important. It's a contrast to the stoniness of the church. It emphasises the disembodiment of the volume. It's very important to the principle of this building that you read it as a plane in space, not as a volume. What would be destructive is an obtrusive volume.' But the mirror-building has other important meanings. It fits into the environment by reflecting it. It provides a precious, sparkling quality akin to the use of gold and stained glass in previous periods. It works both literally and metaphorically as a sign of narcissism. Lastly it is oxymoronic in its very nature, providing the ultimate contradiction 'truth/falsity'. It holds 'a mirror up to nature' truthfully, but at the same time creates a *trompe l'oeil* and distortion.

HENRY COBB & I M PEI, *John Hancock Tower*, Boston, 1968 and 1973-7.

JOHN PORTMAN, *Bonaventure Hotel*, Los Angeles, 1974-6.

KEVIN ROCHE & JOHN DINKELOO, *One UN Plaza*, New York, 1974-6.

PHILIP JOHNSON & JOHN BURGEE, *IDS Centre*, Minneapolis, 1972-5.

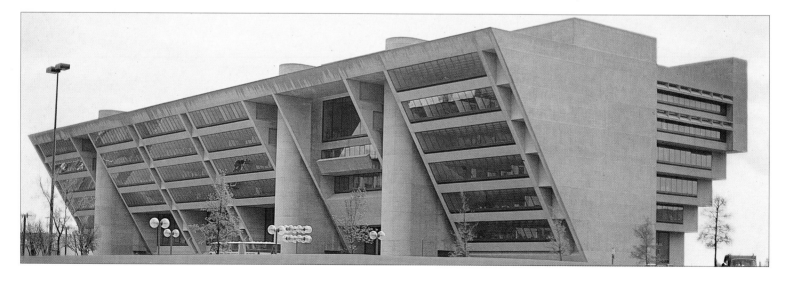

Sculptural Form and Hyperbole

Following the lead of Le Corbusier's Ronchamp (1955) Post-Modernists started to develop a metaphorical architecture, while the Late-Modernists took off in a more purely sculptural direction. During the sixties they used reinforced concrete in a very expressive way and this trend continued to develop into the seventies. Sometimes the results are overwrought and confusing; most often they make use of the rhetorical device hyperbole, extravagant forms meant to impress by their grand, overpowering sweep. One finds this sort of architecture at World Fairs, Olympic stadia, airports and city halls. Kenzo Tange's buildings for the 1964 Olympics contrasts two sets of sweeping forms, hanging in a gentle catenary curve, with a taut tension member and then an emphatic concrete mast, smacked into the ground like an imperious exclamation point. This too is slightly curved in a 'Japanese' way, so the whole is an extravagant statement of national identity. Eero Saarinen's Dulles Airport is more confused in its historical reference, but equally dramatic in its use of curve and counterthrust. The rhetorical figure, developed from an earlier scheme of Le Corbusier, sets an inward hanging catenary curve against an outward pushing row of zoomorphic columns. The way these break through the roof plane and both push and hold, reminds one of arms and heads and craning necks, clearly hyperbolic figures.

A more extreme use of a structural shape is I M Pei's upside-down pyramid in Dallas. This city hall also relates to earlier structures of Le Corbusier in reinforced concrete but treats the material with a hard, flat, precise surface more like steel than masonry. All sorts of extravagant figures are combined with this extraordinary shape: smooth glass walls incline on the same inward slope of the concrete giving a paradoxical identity to these two materials. Strong verticals smash through the slope to emerge on the roof and set up a basic antithesis to the horizontals. Then three different marching figures are juxtaposed – the stagger to one side mounting towards a heavy cantilever, and the two front diagonals, one in alternating bands, the other in indented blocks. All these create a predictable climax at the heavier cornice.

If Pei is here using form more as hyperbole than to communicate specific ideas or functions, this is also true of his Christian Science Church Center. This work has an excessive degree of drama, like St Peter's, and functions in a comparable way to the Vatican for the Christian Scientists although on a smaller scale. Landscaping literally becomes part of the buildings. Water is treated as a flat, architectural plane to double the images, and extensive linear forms are taken up in the Sunday School Building. This last has a huge double cornice surmounting a colonnade and flare, finished with a steel-like concrete. Precisionist concrete is the oxymoronic figure most identifiable with Pei.

Denys Lasdun also has developed the late style of Le Corbusier in a highly sculptural direction. His National Theatre achieves its fitting drama with a series of highly contrasting figures: four strong horizontals, earth-like strata for Lasdun, are punctured by three emphatic verticals, two of which merge at the top. This combination of smash and elision, of the dynamic and peaceful, is played in other keys. For instance flat, quiet walls are placed on a frontal axis to be offset by the buzz of coffers and lift shafts placed on the diagonal. All of these emphatic contrasts are made even richer by the overall *contrapposto*, the play of heavy forms placed in an asymmetrical, moving balance. It's a grand, abstract drama quite appropriate for England's national theatre.

DENYS LASDUN, *National Theatre*, London, 1964.

I M PEI, *Christian Science Church Center, Sunday School Building*, Boston 1964 and 1971-3;

KENZO TANGE, *National Gymnasium*, Tokyo, 1964.

EERO SAARINEN, *Dulles Airport*, Chantilly, Washington DC, 1962-4.

I M PEI, *Dallas City Hall*, 1966-78.

Unintended Humour – Malapropism

Late-Modernism, like most periods of architecture, has not consciously sought architectural wit. Nonetheless there are moments of humour, especially when the architect is in deadly earnest and trying hard to make the great architectural statement. This loosens the critical faculties that usually bind him and something amazing issues forth. It may be 'Pereira's prick' rushing skywards from a heavily trussed base, or 'Bunshaft's donut and pill box' for the Hirschorn collection in Washington, or 'Bunshaft's travertine printer/calculator' for the LBJ library in Texas. This last also resembles an Egyptian tomb (with its ramp and battered walls) and a portrait of the late president in a grim mood. 'Watanabe's dragster' is clearly trying to be funny with its extended exhaust pipes, captain's deck and upward tending balconies; Japanese have seen it as a 'rooster' and a 'sinking ship'. Finally two great Late-Modern malaprops together at Yale, 'Saarinen's whale eating Johnson's tootsie rolls', quite conventional labels attached by the students. In all this work we have a combination of reduction and hyperbole, two rhetorical devices leading unwittingly to a third, malapropism, an endearing trait to have.

*   *   *

If we summarise the major rhetorical devices of Late-Modernism we find them focusing around a set of recurring figures. Extreme repetition, with its attendant qualities of alliteration and assonance, sometimes leads to boredom, but it is intended to produce feelings of awe and the sublime. Repetition is mostly of structure as ornament. Extreme articulation, with its strong contrasts, forced harmonisations and syncopations, sometimes produces verbosity but it is intended to enliven the surface of a building and communicate the complexity of functions within. Synecdoche, a substitution of part for whole and whole for part, is evident in the all-over use of a single material and module. It is often combined with reduction, ellipsis and oxymoron, the paradoxes which result from the use of new materials ('transparent/opaque' glass) and new structures ('safe/unsafe' hyperbolic-paraboloids). Also sfumato, the indistinct movement from light to shadow, results from the new glass technologies and the slick skin plastics. The new spatial type, extreme isotropic space, leads to a host of rhetorical qualities: redundancy, simplicity, ellipsis and reduction. Metaphor is sometimes intentional in the Second Machine Aesthetic with its 'exoskeleton', its 'skin, bones and arteries'. Hyperbole and malapropism are at least implicit in the emphasis on sculptural form divorced from conventional meaning.

If we attend to these major rhetorical devices within the language of Late-Modernism we can begin to understand its character. its relative autonomy and concern for purely architectural meanings, and its ambivalence with respect to Late-Capitalism and advanced technology.

WILLIAM PEREIRA, *Transamerica Building*, San Francisco, 1968-72.

GORDON BUNSHAFT & SOM, *Hirschorn Museum*, Washington DC, 1973.

YOJI WATANABE, *New Sky Building No 5*, Tokyo, 1971.

GORDON BUNSHAFT & SOM, *Lyndon Baines Johnson Library*, Austin, Texas, 1968-71.

EERO SAARINEN, *Ingalls Hockey Rink*, 1957 and PHILIP JOHNSON, *Kline Science Center*, New Haven, 1964.

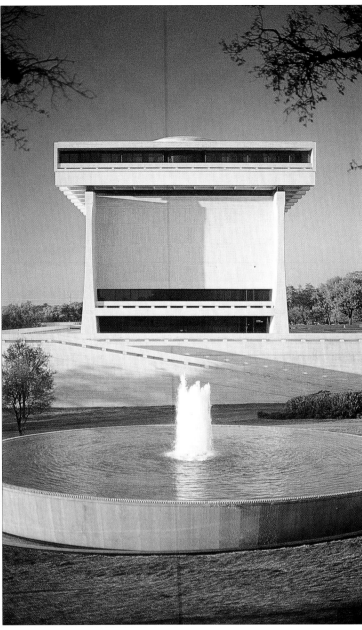

THE HIGH-TECH MANIERA

There are three anomalies to High-Tech architecture which will amuse anyone with a taste for irony. Its major exponents are the British instead of the Germans, Americans and Japanese who, actually controlling most of the high-tech industries, ought to have developed the style. Secondly, a distinguishing feature of the Anglo-technophiles is that they hate the label everyone persists in attaching to the work – as well as the very notion of style. Any finally, High-Tech isn't High-Tech in the sense of the computer or aerospace industries where new products are developed systematically. Rather it's a craft-based tradition which modifies pre-existing industrial systems to achieve one-off, costly (if beautiful) solutions. A corollary to the last point is that, in spite of all appearances to the contrary, it often doesn't work very well.

This, of course, is highly annoying to the public, because the style looks functional. But exposing the structure and services is expensive at the outset and, except for the ease of replacement, expensive to clean and maintain in a pristine shape. When the Pompidou Centre gets dirty, breaks down and corrodes, as sadly all machines must, people feel cheated of the perfectly-working mechanism. Conceived in clear logical diagrams, often rendered in axonometrics which express the 'how and why' of every part, and with each detail designed like a Brancusi, High-Tech promises a perfection which is religious at its core. The statement of Mies (borrowed from Aquinas and Flaubert) that 'God is in the details' expresses the sentiment quite well, and anyone who is not inspired by the way a Foster or Rogers will elegantly solve the details of a structural joint, is probably deficient in some higher spiritual faculty.

The problem, however, is that High-Tech architecture is not presented as a religious or even stylistic mode. Rather it is justified for its supposed functional virtues and presented as a necessity – in short as the embodiment of a materialistic philosophy. This is stupid and a pity. It leads to the ultimate anomaly 'transcendental materialism', an oxymoron perhaps best expressed in Ben Johnson's paintings of these buildings because they have no function whatever except to move us emotionally and intellectually – a form of 'spiritual exercise' for those committed to the higher reaches of the High(Church)-Tech. If only architects and critics would present this work as a matter of cultural and stylistic *choice,* rather than necessity, then its particular virtues could be understood and improved. But virtually all the exponents of the style deny it is a style and admit only to a rational or utilitarian approach.

The reasons for this suppression are both legitimate and unfortunate. Talk of aesthetics and architectural language loses jobs, or worries the client who would rather, in most cases, hear about economic and functional matters. Also an architect like Norman Foster genuinely believes his 'architecture is about people', as he often says, and when 'people questions' are being discussed aesthetics slips into the back-

FOSTER ASSOCIATES, *Stockley Park,* England, 1987-9. High-Tech has evolved, in the late eighties, away from polychromy and exposed pipes and towards a more sober silver or white aesthetic – here articulated by a window-wall of radiant white dots.

ground, or is considered beyond discussion. Hence the style, or formal language of High-Tech, has not reached a very high level of articulation and the rules of its generation and perception have, for the most part, been suppressed. This is a great pity as style is the principal means by which most people perceive and mediate other important questions, those of ambience, function and ideology. Indeed, the label High-Tech causes as much embarrassment among its practitioners as the notion that it is a style, an understandable reaction when one remembers that Modernists have always been reluctant to admit they use conventions and follow each other's example. It thus becomes a particular duty of the critic to make these conventions explicit and open to public debate and choice. Among the few basic rules of High-Tech, the following six seem most essential:

1   Inside-out

The services and structure of a building are almost always exposed on the exterior as a form of ornament or sculpture. This expression of the 'servants' versus the 'served' was formulated by Louis Kahn in the sixties and has been justified by the Metabolists and Richard Rogers for allowing fast-changing technology to be easily modified without disrupting the interior. A prime example is Rogers' Inmos factory, which makes an extraordinary feature of its H-section, top tension members, and ducts, which hover over and jump above two sheds. The long horizontal spans are used for the production of silicon chips and thus require the cleanliness and openness of a giant surgery, something that justifies the exoskeleton. Here the harmony of a central spine and two flanking arms is set off by a cacophony of repetitive incidents – cross-braces, H-masts, silver ducts, steel cables and trusses – which are determined mostly by functional, not visual, logic. From a distance, or very close up, the beauty and sensitivity of design are clear, but as often with High-Tech work the middle-distance view is confusing; a jumble of competing cues.

As for the principle in general, critics contend that exposing services and structure is expensive, resulting in dirty pipes and an inversion of symbolism: the 'servants' have taken over the house from the 'served', technology has dominated living – something that is of course appropriate at Inmos, where the factory wished to express its technological supremacy.

2   Celebration of process

With the emphasis on constructional logic, the 'how, why and what' of the building, its joints, rivets, flanges and ducts, there is an intellectual clarity which is pleasing for both the child and scientist in us. Critics point out that where everything is expressed, nothing is hierarchical, and confusion reigns. This riotous expression, however, has been supported as 'Real-Tech' and 'Wild-Tech', the truthful extravagance of current, complex technology. Jürgen Kunz, who has worked on one of the longest developing High-Tech schemes, the New Medical Faculty Building in Aachen, 1969-84, speaks of the straightforward expression of how things work – 'the boiler-suit approach' – as preferable to the more elevated or rarefied attitude of others.[1] This building, which looks like an oil refinery on top of public housing, expresses its service towers, ducts, red walkways, structure, and glass wall with a matter-of-fact garrulity that is, he claims,

WEBER, BRAND AND PARTNERS, *New Medical Building*, Aachen, West Germany, 1969-84. The 'boiler-suit' approach of High-Tech.

RICHARD ROGERS PARTNERSHIP, *Inmos Factory*, Newport, Wales, 1982, exterior. Its H-section, top tension members and ducts hover over and jump above two sheds.

popular with the patients and doctors. The results are indeed 'wild' and tough, the kind of honest expression of organisation he admires in the work of Hannes Meyer, and one alleviated only by the staccato use of a De Stijl colour range.

The celebration of process often extends to things that are seen to work, and in High-Tech the mechanical plant and travelling crane are as omnipresent as the pediment and keystone are in Classical architecture. At Lloyd's, blue cranes give the impression of a building site undergoing eternal construction, while at the Hong Kong Bank grey maintenance cranes are powerful visual metaphors, especially when they all point in the same direction like anti-aircraft guns on a battleship.

An impressive feature of Norman Foster's work, more pronounced than with any other living architect, is the way he will come up with an ingenious idea and remodel it time and again until it both works, and looks, like a perfected mechanism – an industrial component modified by years of patient research. A case in point are his famous sunscoops on the Hong Kong Bank, a computerised set of motorised mirrors on the south side of the building which follow the sun and bounce it on to a further set of reflective surfaces. These are aluminium with a low brightness so that the bankers and their customers will not be blinded. The concept of providing natural light to the nave of this cathedral of commerce is brilliant. However, in practice, the results are less impressive, producing a dim, metallic, rather than sunny, glow. The way the internal reflectors hang in space gives rise to equally mixed feelings. Here, an extraordinary piece of industrial craftsmanship is made dramatically visible on both sides, designed 'all the way through' and looking like the cross-section of a Futurist double-dome combined with a biplane. Unfortunately it cuts through a cross-brace visually and gives an awkward, bent profile to the top of the nave. Thus the sunscoops' virtues and faults are apparent and it has to be asked whether, at several million pounds, they really provide 'value for money' – a question only the client can answer.

Nevertheless many hostile critics presume they know the negative answer. Buildings which promise technical proficiency and celebrate process invariably over-spend on flexible partitions that are never moved: travelling cranes which rarely lift a window-cleaner; triple-glazing (at Lloyd's), a six-million pound extravagance with the debatable social purpose of equalising the air and heat inside the whole building; photo-sensitised cells and motorised louvres (at the Sainsbury Centre these give a nice light for viewing the art, but also a visual and acoustic buzz); all-over aluminium panels (which at the Sainsbury Centre have now corroded and will have to be put right at a cost of two million pounds, the original building cost being three million). All buildings deteriorate and suffer continual problems, but those which symbolise technical excellence and innovate on so many levels at once are particularly prone to censure when things go wrong. There's no conclusive proof that High-Tech buildings have more problems than others, but there's certainly much evidence that people feel let down when, inevitably, some mechanisms fail. Here we come to the heart of the problem: by celebrating and symbolising process, High-Tech promises more than any technology can deliver – perfect functioning and long-term efficiency.

3 Transparency, layering, and movement

These three aesthetic qualities are dramatised almost without exception. Extensive

FOSTER ASSOCIATES, *Hong Kong Shanghai Bank*, Hong Kong, 1980-6, maintainance cranes. Powerful visual metaphors all pointing in the same direction like anti-aircraft guns on a battleship.

Hong Kong Shanghai Bank, internal aluminium light reflectors. A computerised set of modernised mirrors which follow the sun and bounce it on to a further set of reflective surfaces.

RICHARD ROGERS PARTNERSHIP, *Lloyd's*, London, 1979-80. A well-proportioned repetition of horizontal ducts tapering as they slide past the smoothly finished concrete column.

use of translucent and transparent glass, a layering of ducts, stairs and structure and the accentuation of moving escalators and elevators characterise the High-Tech building. At Lloyd's and the Hong Kong Bank the intricate mechanisms of the see-through escalators are a delight to watch as they roll effortlessly on, although they have an unintended effect of making one feel on the perpetual treadmill of business.

With Shin Takamatsu, the Japanese designer, movement systems are frozen in sculpted steel and given a slightly menacing imagery: for a dental clinic he crosses a bullet train, gunboat, and washing machine, perhaps intending to reveal the aggression latent in having one's teeth pulled. By contrast, Richard Rogers at Inmos breaks up the structural mass into a filigree of densely layered and cheerful elements. The repetition of blue trusses, green ducts, red doors, and grey structure make the space shimmer and dance with a staccato beat close to jazz. The effect is like being inside a Rococo church made from Meccano parts – no wonder the readings of this kind of architecture are divergent.

Critics invariably contend that contemplative areas are hard to find when transparency, layering, and movement are accentuated – a criticism it's hard to refute. What this suggests is the development of High-Tech towards an architecture of contrast. Perhaps in the future these designers will also provide quiet, balanced rooms and even incorporate fabrics and furnishings which dampen the sound and welcome the body. Such oppositions would forestall criticism and actually heighten the sharp intensities so essential to the style.

4 Bright, flat colouring

At the Pompidou Centre and Inmos, Rogers uses bright colours in much the same way engineers do – to distinguish different kinds of structure and services and allow them to be easily understood and effectively used. These distinctions, which make great sense in an oil refinery and the engine room of a ship, have led virtually everyone to compare the High-Tech building to these two industrial types, as if these were the only ones relevant. They have also led Rogers and Foster to simplify the colour-coding of their later buildings towards the Silver Aesthetic and integrate ducts and structure within a palette of greys.

But this use of colour has an associational component which is as strong as its functional necessity in engineering. Bright yellows, red, and blues are the colours of industrial machinery, sports cars, ships, and tractors, indeed most technical objects of the present. These colours are thus associated with the present and future tense, a world of objects free from the restraints of the past. Foster's 'umbrella columns' for Renault refer, of course, to Renault yellow, but they are also uncontaminated by any reference to past architecture, to masonry columns. Instead of having a base, shaft and capital, each column has become a mast of joists and cables articulated, of all places, near the middle. The canary yellow further displaces the structure from tradition and, by extension, from the hidebound conventions of class and etiquette. This is an architecture of ships and holidays, of activity liberated from the weight of a past felt to be crushing.

Critics naturally point out other associations, the bright yellow of car clamps or the dehumanised repetition of factory work, and aver that flash colours are *démodé*, brash,

SHIN TAKAMATSU, *'Ark' Dental Clinic*, Nishina, Japan, 1982-4. Movement systems are frozen in sculpted steel and given a slightly menacing imagery.

FOSTER ASSOCIATES, *Renault Distribution Centre*, Swindon, England, 1982-3. An architecture of ships and holidays, of activity liberated from the weight of a past felt to be crushing.

and tiring. Clearly colour in High-Tech is highly politicised. When Prince Charles compared BDP's Plessy factory to a Victorian prison, the company decided to re-paint the bright red columns a metallic grey to blend in rather than contrast with the aluminium cladding.[2] After trees grow up around the factory the architects hope to restore the original colour.

5   *A lightweight filigree of tensile members*

The thin steel cross-brace is the Doric column of High-Tech – its visual sign and ordering device – and has been so ever since Foster and Rogers completed the Reliance Controls Building in 1967. A cluster of cross-braces in the air can look like a cat's cradle of spindly lines, making them often the most expressive device in a shed-like structure. The tent shape held by cables, especially influenced by the work of Frei Otto, is second only to the cross-brace in popularity and like the bright colours, is valued for its associations with sailboats and ephemeral, informal living – again in opposition to traditional masonry.

Michael Hopkins, for instance, has covered the Schlumberger Research Centre in Cambridge, England, with white translucent fabric hung from black steel cables. The double curves and puckered points of this surface present an extreme contrast to the hard steel, so much so that – if we are allowed to have anthropomorphic feelings here – it looks like a rather painful experience for the skin. Critics fault such structures because they dissolve mass and don't define positive space. That is, of course, their point. They imply endless extension and openness to change, a flexibility and free movement which are supposedly impossible with contained space. In particular, at Hopkins' research centre, the open plan is meant to provide the 'maximum contact between scientists of different departments' and as much 'activity on display' as possible.[3] In this case the tensile cables and translucent fibre-glass membrane are well justified.

6   *Optimistic confidence in a scientific culture*

Underlying High-Tech building is the Futurist promise of an unknown world waiting to be discovered. This results more in a method of working – an attitude towards materials, colours, and invention – than a compositional principle. However, this often leads to open, indeterminate space and picturesque fragmentation or, at worst, a chaotic massing and confusion of cues. When High-Tech fails as architecture it does so because too many inventions are attempted at the same time, and multiple options and flexibility are taken to an extreme. Furthermore, the emphasis on teamwork and the simultaneous creation of separate parts of a building means that sub-assemblies tend to dominate over considerations of the building as a whole.

*   *   *

Since High-Tech architects have not formulated an explicit aesthetic, or any rules of composition, their overall designs either remain rather primitive – a vague Classical symmetry here, a stepped profile there – or jumbled, especially at the top and bottom of a building. Lloyd's and the Hong Kong Bank are both crowned with technical

FOSTER ASSOCIATES, *Hong Kong Shanghai Bank*, Hong Kong, 1980-6.

MICHAEL HOPKINS, *Research Centre for Schlumberger*, Cambridge, England, 1985-6, and *Mount stand at Lord's Cricket Ground*, England, 1985-7. Sports and research and development are two activities which in our time have conventionally adopted a High-Tech manner.

elements – cranes, mechanical boxes, and a heliport – but from most angles these tops are a buzzing confusion of indeterminate forms, a direct consequence of representing indeterminacy. At the base most High-Tech buildings hit the ground abruptly with no transition. The knife-edge joint, the clean contrast, the absence of podia, mouldings and transitions are all a clear consequence of the anti-Classical assumptions. But the avoidance of certain formulae does not necessarily create anything positive.

What comes through in the best designs, however, is an exuberant optimism about the future of a scientific and technological culture. The Hong Kong Bank is seen by a critic as 'A Building for the Pacific Century', reflecting the Pacific Rim's growing dominance of world trade; moreover, many of its sub-assemblies, such as the flooring panels, were specially designed systems adapted from space technology and the aircraft industry.[4] Stansted Airport, designed by Foster Associates and Ove Arup and Partners, represents the conjunction of this optimism with a building type suited to it: a clear, elegant engineering solution for a function that is plausibly in a High-Tech style. Other appropriate types are those micro-chip factories and research centres mentioned above and the many industrial commissions which Foster, Rogers, Hopkins et al have managed to build or currently have on the boards.[5] It's worth stressing that most often High-Tech is indeed used on stadia, sports halls, airports, factories, and large multi-purpose centres – jobs for which society acknowledges it is 'the right style'. The conflict arises when it is applied to offices, housing, schools, or traditional building types, or used near landmarks such as St Paul's Cathedral. Here there is a problem. High-Tech architects are reluctant to admit their approach isn't universal and only too quick to condemn anything that looks remotely familiar as lacking in confidence and vigour. If, however, they actually seek universality, then their buildings will finally address questions of style, composition and suitability to context which have heretofore been suppressed.

FOSTER ASSOCIATES WITH OVE ARUP AND PARTNERS, *Stansted Airport*, England, 1986. A clear, elegant engineering solution for a function that is plausibly in a High-Tech Style.

FOSTER ASSOCIATES, *Hong Kong Shanghai Bank*, Hong Kong, 1980-6. Exuberant optimism about the future of a technological culture – 'A building for the Pacific Century'.

BEN JOHNSON
AND TRANSCENDENTAL
MATERIALISM

Most Westerners are brought up to believe that the spirit is noble and the flesh is weak. This elevated idea the Christians took over from Plato and it enjoyed a long, two thousand year reign until in the nineteenth century, with the advent of perceivable material progress, the doctrine was inverted. For a century, philosophers and Darwinians questioned the reigning idealism and tried to establish a form of materialism – dialectical, historical or evolutionary – in its place. Their efforts had some success – the mass-produced Ford, the Russian Revolution and today's genetic engineering – but by and large Westerners continued to believe in their various types of idealism. The point of Plato's parable about the cave is that truth is hidden and the ideas behind things can only be discovered by enlightened reason. Ideas are transcendent and universal and only reveal themselves after much intellectual effort, whereas things of this world, 'shadows on the wall', are evanescent, a matter of opinion and probably dirty as well. Ideas are permanent and beautiful; things are plural and ugly.

This *idée reçue*, while questioned by Karl Marx and American consumer society, has had unexpected support recently, at least of a negative kind. For twenty years the West has become increasingly aware of the limits of progress and since the 1960s there have been pressure groups of the most specialised kinds devoted to stopping the negative consequences of material growth. Materialism now means car graveyards, Chernobyl and the imperial power of Japanese multinationals. Technical progress has become a goal of national survival, an all-too-real Darwinian struggle, not something to be enjoyed. Hence the rarity of that nineteenth-century breed, the technological optimist, the Brunel and Paxton, the engineer who could produce the poetic expression of the latest technology and at the same time innovate pragmatically.

In England, of all unlikely places, the High-Tech style is more highly regarded professionally than elsewhere, even America and Japan. Norman Foster and Richard Rogers, Gold Medalists and Royal Academicians, are undisputed world leaders of this approach, but there is also a group of eminent followers such as Nick Grimshaw and Michael Hopkins. Ben Johnson is the artist equivalent of these designers and like them he stands above his foreign competitors in the same genre, for instance the photo-realists, Robert Cottingham, Jack Mendenhall and Ron Kleeman. The only American who achieves similar controlled effects is Richard Estes and his *Escalator*, 1970, might have been painted by Johnson; but Estes is ultimately interested in the ambiguity of urban reality, Johnson in its transcendence.

Festival Building, 1988. Acrylic on canvas, 200 x 200 cm (80 x 80")

105

An ironist would explain this strange historical situation by the theory of compensation. Since England was the first to have, and then the first to lose, industrialisation and its benefits, it inevitably would produce an élite school of painters and architects to reflect on these former glories and compensate for their absence, just as the Romantic poets were the first to celebrate untrammelled nature (as it was going under). This McLuhanite explanation has something to recommend it, but I think there's a more powerful reason: the persistence of the Modernist tradition.

Ben Johnson, like the High-Tech architects, was brought up on a diet of Le Corbusier and Fernand Léger, Purism and the Precisionism of the American Charles Sheeler. It is true there was variety in that diet, for Johnson the Expressionism of Max Beckmann, but it had one overpowering ingredient: the promise of technical beauty. This, of course, is more than the engineer's aesthetic, 'truth equals beauty': it is basically a spiritualisation of the machine, a transcendental materialism. People who fail to see the difference between this and functionalism will miss the point of Johnson's work (not to mention Foster et al). Spiritualisation of matter, transcendental technique, is a criticism of utilitarian architecture as well as other approaches. In Johnson's paintings, for instance, one will find no people, no evidence of society, time, use or all the contingent signs that make every-day reality so real. This 'otherness' or estrangement relates his work to the Magic Realism of the 1970s, which is also unreal with realistic means, but it has a polemical edge as well. The absence of clutter, Johnson's scrubbing of Paxton's Crystal Palace or editing of Foster's swimming pool is like Ozenfant and Le Corbusier's 'vacuum-cleaning period of architecture', a moral purification rite. He has taken out the notice boards, danger signs, weathering and grease spots (it is a Plant Room!) and intensified the architect's idea of purity even more. Where Foster is abstract and repetitive with his structure, Johnson is positively dazzling with his jazzy geometric green coffers and staccato grid. The dance of these thin horizontal and vertical lines is an intense vibration and it is all contained within a classical one point perspective oriented frontally to the picture frame. The water is as well behaved as the machinery, becoming a perfect mirror, or even the abstract plane of the canvas.

Johnson thus implies a relation between his virtuosic technique and the subject of his painting. Both are based on detailed description and knowledge, creating an image or building with the aid of working drawings and photographs and painstaking labour. Johnson may use a spray gun to give buildings the desired resonance of colour, while Foster will, characteristically, borrow techniques from a variety of specialised sources, but they both conceive of technique as transcendental, as the equivalent of St Ignatius' Spiritual Exercises. Johnson's studio in West London is as clean as a laboratory and spare as a Calvinist meditation room. Foster hangs Johnson paintings of Foster buildings above his ultra clean floor of Pirelli rubber. Evidently we are dealing here with something more than professional practice and less than a cult.

There are certain recurrent stylistic trademarks. Most Johnson views are

The Crystal Palace Reconstruction 1, 1984. Acrylic on canvas,101.6 × 152.4 cm (40 × 60")

Poolside Reflection, 1984. Acrylic on canvas, 159 × 217 cm, (62.5 × 85.5")

cropped and focused down on a small area of space, the view through a narrow-angle Hasselblad as it were, and the lighting from one side casts crisp shadows. The High-Tech, whether Paxton's, Foster's or Arup Associates', is lightweight steel and there's usually a filigree of cables, tension members and thin mullions which buzz about with cheerful complexity. This is *British* High-Tech, not the robust concrete of Le Corbusier or the chunky gear-wheels of Léger or the flues and grain silos of Sheeler. The time is 6.30 on a clear Summer afternoon of eternity, or night-time at Roger's Inmos after everyone has gone home and one is alone to confront the austere beauty of industrial truth. It is a time before deterioration has set in, before the Pompidou Centre has rusted and been coated with Paris soot, a time even before the Crystal Palace has burned down (although a hint of the fire can be felt in the orange glow welling up from the bottom of the structure). It's a time of promise, of belief in the destiny of the Modern Movement before it all went horribly commercial. It's a time when we could still believe the Victorian engineers were the counterparts of the ancient Greeks: heroic, virtuous, and in control of industry. Time is suspended as a fragment of tough, distanced industrial reality brought into focus for our contemplation.

It may be *Goodman's Yard,* an ambiguous sea of glass and cat-walks, or the repetitive ridge and furrow roof at the Palm House, Kew; a fountain pen *(Mark VI)* or *Castings* or the yellow spider structure of Foster's Renault Centre but whatever the object or place, it is removed, modest, impersonal, almost alienating, but certainly 'other'. These are not the subjects of conventional Still Lifes, nor with the exception of *740/760* (the cross section of a Volvo) the subjects of consumer interest. Rather they are the anonymous beauties of industrial man, the modest and hidden icons for a religion which doesn't exist.

Johnson has been compared by Edward Lucie-Smith with the architectural painters Canaletto, Panini and, even more justly, with the severe abstractionist of Dutch building, Pieter Saenredam. These parallels bring out the common preoccupation with precise forms seen under clear light, the Classicists' ideal, but they also suggest a fundamental difference. Johnson, unlike the Classicist, is not concerned with the social setting and the drama of architecture as a humanising language with its proportions and details related to the body. There are no people in Johnson's work; they aren't good enough. Instead, as in the Still Lifes of William Bailey, objects have taken over the role traditionally reserved for humanity. Bailey has said that his limitation to Still Life and the occasional portrait springs from the agnosticism of the present age which has no 'shared myth'. The bowls and coffee pots depicted in his work are meant, like Morandi's, as a substitute for the significant acts of great men, the most elevated subject matter of traditional painting. He gives these pots a heroic dignity that has an uncanny presence, as if each object were a Renaissance character imbued with a purpose.

In a similar manner, Johnson gives this presence to architecture, at once intelligent and dignified, a substitute for the human realm which is so clearly

Goodman's Yard, 1985. Acrylic on canvas 57 x 86 cm (22.5 x 34")

East Mast with Grid Lines, Beams and Outriggers, 1986. Acrylic on canvas, 95.5 x 119 cm (37.5 x 47")

Central Spine (Inmos), 1985. Acrylic on canvas, 115 x 150 cm (46 x 60")

missing. The 'presence of the absence' of people echoes through these lonely spaces as it does in a Cistercian Church which is no longer used, and one suspects the real root of Johnson's work is not so much architectural as religious painting. Every object is treated with a reverential care and often placed in a grid of space proportioned to the golden section. The geometry of the architecture is painstakingly resolved with the vanishing points and the play of light reminding us of the Gothic fascination with harmony and light metaphysics. With Johnson, these concerns are absolutely obsessive. But here is a paradox; for the subject matter is so obviously secular. Why expend so much devotional zeal on utilitarian objects, is God really in the details of a *740/760 Volvo*?

Such questions have to be asked of Johnson and Foster, the whole High-Tech enterprise and what remains of Modernism in general. Inevitably the answers are sceptical, one can't believe in this faith, however full of promise it may look. Transcendental Materialism is just another chimera, although a highly attractive one to the youth and the large corporations. It is probably the natural ideology of Late-Capitalist and Socialist Society and will continue to flourish well into the next century. But its success brings, as we are all aware, a concomitant failure – progress begets pollution, expectations of transcendence in such an environment bring inevitable frustration. Johnson's paintings might deal with such ironic, indeed tragic consequences in the future as his vision deepens and becomes more complex. As it is now the vision is pure, and a salutory reminder of what it was like to believe in the future before it became the Brave New World, a form of spiritual art which is today all too rare.

Mid East Looking West, 1989. Acrylic on canvas, 120 x 180 cm (48 x 72")

Glazed Arcade (North Harbour), 1986. Acrylic on canvas, 200 x 300 cm (80 x 120")

740/760, 1986. Acrylic on canvas, 198 x 297 cm (78 x 117")

MADELON VRIESENDORP and REM KOOLHAAS, *The Floating Swimming Pool*, 1977. In a serious satire, of which this is the penultimate stage, Constructivist architects escape to freedom and New York in their amazing machine – it is propelled by their synchronised strokes. Ironically, in a new dialectic, 'they have to swim toward what they want to get away from, and away from where they want to go.' When they get to New York this floating pool, an architectural thermometer, is inserted into all the trite, complex and contradictory architecture and, with Neo-Mod simplicity, 'takes the temperature of its decadence'.

SECTION II
SERIOUS JOKES

IRRATIONAL RATIONALISM
THE RATS SINCE 1960

The philosophical problems with Rationalism have long been known, especially in the Anglo-Saxon world. Hence its recent re-emergence as an architectural movement is apt to raise eyebrows. Can these designers really propose a return to principles we know to be questionable and furthermore, ones which have had such a deleterious effect in this century? (Abstract form, endless right angles, and architectural 'truths' which are supposedly universal).

The answer to this question is by no means clear. On the one hand, the architects (known affectionately as 'Rats' since at least 1975) share some of the defects of the Rationalist philosophy – dogmatism, élitism, reductivism – but, on the other hand, they have given this philosophy a new twist so that it often appears ambiguous, surreal and sensible by turns. Like any architectural movement it is made from a heterogeneous corpus of styles and ideas which are only loosely grouped around a common banner. No doubt, some of these architects wish the movement had a different slogan and pennant under which they could fight. A name, a tag, influences the way people look at architecture which is why I propose, half-ironically, the prefix 'irrational'. This Rationalism has always been, in part.

As a philosophy stemming from Plato, Descartes in his more Jesuitical moments and Kant, Rationalism emphasises truths known intuitively to the mind, without any reliance on experience. The *a priori* truths of mathematics, the categorical truths of space, time and causality don't, it was argued, depend on knowing anything about the external world. These self-evident propositions ($2 + 2 = 4$, the laws of geometry and logic) could generate a whole series of deductive truths as long as correct reasoning was followed.

By the same token, Rationalist architects would generate wholly consistent and 'true' buildings if they followed certain general principles in a rational way. The Abbé Laugier said 'if the problem is well stated, the solution will be indicated', a slogan Le Corbusier and other French architects liked to quote. Laugier hoped to generate truthful architecture from the elements of a primitive hut built out of wood. 'Let us never lose sight of our little hut', he needn't have urged. The next hundred and fifty years were spent looking at primitivist construction, designing primitive huts in first-year studies at the Bauhaus and in woodlands away from the city.

'An architect must be able to justify by reason everything he does', Laugier also averred, and it was this proposition which really proved so fatal to the Rationalists. Their assumed truths, like the primitive hut or the grid used for all planning, have always seemed embarrassingly absurd. How could one possibly base a sophisticated urban architecture on such simplistic notions? The successive attempts by Rationalists to find new, indubitable propositions were equally bizarre. An eighteenth-century architect

ALDO ROSSI, *Casa Aurora*, Turin, Italy, 1984-7, view of corner, ground floor and facade detail. Rossi takes up the classical hierarchy in the use of stone-facing for the first floor and the arcaded shops at ground level. Local bricks and stone fit into the Torinese tradition.

SIR THOMAS TRESHAM, *The Triangular Lodge*, Rushton, 1595. With certain historical licence I illustrate this essay in Catholic symbolism as a Rationalist building. Like other buildings of its time, it is an absolutely clear expression of a single idea, in this case the Trinity. Rationalist architecture makes a virtue of reducing form to the expression of a powerful idea which is held dogmatically – witness Boullée, Ledoux, Le Corbusier and Aldo Rossi. Here three triangular gables on each of three sides surround a central triangular chimney. The windows are built from trefoils, so is the door-head with its inscription announcing the theme *tres testimonium dant*. Three floors, countless plays on the owner's name (*tres*-ham) and various other hermeneutic symbols of the banished Roman Catholic mass made this a sermon of high treason. Rationalist buildings are often just as symbolic and geometric.

wrote 'Gothic architecture improved' and tried to do just that by rationally turning the Gothic pier into a Classical Order. Another eighteenth-century Rationalist sought the 'Natural Model' for architecture and inevitably came up with man's ancestor, monkey-man, living in caves. In the twentieth century the same pursuit continued as architecture would be indubitably founded on the firm rock of function, logic, economy and structural determinants. All these vain attempts were motivated by the search for *certainty.* And here we have a deep, underlying psychological motive which runs through all the Rationalists, no matter what their particular truth happens to be.

Before discussing the Rats, I should like to mention the pitfalls of the basic philosophy. In architecture, as indeed most science, it is clear Rationalism won't take one very far since a large part of its creation and realisation consists of endless empirical data. Interviewing clients, using material at hand, modifying design endlessly according to *ad hoc,* contingent requirements – Rationalist architects have always proven themselves weak on these things. In general they are hostile towards public opinion and contemptuous of anything that would disprove their basic assumption. In short they are 'fact-proof', hermetically sealed off from the pollution of reality like a good air-conditioned building. These architects might be called 'reinforced dogmatists'. Their ideology continually reinforces the evidence to which they attend thus strengthening their original belief, much the way reinforced concrete gets stronger and stronger if heated and battered.

Admitting all this quite candidly (unlike their predecessors of the 1930s, the Rats are disarmingly frank), they might point out the following virtues in their position. It is clear, consistent and unlike other architecture, quite passionate and convincing. If architecture is an art that should move and persuade us, then Rationalism is the best style. It is not botched and bungled by petty requirements. It can be quick and decisive, cutting through all the indecision and fog of more democratic design. Finally, in a Rationalist Age, the Age of Science, when all positions are unprovable, it becomes the most credible. People, especially leaders of a field and academics, are most credulous towards anything offered up as rational.

This last argument, however pragmatic, is tasteless and needn't be dwelt upon. The devastating critique of Rationalism is quite enough, and it has been made by Karl Popper.[1] Basically the critique shows that no propositions are self-evident and unquestionable. Contrary to what the Rationalists contend, science develops by subjecting its 'truths', or hypotheses, to constant criticism, or refutation, and it is this continual process of conjecture and refutation which eliminates errors. The Rationalists rarely, if ever, try to refute their own theories; they wouldn't for instance, conduct market research on one of their housing estates, because its truth lies outside society and everyday experience. They have no use for Popper's *Critical Rationalism,* or what is now called the 'sophisticated form of "falsificationism"'. This latter kind of Rationalism tries to falsify its truths and tentatively keep only those which have withstood this test. Rationalist architects have not been prepared to do this.

Hence the Rats are doomed to a kind of beautiful irrationalism, the lyrical and clear expression of propositions which are often as unlikely as Laugier's 'primitive hut'. The beautiful style, which has been going on since at least Boullée and Ledoux, appeals particularly to an élite – a small but coherent group of architects and critics. They have, in this century, produced the supreme expressions of organisation that appeal to the mind: the sublime idealism of Leonidov's structures, the grand organisational sweep of Tony Garnier's *Ideal Industrial City* where every function has a logical place, the well-ordered, and well-scrubbed housing blocks of J J P Oud, almost all the work of Le Corbusier and some of that of Nervi – these are the triumphs of *the style that appeals to thought*. If the Irrational Rationalists have a justification, it isn't in either their truths or their method, but in their ability to make diagrams of ideas exact and exciting.

Many of the themes and problems of recent Rationalism were worked out by the Italian architects in the twenties and thirties. Guiseppe Terragni and the MIAR *(Movimento Italiano per l'Architettura Razionale, 1927)* stated the abstract qualities to be sought: 'The desire for *sincerity, order, logic* and *clarity* above all, these are the *true* qualities of the *new* way of *thinking*' (my emphasis). The 'call to order' is a recurrent call: Paul Valéry made it in his dialogue on *Eupalinos or the architect,* an article which Le Corbusier and other Rationalist architects continually cited. The desire to put architecture 'in order' corresponded quite directly to attempts to order the political universe in the twenties, so it was not surprising that the MIAR often looked to Fascism to give the lead. In fact several Rationalist exhibitions and manifestos were explicitly dedicated to Mussolini, and Terragni's best work – the Novocomun and Casa del Fascio – were implicated in reactionary politics. This sad and confusing connection of Italian Rationalism with Fascism has been well documented by Guilia Veronesi and Leonardo Benevolo and I will not dwell on it except to point out the psychological connection.[2]

Rationalism has *sometimes* proven weak on totalitarianism because they both emphasise order, certainty and clarity, and they both tend to look to a Classical past for inspiration. These common tendencies don't of course mean that Rationalist or Neo-Classical architecture is 'Fascist', but it does mean that in our century they have *tended* to go hand in hand. This connection poses a great semantic problem for architects such as Aldo Rossi, because try as they might to dissociate themselves from Fascist architecture of the thirties, their style is historically tied to it. We know that one dimension of architectural meaning is always historical association, and no one can escape this. All the Rationalists try to resemanticise their style, but they are only partly successful. There is always a tinge about it of Mussolini's Third Rome.

Universals and right angles

The Rationalist architecture of the early sixties was carried on by Mies van der Rohe, Mathias Ungers and his students in Berlin, James Stirling and Louis Kahn. At least, in retrospect, these seem to be the major exponents of ideas and a style that was later to be named in the 1973 exhibition 'Architettura Razionale'.[3] This exhibition took place at the fifteenth Milan Triennale, forty years after the last exhibition with this name.

Mies' work put forward the notion of 'universal space', a neutral, flexible sandwich of space with movable elements that could supposedly incorporate all functions. It also promoted the ubiquitous right angle, a natural result of post and beam construction.

The underlying notion which justifies this, the *a priori* truth of the right angle, is not just based on constructional truth – on vertical loads and horizontal surfaces – it also is one of the ordering systems most easily grasped by the mind and hence claims a

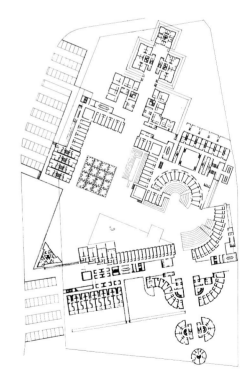

O M UNGERS, J SAVADE and J F GEIST, *Student Hostel Competition,* 1963. Like Hadrian's Villa, a series of different unit shapes are repeated on a series of axes that cross and sometimes collide. Multiple geometries, dissonant angles and a subtle *public* order emerge.

certain psychological universality. Furthermore it is simple. For these sorts of reasons Louis Kahn often started his design with a square plan – what he called the preform or FORM. He would then look for circumstances in the particular brief which distorted this Platonic form – what he called DESIGN. Thus any of his buildings would be a mixture of Rationalist forms (triangles and circles were added) with empirical twists and turns. The particular style he used to represent these buildings in model form was very reminiscent of Palladio's drawings, those flat, smooth surfaces punctuated by dark square holes. Kahn's models looked like Palladio's farmhouses, and they were so starkly seductive that the style of 'cardboard architecture' was formed, influencing greatly the whole Philadelphia School and the New York Five. Even Robert Venturi whose later work was in an empirical style, whatever the local vernacular, practised cardboard architecture.

Another great influence of the early sixties was Hadrian's Villa, an example of urban planning which fascinated not only Kahn, but Colin Rowe, Vincent Scully and Mathias Ungers. Projects began appearing by 1963 which showed the mixture of varied and clashing geometries of this Roman villa.

Hadrian had done in the second century what modern planners could do now: use a limited repertoire of six or eight geometric units and their extensions and then smash them together in a 'juxtaposed manner' (a favourite phrase of the time). Colin Rowe was later to write a book around this compelling image and method, which he called 'Collage City' and 'Collision City'.[4] Part utopian and absolutist and part historical and accidental, Collage City, like Hadrian's Villa, could incorporate anything into its pattern without being destroyed, because its pattern was already rich and fragmented, *but* geometric. It is worth emphasising that Rowe's approach was much more universal than Mies' and other Rationalists' because it was made from a richer repertoire of primary elements and more open to distortion and accepting new uses.

The work of Archizoom and Superstudio in the late sixties took the collage approach and streamlined it back in the direction of Mies. Back was the ubiquitous grid; in fact, 'No-Stop City' and the Continuous Monument had three-dimensional gridded space that was to zoom around the whole world, uniting all activities in a common white rectangle. Superstudio spoke, with barely discernible irony, of the 'sweet tyranny' this would induce in people admiring the grids. Archizoom spoke about 'isotropic space', homogeneous sandwiched space which would be well serviced like a supermarket and just about as neutral and boring. They considered this a subversive proposition to a consumer society – taking its ultimate building type and the pressures towards conformity to their absurd extremes. Rationalists have always loved an argument pushed to absurdity, especially if it starts from a self-evident truth.

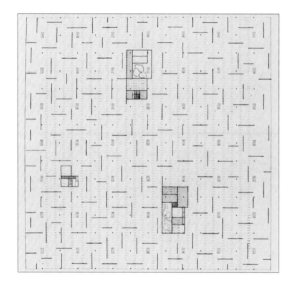

ARCHIZOOM, 'Homogeneous Living Diagram' *No-Stop City, A Climatic Universal System*, 1970. An endless Cartesian space with recurrent partitions, columns and services. The models of supermarket and parking lot are used with a mixture of irony and love. Isotropic space is both the death and resurrection of architecture.

SUPERSTUDIO, *Collage*, 1966. Continuous Monument in Spain, and *Diagram*, 1966, the 'sweet tyranny' in admiring the grid.

Reduction to archetypes

About 1968, Aldo Rossi's projects started to have a great influence in Italy, and elsewhere in the student design world. In a sense they had a profound impact for precisely the reason that the schemes of Archizoom, Superstudio and the New Brutalists did: for pushing the nihilism of consumer society so far that it actually became poetic. This paradox of meaning through anti-meaning is underlined by all critics of Rossi whether they praise or attack him. They all respond to the ambiguity of

Il gioco della morte.

Il cimitero di Modena – Aldo Rossi 1972

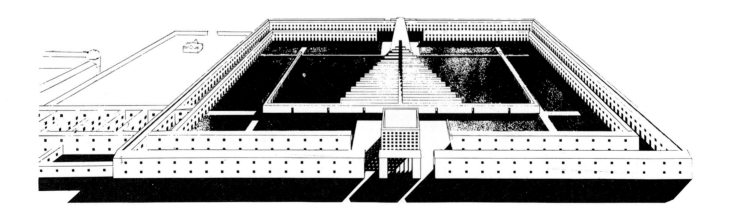

portraying death, silence and alienation with such ruthless consistency and remorseless repetition that these primary meanings are partly transformed.[5]

The experience of the Modern architect in Italy has always been closely associated with death. Several Rationalists were killed in concentration camps, others designed monuments to patriots, so it is not surprising that mortuary themes and death-camp overtones constantly inform their work. One of Rossi's most important schemes, the project for the Modena Cemetery, 1971, is next to the Lager of Fossoli, a place of commemoration for those who died under Fascism – and this cemetery has a sanctuary for the war dead and the partisans. It's a cube with black square windows opening on to a void – sort of mass housing for the dead, in a De Chirico style (even with a pitch black shadow drawn in the empty piazza). Endless straight lines and repeated arcades enclose this sacred image of stillness. A squat cone juts up on the main axis, reminiscent of death-camp chimneys, but this awkward cone is not for 'the final solution' – it's a monument to 'the common grave'. The fury that such ambiguous images can inspire in people should be compared with the anger that Lena Wertmuller's *Seven Beauties* generated. She also used the images of an extermination camp for their ambiguous beauty, and like Rossi, is inspired by a kind of metaphysical gloom.

Rossi's images are not necessarily pessimistic, although they have been compared even by favourable critics such as Vittorio Savi to mental hospitals; Rossi himself is inspired by galleries, arcades, silos, factories and farmhouses in the Lombard country-side. In his additions to the working-class area in Milan, the Gallaratese neighbourhood, he has produced a Modern version of the traditional tenement corridor, which, he says 'signifies a life-style bathed in every-day occurrences, domestic intimacy, and varied personal relationships'.[6] The only problem with this characterisation is that few people would see it; most would compare it with engineering works, tunnels or roadworks, as Rossi has admitted in the same article quoted above. Or they might say it signifies 'barracks', 'social deprivation' and *'l'homme machine'*. In point of fact Rossi's language is so reduced in signification that it is read in diametrically opposite ways: by the élite, by critics such as Manfredo Tafuri, as 'emptied sacredness', as 'a discourse on itself', and by the public or hostile critics as 'quasi-Fascist' and 'cemeteries and prisons'.

Tafuri answers these critics with a kind of miraculous escape clause contending that Rossi can rise above historical associations, like an architectural superman, because his architecture is autonomous, free from contamination: '. . . the sacred precision of his geometric block (the Gallaratese) is held above ideology and above all utopian proposals for "a new lifestyle";' or: '. . . The accusations of Fascism hurled at Rossi mean little, since his attempts at the recovery of an historicising form exclude verbalisations of its content and any compromise with the real.[7]

How does Rossi manage this disappearing act, this superhuman feat which has eluded every other architect? By using a 'syntax of empty signs', by 'the law of exclusion', by reducing the Classical language of architecture even beyond the purity of Fascist Stripped-Classicism. Such extreme nudity ravages the mind of certain critics and makes them suspend their usual scepticism in a conversion that can only be termed religious: 'emptied sacredness', they aver.

Well, it may be too obvious to mention, but Rossi's forms *are* bivalent: sacred and

ALDO ROSSI, 'House of the Dead', *Modena Cemetery*, 1972, and *project for the Modena Cemetery*, 1971. Along the four massive walls and under them is the columbaria; in the centre, stepped shapes are the ossuaries; in the green patches the burial ground. The cone represents the common grave while the sacred cube is for the war dead and partisans. The symbolism is as strong in its own way as Thomas Tresham's triangle.

all too real, sublime and prison-like, heaven and the concentration camp, and I don't see any point in denying both aspects since Rossi himself so clearly plays on both sets of meanings. This duality of extremes is slightly titillating, if not provocative, and I personally find his work full of a terrifying loneliness and claustrophobia which is not undesirable in a painting. Some of his best architecture is painting. The same is true of another Rationalist, Massimo Scolari, who also claims the 'autonomy of architecture' from ideology and historical contamination.

Such autonomy is possible only under extreme and artificial conditions: when the perceiver abstracts himself in time and space from a building, brackets off its contextual setting and concentrates on the distortions of the language itself. Within these limits he can experience the building as a unique aesthetic act, an act which furthermore just refers to itself, or to its own internal relations (void against curved barrel vault etc). It is this kind of meaning towards which Rossi and Scolari aspire, hence their celebration of the monument as the most architectural of building types. 'Distributive indifference belongs to architecture . . . the architecture of maximum precision – ie that of monuments – offers potentially the maximum freedom.'[8] We are thus back in the Surrealist world of Mies where any function can be poured into the same semantic form.

Historicist Rationalism

The one area where the Rationalists aren't altogether irrational is in their treatment of urban form. Several of them, particularly two brothers from Luxembourg, Robert and Leon Krier, have mounted well observed attacks on the devastation of city fabric. They criticise all the forces, whether economic or ideological, which have destroyed the texture of cities and they have proposed quite elegant alternatives which patch it up or create new wholes.

> The debate which both Robert Krier and myself want to raise with our projects is that of the urban morphology as against the zoning of the planners. The restoration of precise forms of urban space as against the wasteland which is created by zoning. The design of urban spaces, both traffic and pedestrian, linear and focal, is on the one hand a method which is general enough to allow flexibility and change and on the other hand precise enough to create both spatial and built continuity within the city.[9]

Basically the Krier brothers follow Camillo Sitte's notions of articulating continuous urban space as a negative volume that flows and pulsates and reaches a crescendo around public buildings. This, as against functional separation and the forces that tend to make each building a freestanding, embarrassed monument. At Echternach Leon Krier inserts a traditional arcade and circus, using the existing morphology of the eighteenth century to create an identifiable spine to the town and a culmination of the entrance route on the existing abbey. Height, scale, silhouette, building material are all compatible with the existing fabric, although accentuated to give a new emphasis to the public realm. Leon Krier uses the traditional aerial perspective of tourist maps to stitch these forms together. The image which results is reminiscent of eighteenth-century Bath and it is with such master builders as the Woods that the Krier brothers bear comparison. They are inheritors of a great tradition which was broken in the twentieth century by, among others, the previous Rationalists.

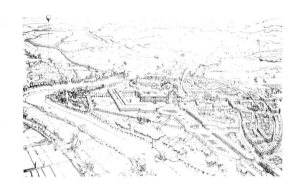

LEON KRIER, *High School at Echternach*, 1970. Krier takes this medieval and Baroque city and accentuates its fabric sympathetically as shown by this tourist perspective. The existing Baroque school is doubled and a glazed corridor is placed between the two halves. Then this Baroque facade is varied to form a main entrance boulevard that focuses on the existing church (which is transformed into a community house). Sportsground, park and a circus are added. Note the quaint 1920s technology, the bi-plane and balloon monument to Leonidov – typical Rat symbols.

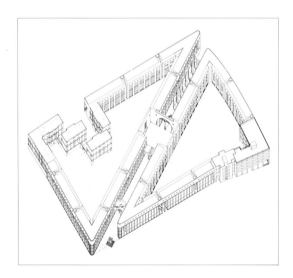

LEON KRIER, *Royal Mint Square Housing project*, 1974. A very sympathetic bit of city stitching and patchwork that nevertheless has a grand urban scale reminiscent of Bath. A diagonal route bisects the site, saving several existing buildings, keeping the street fabric and creating green triangular courts. A 'public room' with entrance portico on one side and gate to a car park on the other is in the centre of the pedestrian way. Various 'poetic' elements are placed along this route such as the cypress trees and four telephone booths.

Leon Krier's competition entry for the Royal Mint Square Housing, 1974, is in my view, the most sympathetic urban scheme of the Rationalists. It preserves traditional London street patterns and a few existing buildings, and incorporates those elements in a new pattern which cuts diagonally through the block. Thus two triangular courts and a central avenue are created which remain free from motor traffic; and the public realm is very subtly introduced in the form of arcades and a public square in the centre. Krier introduces several touches reminiscent of Le Corbusier and his *objets à réaction poétique:* a set of four telephone booths grouped together as a raised altar, existing trees, a gate and portico entrance to the 'public room' and a row of cypress trees. These elements are set along the avenue to punctuate its otherwise rather repetitive syntax. Like all the Rats, Krier is obsessed by long, linear sight-lines as if the city should afford endless opportunities for target practice.

Both Kriers extend their historicism to all periods including the recent past, so their buildings tend to be ironic juxtapositions of various references rather like the collage cities already discussed. The work of Le Corbusier, James Stirling, Palladio, Leonidov and De Chirico is incorporated or transformed in fragments to provide hermeneutic texts for the initiates to decipher. In-group jokes (a head-waiter serving up Le Corbusier's head, like Holofernes, while James Stirling scratches his head in consternation) as well as barely disguised Communist slogans decorate their public realms. Robert Krier, in his Siemer House near Stuttgart plays with Expressionism and the black and white architecture of the twenties. Black-edged skylights and black voids punctuate white stucco cubes with a nearly complete symmetry. The Rats have reintroduced symmetry ironically, along with the white International Style that had previously banished it.

The most successful historicist, at least in terms of public recognition, is Ricardo Bofill and his group from Barcelona (Giscard d'Estaing described him as 'the finest architect in the world' and Bofill is not even French). They have produced housing in a variety of historical styles varying from neo-Gaudíesque through neo-vernacular to neo-Gothic (housing in the shape of a cathedral – what occupies the high altar? Nothing). Bofill and his partners have consciously embraced the Rationalist position, so that now one can speak of a Paris-Rome axis to the movement that includes peripheral centres in Berlin, Barcelona, London and New York.

For Bofill the Rationalist historicism means the free use of endless Roman arches, peppered with a few columns, Gothic windows and cypress trees. At Walden 7 (a hill of housing satirising the dystopia of B F Skinner) Bofill has used a very intricate geometry on a vast scale to induce true basic responses: claustrophobia on the inside and agoraphobia on the outside. When one is on the eighteenth floor, on one of the bridges overlooking a fountain at ground level, and the wind is whistling through a twelve-storey opening cut into the hill, then vertigo is the proper response. Bofill has proven popular because he makes picturesque use of the Rationalist style, always varying the surface and usually painting it a strong colour, so his work contrasts strongly with the grey mass housing it is meant to supplant.

Very often Piranesi's prison sketches are invoked as a source of Rationalist poetics, and with Bofill more than the others, you feel you are back in this delightful madhouse of the eighteenth century. Appropriately his office is moving into one of these phobic

RICARDO BOFILL, *Walden 7*, Barcelona, 1972-5. A man-made hill of twenty storeys with twelve storey holes punched through it and precipitous bridges across the open courts within. The red tile and repeated curves set up a very sensual rhythm.

PETER EISENMAN, *House 11*, an example of 'cardboard architecture' finished in 1969 for Mr and Mrs Richard Falk, Hardwick, Vermont. A structural square grid and a virtual grid interact along with a series of logical (but arbitrary) rules: diagonal sheer, inversion of themes, gradation of partition size, graded ascension of floor levels from one side to the other. Some of these rules are 'marked' on the outside for those who care to read the building with the transformational diagram in their hand.

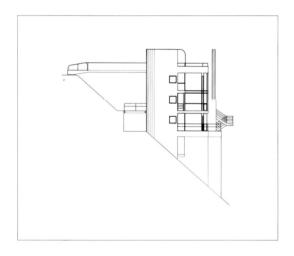

RICHARD MEIER, *Douglas House*, Harbor Springs, Michigan 1971-3. Using a Corbusian syntax of independent structural frame, entrance ramp and double height space, this building, like Eisenman's, represents layered space on its facade. Mullion lines take up, for instance, balcony points and column lines. Meier has given a bent wall on the entrance side which allows space to flow vertically and sideways across four levels – outdoing Corb at his own game.

RICHARD MEIER, *Douglas House*, Michigan, and *Smith House*, Connecticut, 1965-7. Layered space, distorting syntax, or architecture making a comment on previous architecture.

buildings, a converted concrete factory that already is *The Architect's Dream* come true (endless vistas of pure form, grand space and cypresses, cypresses, cypresses on the roof!).

In America, Rationalist historicism got a champagne breakfast with Arthur Drexler's exhibition at the Museum of Modern Art entitled 'The Architecture of the Ecole des Beaux-Arts' (October 1975 - January 1976). Here was MoMA, the mother of the International Style in the USA almost polemicising a return to all the bad old virtues of the nineteenth century: ornament instead of pseudo-functionalism; urbanism and public buildings instead of mass housing; axes and heavy arcades and even heavier cornices as against airy transparencies; a love of detail, colour and history instead of the eternal, black and white present. Such were the implied alternatives. Unfortunately as a coherent polemic Drexler's exhibition never finally took a stand and engaged the present, as it might have done if put on by a Krier or Rossi. But it gave a good indication of which way the wind was blowing up Fifth Avenue, from the IAUS to the MoMA.

Architecture about itself

The acronym IAUS refers to the Institute for Architecture and Urban Studies, an institute run more or less by Peter Eisenman which has been a centre for Rat study for five years. Not only do many of the New York Five meet there, but also Rem Koolhaas, Mario Gandelsonas and Kenneth Frampton, all sometime-Rats, work there. The house magazine, *Oppositions,* always carries one or two articles on international Rationalism by Manfredo Tafuri, Colin Rowe and others.

Eisenman's work, when it is not called Rationalist, is termed 'White' (which it almost always is when not black); 'Structuralist' (concerned with the relation between deep structural grids and surface structural representation); 'cardboard' (not only looking like this homogeneous cardboard, but also like a model); 'virtual' (in the sense of conceptual rather than just perceptual), and 'Corbusian' (actually more like Terragni). There are many labels under which a discussion of Eisenman's work can proceed and all of them are esoteric. He claims to be an élitist, indeed an anti-populist, making architecture more complicated than it has to be in order to engage the mind (and torture it into submission).

His logical diagrams of the way the building is 'generated' (key word borrowed from Chomsky) would please any scholastic; they're more complex than the generation of rib mouldings from fan vaulting. And he presents the finished building as an illustration of the generation! Yes, the buildings are *about* the making of architecture, a process not a result. That is, they represent on the surface very hard to perceive transformations which the interior geometry has undergone.

Ideally speaking, Eisenman would like to show the several arbitrary *rules* which have determined the building: the moving of volumes about on the diagonal, the rotation and inversion of lines and planes, the layering of space and so forth. In short only the *syntactical* elements are represented (or 'marked' in Eisenmanese). The basic marking is that of the surface structure which represents two or three different deep structures (grids, rotated and sheered grids). The basic problem is that no-one, not even Colin Rowe who has greatly influenced this process, can actually understand the markings. They are too ambiguous, and coded with too many possible referents to choose

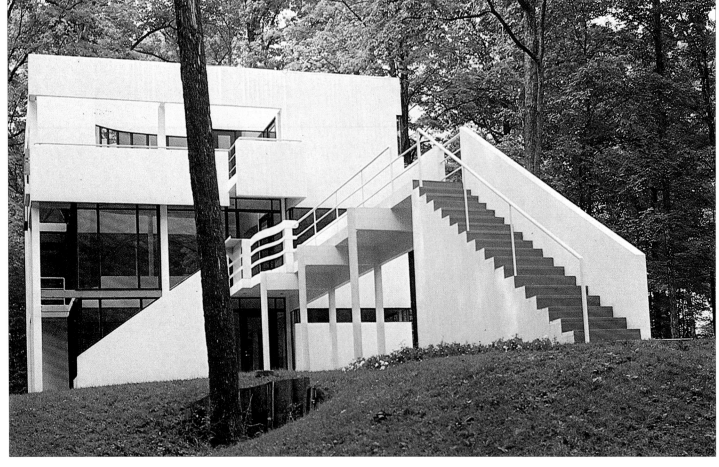

between several readings. Thus the glass bead game, which is seductive to play in the case of an architect like Palladio, is ultimately frustrating. Rationalism pushed into a reductive corner proves once again irrational. To say this, however, is not to condemn it as expression. Eisenman's houses actually absorb a lot of *semantic* content – they are experienced as elaborate structural symphonies, as the white, light-filled architecture of Le Corbusier and Mykonos, as playful games of nonsense poetry. One client fell in love with his structuralist games even though a transformation in the rules drove a column smack through his marital bed. Another client hated the transformations and lived in the basement before he moved out (a mathematician who *understood* Chomsky). No matter, Eisenman goes on and on with his logical convolutions until they dazzle the mind through sheer excess. As William Blake said of methodologists 'if the fool would persist in his folly he would become wise' *(Proverbs from Hell,* incidentally).

On this score, Richard Meier isn't quite as wise, or excessive, as Eisenman and his buildings are really just about some schemes Le Corbusier left unfinished or never bothered to fully work out. Meier, one of the Five (along with Michael Graves, John Hejduk, Charles Gwathmey and Eisenman) confines himself to the early twenties syntax of Le Corbusier before it became more curvilinear and Brutalist. As he says of his Smith house, it is Le Corbusier's Citrohan on one side, Maison Domino the other and, one might add, a collage of what's left over in between. The emphasis, again, is on layered space and distorting syntax, of architecture which is making a comment on previous architecture, and the surprising fact is, given the rarity of this game, that it is neither pastiche, nor uncreative. Meier actually continues the Corb tradition, even if he bends it in the direction of *House Beautiful* and the Jet Set. Like many of the Five he has found clients among the *nouveaux riches;* white Rationalist architecture in America is, semantically speaking, the counterpart of the Neo-Classical style. You don't ask for a Palladian villa now, but a Corbusian one.

Meier has recounted, apparently with a straight face, how the Douglasses wanted another 'Smith House' like the one they saw in *House Beautiful.*[10] After persuading them to have a new improved model, Meier found the local citizenry wouldn't accept anything but wood finish. He tried 'thirty different shades of white-grey and buff coloured paint – in an effort to resolve this issue'. But the answer was 'no'. The Douglasses built their white jewel elsewhere.

If Eisenman's architecture is about a logical design process, then Michael Graves' is about certain architectural elements – particularly doors and points of entry.[11] He 'foregrounds' these elements, calls attention to them by dislocating them from their habitual context. For instance in the Hanselmann House, the public entrance is raised, pulled away from the main body of the house and given an extra articulation of columns, thus creating a screen, or billboard effect. Key to Graves is the opposition between 'sacred and profane' space and the transition between them particularly pronounced in Baroque church architecture. The Hanselmann House has some of this quality.

You approach the frontal planes directly on axis, and the procession towards the more private areas is articulated by a series of implied and real planes set at right-angles to your movement. This layering of tight space was a theme of Corbusier's Garches as Rowe pointed out (in an essay that influenced all the Five's buildings[12]). Graves,

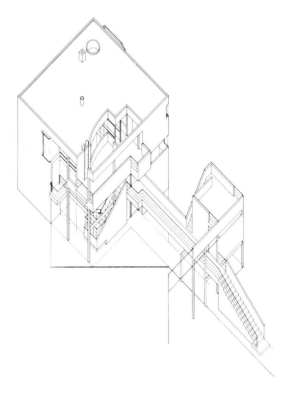

MICHAEL GRAVES, *Hanselmann House*, Fort Wayne, Indiana, 1967-8, axonometric, and (opposite) entrance to living room and street facade. The entrance from the southeast is up some stairs, over a bridge to the middle of the house. The gate of columns and entablature, if built, would have given a pronounced sacred feeling to entry – in effect a double doorway – the first one a public symbol of the second.

however, plays the game quite differently. By pulling away the entrance and making it ceremonial, he creates a big outdoor room, a public space which is in fact a cube of empty space identical to the positive volume of the private space. Thus a certain drama and significance of entry is created, so potent that the house could be more appropriately used as a shrine.

After you reach the ceremonial bridge, you head straight at the centre of the cube noticing such distinctive features as a diagonal to the left (indicating the stairs down to the children's level) and a balcony overhead (articulating the second entry). Certain Corbusian elements are exaggerated: steel tubing and white picture windows framing the sky, a slight curve recalling the ever obsessive guitar shape of Cubist paintings. Even the underlying Corbusian order of columns detached from white planes is emphasised.

You open the front door, arrive at the public level, and are confronted by stairways at right angles to each other and an idealised, Cubist mural of the house – a kind of totemistic representation of the whole thing. The mural is then a transformation in two dimensions of your experience in three – rather like an Eisenman drawing, except elements are even further fragmented and made more complex than the architecture. Another notation is set up in terms of colour – blue for sky, green for nature – thus, if you are aware of it, underscoring views out of the house. (Graves has written on the 'celestial soffit' and he often curves this element making a visual pun on clouds in the sky.) In all of his buildings, there is a heightening of the vertical dimension: the sky is always brought in by frames, by columns and beams reaching out into space.

In fact there is always an ambiguity of space, perhaps best seen in his Gunwyn office conversion where elements are so tightly packed that you have trouble distinguishing foreground from background. Essentially space is collapsed in two dimensions to appear as a Juan Gris still life (the Cubist Graves most admires). The movement through portal frames is so rich that it foreshortens the experience into a single flat plane. Everywhere you look mechanical, structural and wall elements compose into a two-dimensional collage. The trick, like all good architecture, calls attention to itself and takes time to experience.

Obvious doubts arise. Why should Graves confine himself to a 1920s semantics? Clearly his emphasis on the significant points of architecture – doors, windows, walls – is valid and exemplary at this time, but he refuses to perform an essentially traditional role with a traditional syntax. No mouldings, capitals and pediments, no popular signs which would have a wider resonance of meaning. Furthermore the symbolic cues necessary for an understanding are essentially esoteric. For instance in his Benacerraf House, you need a Reader's Guide to understand that a blue balustrade is really a 'column lying on its side'. There is an infinitude of such hermeneutic meanings in the Five's work.

Influence of the Rats

The work of the Five and the Italian Rationalists has had an enormous influence on architects who aren't directly in the tradition. Arata Isozaki has, since 1970, been producing variations on cubes and grids and Palladian plans. His Gunma Museum is a sequence through an implied deep structure of large cubes, which is everywhere articulated by a surface structure of small grids. Isozaki even elaborates the Rationalist

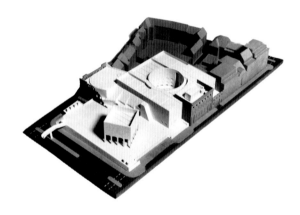

JAMES STIRLING, *Düsseldorf Museum project*, 1975. The open circle becomes the covered square. Like Kahn and Rossi, the architect is fascinated by these basic primitive forms conveyed with a stripped Classicism. The building fits, on one side, very neatly into the city fabric, taking up the street facades and cornice line. Then the square element, raised on a podium is turned to the side, picking up major site lines and acting as a symbolic entrance.

CESAR PELLI AND GRUEN ASSOCIATES, *Pacific Design Center*, Los Angeles, 1975-6. Transparency, reflectivity and translucency.

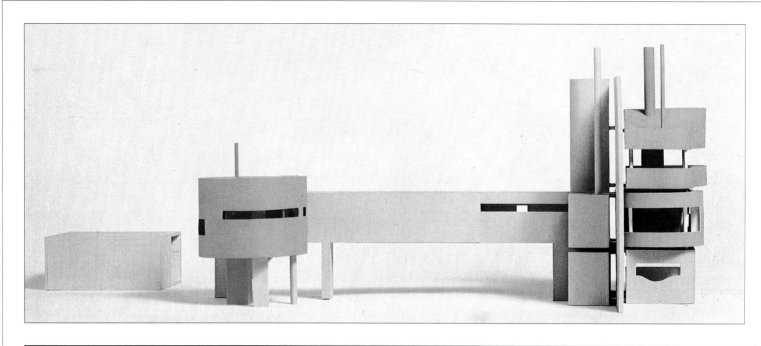

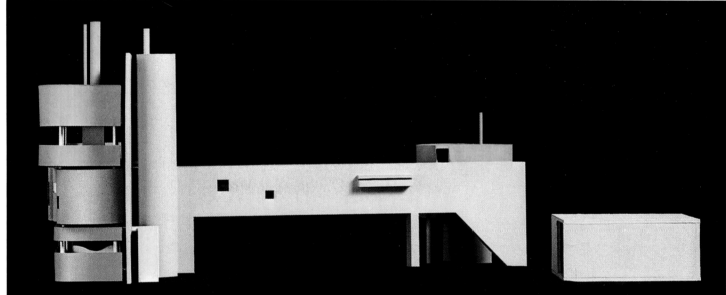

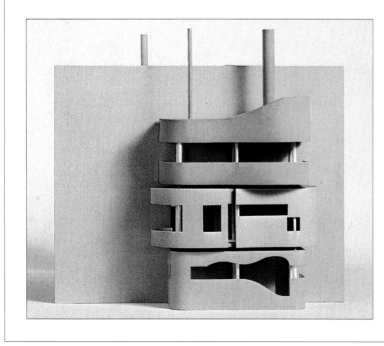

style – the non-joint joint, the window or door opening as 'absence of wall', the smash together of grids without any mouldings or visual junctions.

Cesar Pelli and the 'Silvers of Los Angeles' have been developing their own version of spatial ambiguity based on refinements of the curtain wall which bring transparency, reflectivity, translucency in a sequence of views.[13] The Silvers also reify the grid.

In England, Alan Colquhoun and John Miller use a restrained form of Rationalist style reminiscent of the work of Max Bill, while James Gowan produces a kind of Neo-Neo-Palladianism and James Stirling, slightly influenced by his former draughtsman Leon Krier, practises a type of Modern Neo-Classicism.

Stirling's shift in this direction, noticeable since the Derby scheme of 1970, is interesting because it indicates a general move of many architects towards urban and historicist meanings. A building as a part of the historical fabric, rather than as a discontinuous monument, becomes a prime focus. His museum scheme for Düsseldorf shows much of the Rationalist historicism I have already mentioned.

In volume, Stirling's museum scheme fits into the city fabric and gives a very enjoyable twist to the existing pedestrian street: it becomes first an open outdoor room to the sky, a circle, and then a glass roofed portico, a square. Positive square, negative circle, conceptually one tries to square the circle. The same opposition can be found in Aldo Rossi's urban projects, although made with less tension and irony. In fact the ironies of this Düsseldorf scheme becomes a bit black when one reflects on certain references. The windows of the open circle recall the Nazi work of Albert Speer and they seem to sink into the ground. They are placed way below the roof line and emerge half above the ground implying that Nazism is still present, but that it is sinking (or is it rising?). The only remains of the old Stirling, the Futurist, are in the ramps and curved, patent glazing. All in all it shows how strong the Rationalist influence has become (although as mentioned Stirling himself created an aspect of this in the sixties).

King Rats or Rat Killers? – Surrationalism

We have seen that Rationalism taken to an extreme becomes absurd, and that practised as a half measure it's simply irrational. Of course its twin, functionalism, was never functional and there are few movements that live up, or down, to their slogans. This is not altogether a bad thing since any doctrine is bound to be simplistic and its followers will therefore spend much of their time trying to balance if not altogether refute it. Thus it is appropriate that from within the movement come two supreme ironists whose Rationalism is so explicitly extreme and thorough-going as to make all the pitfalls and beauty of the approach abundantly and deliciously clear. They push Rationalism so far it becomes surreal or Surrationalism: they are the King Rats or Rat Killers, depending on where their extremity leaves the movement. Either way it can't go on any more pretending to be straightforward and sensible. Either it evolves towards an empirical base and becomes *Critical* Rationalism, or it evolves in more absolutist directions towards the Surrationalism of these two Kings.[14] Both have been influenced greatly by Surrealism and both, not surprisingly, haven't built anything – but their projects are no less persuasive for that.

Big John Hejduk, who must be over six foot six and who speaks like a John Wayne from the Bronx, likes to build little, tiny, minuscule models of his unbuilt houses (some

JOHN HEJDUK, *Bye Residence*, 1972-74. Basically living space on one side of the wall and functional space on the hall side of the wall, periscopes over the top. The guitar and the stomach-shaped rooms are painted in muted primary colours. At one point Hejduk was considering that these rooms should be rendered like an architectural drawing with scratchy shadows. It took Hejduk two years to make working drawings for this house which was never built.

are $1\frac{1}{2}$ inches small). I'm not sure why he likes this massive disjunction in scale (he does of course carry the models in his pockets) but it is entirely fitting to the rest of his message which thrives on absurdity and paradox. Magritte is one of his exemplars.

Hejduk will take an essentially prosaic and normal idea and then belabour it so long that it becomes extraordinary and abnormal. First, in 1954, he worked over Palladio, planning houses based on nine squares until he had exhausted much of the magical potential for filling these squares with columns and chimneys. This research on pure geometric relations and a trabeated, cated system of space lasted until 1962 when – miraculously like Theo van Doesburg – he rotated his geometry by 45 degrees. The result? 'Diamond Houses'. For the next four years diamonds were to be explored. All sorts of diagonal properties were discovered which Mondrian and Van Doesburg only just touched on: the meshing of two grids produced no end of nice collisions. Space seemed to whirl about like a centrifuge, stairways and chimneys went into 'three-dimensional torque', the edges or corners became 'charged and filled with maximum tension'.[15] The effect was so mesmerising that Ken Frampton used this formal twist as the second theme of his justification of the Five, an article he called 'Frontality and Rotation'.[16] This was rotation all right, every corner of the room reminded you of the fact. For initiates into the hermeneutic code of the Five, there were also other cues. Whenever one saw a round column one was meant to think 'rotation'. When one saw a square column one thought 'frontality'. As Hejduk said of Le Corbusier's Carpenter Centre – 'the shape of the structural columns is round, indicating a centrifugal force and multi-directional whirl'.

Or as Frampton said of Eisenman's 'House I': '. . . The unresolved tension between frontalisation and rotation [is created by] the presence and/or absence of stainless steel cylindrical columns.'[17]. Oh, those absent square columns are just so . . . frontalised! This is all very interesting and it reminds one of the traditional Japanese, indeed Shinto, distinction between round, untreated cypress columns symbolising tree (nature) and squared-up wooden beams symbolising man-made (culture). But of course this Japanese code was neither so esoteric, nor based on *missing* cues for its interpretation.

Anyway, Hejduk moved on from his diamond fixation to concentrate on what he really came to love – walls. He designed one project, somewhat racist in overtones, which consisted of two houses, one black, the other white, which were separated by a high wall. Then he provided holes and periscopes so these opposite neighbours could surreptitiously monitor each other – the wall uniting them in a mutual obsession. Hejduk then looked at Philip Johnson's wall houses and the canonical Rationalist building Hadrian's Villa, with all its types of wall, and of course Hadrian's Wall itself.[18] By 1964 he was really into the wall in a big way and he started designing houses whose drama consisted in constantly penetrating through an outside wall to find yourself – outside.

For instance, on one side of the Bye Residence there are three superimposed rooms of living, sleeping and dining which are separated by a flat (frontalised) wall plane from bathroom, stairs, study and long linear hall. A periscope is thoughtfully provided. Putting a large, structured wall, a shield between these two types of room (rendered in Cubist shapes and pale primaries) gives them a felicitous kind of schizophrenia, as if they belonged to two different families (one horizontal, one vertical). It also increases the drama of transition and, a functional point Hejduk might not like to make, is very sensible if there is a lot of traffic and noise on the garage side.

The fascination for walls ('Wallism' – a well-known disease of bad neighbours)[19] reached a pinnacle (if that is the right architectural word) with his project for the Venice Biennale in 1974. This was called a 'Cemetery for the Ashes of Thought', a kind of museum or mausoleum for thoughts that weren't quite dead, or at least ones that Hejduk wished to commemorate. Hejduk made it an explicit commentary on Rationalism, since it was a project for Italy, a 'commentary on and answer to the architecture of death', those schemes of Aldo Rossi which appear so quiescent and necrophiliac. His answer was a lot of wall. Many (it's hard to count because of optical vibration) walls to be twleve feet high, to be placed four feet apart and run straight for six hundred feet. Six hundred feet of wall, one side black, the other white, holes every two or three feet! You'd feel like a termite lost in a straightened Bridget Riley.

What was the point? Hejduk said that various plaques and cubic gravestones would be placed throughout giving the titles of old thoughts (eg *Remembrance of Things Past, The Counterfeiters,* various titles of books he admires). The main house, an abandoned factory, would be painted deep black, would have more plaques, now with the authors' names, and it would be inhabited from time to time by a visiting dignitary (who presumably would spend his time recalling those previous moments of time past, *Death in Venice,* etc).

Hejduk spent a whole month colouring in the spaces between the walls. Such projects starting from a Rationalist concern with first principles, and architecture about itself, render the principles authoritarian. They grow to consume everything else. Like a traditional Surrealist, Hejduk focuses on everyday aspects of reality, but then gives them an independent life of their own, cut off from their original function. Doors, walls, triangles, chimneys, linear halls dominate everything, like Magritte's apple that expanded so much that the inhabitants were forced to flee their room. This impossible likelihood, like magic, forces us to reconsider the prosaic, and the assumption of what really is rational.

That other Rat Killer, or King Rat, Rem Koolhaas and his team of metropolitan enthusiasts, is also very influenced by Surrealism – particularly the 'paranoid-critical method' of creativity practised by Salvador Dali.[20] Central to this method is the projection of dreams, phobias, ideologies and obsessions onto the real world, until they become true by sheer force of repetition and will-power. The history of civilisation, and particularly that of New York City, looks from this angle like a sequence of such projections. Koolhaas says of Manhattan (and he quickly turns this *apercu* into a philosophy, Manhattanism), that it was 'a compression of all the best of Europe'. It was a successful paranoid projection of the Dutch phobia – 'New Amsterdam'. Its history has suffered successive projections, those of endless ethnic groups and paranoid Rationalists such as Le Corbusier, until each part of it represents the distillation of some ideal dream. To take this tendency even further and bring it to self-consciousness, Koolhaas has designed 'The City of the Captive Globe'.

This project gives to each city block a self-consistent and self-referring style and ideology – or 'mania'. Thus Le Corbusier's serrated towers stand next to Expressionist pointed arches, Malevich near Superstudio, the ever-present globe and needle (1939

World's Fair) is next to what looks to be the Plaza Hotel and Mass Housing. Other Rationalist icons are strewn about – the World Trade Center looks down on 'the captive globe' at the centre.

The point of these blocks, like the paranoid-critical method, is to banish any reality which does not serve the original mania – what could be a better critique (and celebration) of Rationalism. In Koolhaas' words (and he is the son of a Dutch poet):

Each science or mania has its own plot. On each plot stands an identical base, built from heavy polished stone. These bases, ideological laboratories, are equipped to suspend unwelcome laws, undeniable truths [sic], to create non-existent physical conditions to facilitate and provoke speculative activity . . . The changes of this ideological skyline will be rapid and continuous, a rich spectacle of ethical joy, moral fever or intellectual masturbation.[21]

In a sense this is just real New York intensified.

Koolhaas and OMA developed their theories in 1972 with a study of the Berlin Wall (walls again), and their scheme for London called 'Exodus, or the Voluntary Prisoners of Architecture'. When I pointed out to Hejduk the remarkable similarity in wall obsession he drew back in disdain. Obviously there is no place for two King Rats occupying the same territory, but the similar obsessions turn out, in this case, to be fortuitous (although perhaps psychologically connected).

Is it true that people, not only designers, love to be 'voluntary prisoners of architecture'? Can the history of architecture really be seen as the self-imposed incarceration into walls, skyscrapers, globes and needles? In a dream-sense, yes, and it's this unwritten dream which Koolhaas wishes to record, and reinforce.

'Every skyscraper in New York wanted to be a sphere and every sphere secretly wanted to be a needle . . .' The drama of 'delirious New York' unfolds like an illuminated nightmare, with the two protagonists, the Chrysler Building and the Empire State in bed with each other. There they lie, the feminine Chrysler curving over to meet the larger Empire State, while the Statue of Liberty holds a flaming lamp above them. Their tryst is over, symbolised by the spent rubber balloon of the Goodyear Tyre Blimp. But then suddenly the jealous RCA building intrudes, and casts its search-light on them. The best of New York skyscraperdom looks on aghast (or is it with an interest in morals?).

What is the message of this *in flagrante delicto?* Out from underneath the bed is born the magical New York Grid, Central Park and the spaghetti of roads, tubes and services (the underground, deep collective unconscious). Manhattan is being killed (by recent architects) and in the next set of drawings we see that the only hope is for more spaghetti, more fanatical obsessions which produced these two former 'largest needles in the world'.

In many such drawings and watercolours Koolhaas and Vriesendorp portray what they call 'the secret life of buildings': 'To introduce explicit figurative, symbolic elements in the urban realm, OMA is developing a quasi-Freudian language to identify and analyse the psychological characteristics and properties which could be ascribed to architecture.'[22] With a kind of remorseless wit Koolhaas shows what psychological characteristics have existed; the evolving globe and needle become more and more sick and finally degenerate into the awful slab blocks. Wallace Harrison, who has been

MADELON VRIESENDORP, *Delirous New York*, 1975. 'A quasi-Freudian language to identify and analyse the psychological characteristics and properties which could be ascribed to architecture'.

MADELON VRIESENDORP, *In Flagrante Delicto*, 1975. The Chrysler Building, female and the tallest until 1931, curls up to the Empire State. This gouache is part of a series 'The Secret Life of Buildings' and the drama continues.

ZOE ZENGHELIS, *The City of the Captive Globe*, 1972. What New York City is trying to be, a distillation of ideologies which have been 'inflicted' on the world. Each block is a complete and pure expression of 'a certain form of madness' – notice the Rationalist block of ice-cool cubes, lower right. The captivity of the globe in the centre is the final subjugation of the reality principle by the 'paranoid-critical method'. All blocks are isolated on rectangular podia which carefully exclude unwelcome truth – the censorship practised in every nation. Incidentally, of all nations, South Africa has the highest level of paranoia; West Germany is second.

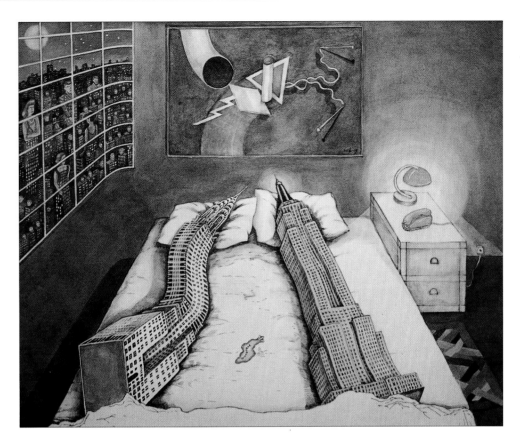

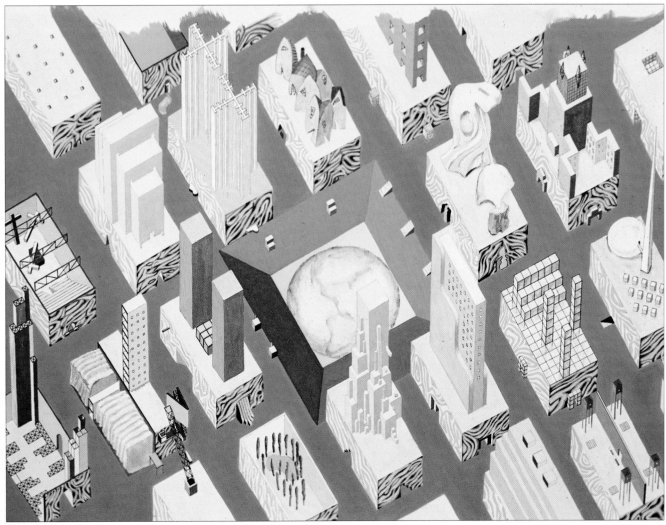

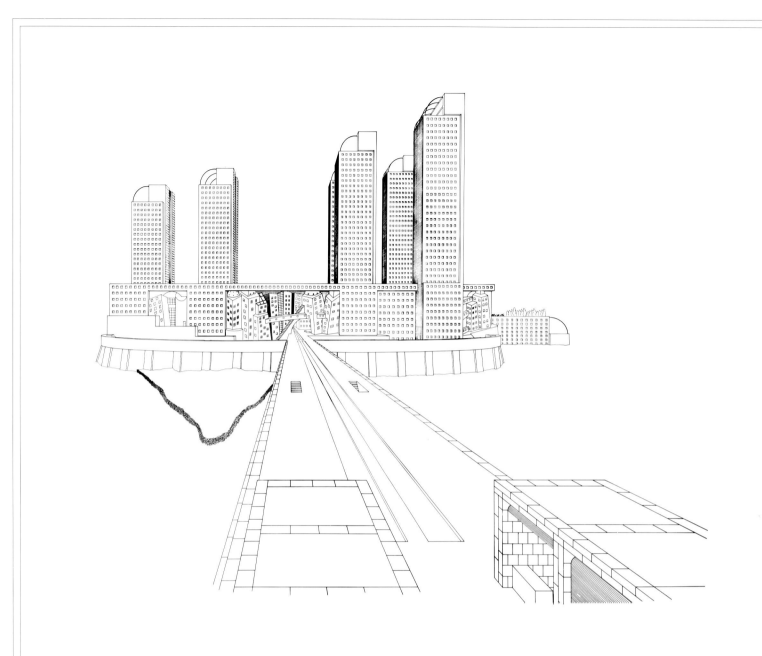

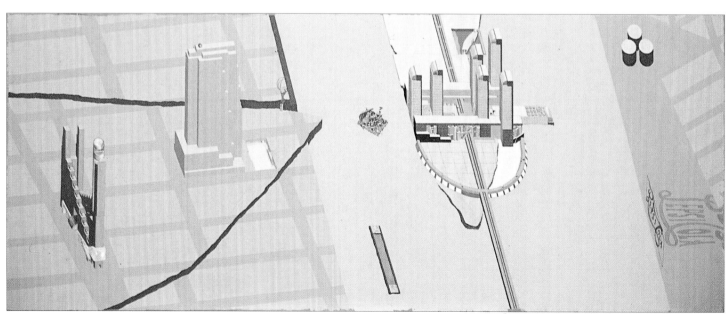

instrumental in this evolution with his RCA and United Nations slabs, still feels a throb of the Manhattan blood in his clotted arteries, so he is capable of utterly inexplicable gestures – such as the slight curve. Koolhaas finds these curves becoming more and more obsessive after the RCA building (he studied Harrison's curves for three years) until they reach a spasmic crescendo in the UN building. The weak curve of Harrison recurs here fifty times! Whatever can it mean? Koolhaas decodes it: 'That means there's something the matter with it. It's the *limp curve of humanism* which betrays the perpetual representation of guilt feelings.' The same limp curve of humanism disciplines Harrison's Opera House at Lincoln Center which is a 'marble cyclotron that twists and turns people until they lose reality'.

This psychoanalysis of architecture is then turned into a utopian paranoid conjecture, a scheme for Welfare Island. The grid of Manhattan and Harrison's limp curve are there as well as other recognisable manias: in fact Koolhaas calls his scheme 'an architectural parking lot, a graveyard for discarded schemes', tinged with the 'humiliating setbacks' he prefigures in his future. The skyscrapers are there with their 'heads' looking at Manhattan and the RCA, while one of them has collapsed on its side as a 'groundscraper'. The Rat emphasis on repetition is there, brought to a new pitch of boredom. So is the Rat jumble of buildings, a collision to rival New York which is also a 'shipwreck of architecture'? To 'take the temperature of this shipwreck', Koolhaas has devised his 'architectural dipstick' in the form of Gericault's *Raft of the Medusa*. This he inserts at various points to see how healthy is the paranoia. The raft is in a sense the perfect image of Manhattanism, a group of survivors from a shipwreck, who cannibalise each other in order to survive.

> According to the Classic Chronicle, their parachute dropped the castaways of the Medusa and their raft on the rescue-ship 'The City'. It appeared like a serene monument bursting with the ornamental frenzy that its inner life provoked. It was an unknown, a new form of life, inside a timeless architecture: an innumerable mixture of activities generated by the ship's hedonistic daily programme. It was a spontaneous Planning Centre governed by the continuous satisfaction and shameless application of human passions. Amongst the protagonists of the inspired state of anarchy, Jesus Christ and the Marquis de Sade were engaged in a mutant form of behaviour which was echoed by the splendid order of the architecture . . .[23]

And so Rationalism born in the paranoid conjectures of an eighteenth-century monk dreaming about the lesson of the Primitive Hut ends two-hundred years later on a wooden raft of Surrationalism, the Rats unable to leave their sinking ship and eating each other to save their lives.

This essay was written in 1976 just as the Rationalists were splitting into Late and Post-Modernists (see note 14). Those such as Eisenman and Meier kept to this direction, while Graves, Bofill and the Kriers became more representational, Classical and Post-Modern.

REM KOOLHAAS, *Welfare Palace Hotel*, 1975. This hotel of towers faces Harrison's RCA building and New York with its glass walls and seven heads. A fault runs through the hotel and one tower has fallen over on its back. The site is a graveyard for discarded schemes, an architectural parking lot full of Rat beauty and monotony.

PHILIP JOHNSON
THE CANDID KING MIDAS
OF NEW YORK CAMP

There he sits on Christmas Eve, Philip Cortelyou Johnson, in his weekend See-Through House turning up and down the outside flood-lights while all around him gentle snow flakes fall, fall, fall – poof, poof, poof – each one picked out and highlit by the floods . . . 'With the lights out inside and the snow coming down, it makes you seem to go up – like a great celestial elevator!'

Philip Cortelyou Johnson ascending into a weekend heaven in his quarter-of-a-million-dollar Glass Box, his cosmic fish-bowl, all tucked in by central heating, shrubbery and plenty of stone walls . . . thinking out the next way he can send up the Modern Movement, outrage the socially responsible, deny the underpinnings of Le Corbusier, Gropius, Fuller, 'Epater le Mouvement Moderne?' After a hundred years of smashing the nerve-endings of the bourgeoisie, Modern architects have found that the old neurons won't fire any more, the synapses are worn out, there is nobody left to shock except a fast-diminishing group of themselves, the last people on earth who still can be surprised, outraged, ethically repulsed.

When Philip Johnson built his See-Through-It-Isn't-There Glass House in 1949, he provided a set of programme notes (like a nineteenth-century Romantic composer) published them in *The Architectural Review* for all the professionals to follow his sources, his eclectic stealing, his architectural kleptomania – seventeen (17!) different sources ticked off. The See-Through House was entirely made up of sources pillaged from the Greats of the Past – nothing original, but all acknowledged right there for everyone to see: 1) site plan and spiderweb walkways taken from Le Corbusier, 2) sliding arrangement of volumes stolen from Mies, 3) asymmetrical composition lifted from Theo van Doesburg, 4) Acropolis planning from Choisy, 5) straight-on symmetry from Schinkel . . . 8) the Glass House from Mies . . . 13) glass walls by Mies . . . 17) open plan from Mies . . . After this building Philip Courtelyou was called Mies van der Johnson because he robbed I-beams, corner details, open planning, tinted glass, chairs, tables . . . English moralist critics love it! The English critic and Defender of the Modern Movement, Sir Nikolaus Pevsner, loves to catch Philip out playing at his eclectic game: '. . . that brilliant rogue Philip Johnson . . . is a virtuoso at playing with stylistic materials old and new . . .' and Sir Nikolaus is a brilliant rogue-finder with his searching out of every possible stylistic source – 'sourcery'! The English critics love to catch Philip playing at sourcery. They come in droves on their pilgrimage to the US to visit Johnson at his New Canaan House, to tour the grounds, to look at his Pop Art collection, to be deliciously outraged at his Camp sensibility.

James Stirling, the English architect committed to a functionalist base, drives up to Johnson's New Canaan compound. 'Look at this', Philip says, pulling out a devastating assault on his work and character from *Architectural Design,* 'you Englishmen always

Glass House, New Canaan, Connecticut, 1949. When first built in the heart of New York's commuter-belt, this see-through house caused a lot of local consternation. Johnson had to build a six foot high stone wall to protect himself from the gaze of the curious, Sunday strollers. But also, to whet their appetite, he would conduct an occasional tour of the open-planned house. Pointing towards an empty space. 'This is the library, Madam, you see it's an *American* library – no books.' When she objected that this open planning was unsuitable for family life – 'It's a nice place but I could never *live* here', Johnson replied, 'Madam, *I* haven't asked you to'.

'Follee', 1962. Cocktails are served in this six-foot high Acropolis. The sylvan silence is broken by a hundred foot *jet d'eau* and a two inch waterfall.

Glass House, New Canaan, Connecticut, 1949. Exterior

Glass House. The function of the glass wall was to minimise the imposition on the beautiful landscape and allow for changing views of the four seasons to become the subject of architecture – 'the most beautiful wallpaper in the world'. Actually, Johnson's love for landscaping and exotic plants equals his love for architecture (see the garden for the Museum of Modern Art).

Guest House with its golden arras and aedicule.

attack my work with such style. It's absolutely fabulous, only an Englishman could have written this':

> One step further along the road to complete architectural decadence has now been taken by Philip Johnson, with yet another addition to his idyllic estate in New Canaan. Although it is passed off by the architect as a 'folly' by virtue of its entirely false scale it is, nonetheless, in its trivial historicism, quite typical of Johnson's recent work . . .

'Complete architectural decadence'! And Johnson likes this attack because of its style? Indeed – his Glass House is a temple decorated to the celebration of style. Besides the sourcery already mentioned there is a painting by the seventeenth-century Classicist Nicolas Poussin – the *Funeral of Phocion* – a life-sized Nadalman portrait of *Two Women* (these two women are chatting and embracing and they are monobosomed and made out of white *papier-mâché*). There is a small Giacometti *Thin Man* inching his way across the floor, a Claes Oldenburg – *Bursting Banana Split* (of course) – and as for the accompanying elements – low cabinet units which look as if they were made out of Chinese teak; shaggy potted plants; a soft, white wool rug which creates a conversation island on the polished redbrick-herringbone floor; a seating pool made up of Miesian leather chairs, reclining couches . . . LEATHER. Johnson loves leather. The only enclosed room in the house, the bathroom, *'la salle de bain'*, is covered in oily, pigskin panels and the tiles on the floor are all leather.

In his Guest House which is located diagonally to his Glass House, Johnson inverts the open, flowing style and encloses two bedrooms in a brick cube which only has small, Peeping-Tom portholes for windows. The effect is inward-looking, protective, womb-like, a 'feeling of cuddle' (Johnson calls it) caused by the warm curves of the hung-plaster domes and the honey-dew arrases of gold and silver which tinkle and caress the indirect light that gently spills and cavorts down them. The wandering-wire sculpture especially designed for the space over the bed is lit like the nimbus of some Byzantine saint but it dims and brightens when Johnson turns up and down the rheostats. With this building and more particularly with its paired column domes, Johnson finally broke with the Modernist commitment to structural honesty and straightforward expression. 'This is my High-Queen Period' Johnson says with a wicked smile directed at the aescetic priesthood of the Modern Movement.

But the building which really brought out their collective wrath was his 'pleasure pavilion', his 'follee', his underscaled forest of pre-cast white concrete columns placed in his *artificial* moon viewing lake in the west part of the Johnson Compound. Here it is, the final insult to functional purpose and everything the Pioneers of the Modern Movement had fought for – relevance, social utopianism, a non-historicist style. To them it would be a practically useless piece of under-scaled wedding-cake whose purpose was, as Johnson put it, 'to make giants of the visitor (an idea borrowed from the dwarf's chambers at Mantua)'. The Classical colonnade, which appears to be twelve feet in height (but is actually half that), appears suddenly even smaller when the hundred foot-high *jet d'eau* explodes into action at the press of a button.

In the 'follee' are gigantic Erie Canals of gushing water ten inches wide that pour over Herculean precipices of two inches, and thunder to the bottom of the lake with a resounding tinkle. This tinkle is then taken up again in a visual form as it reverberates

off the interior of the gold-leaf domes (which are only three feet wide).

The British magazines sprang into action. *Architectural Design* shot out its 'complete architectural decadence', its 'trivial historicism', its condemnation of these 'feeble forms'; *The Architect's Journal* drove in the message: '. . . we all have this ugly romantic urge in us . . . for too many people, this sort of disincarnate architecture is the real thing, and the attempt to ally form with social purpose an irrelevant bore'. The British critic Reyner Banham answered this mounting attack on what he termed 'one of the most sincerely hated buildings in the world'. But the defence was hardly needed. Johnson himself turned the joke back on his critics in an interview presented right in the heart of the debate – on the BBC with Susan Sontag:

> Philip Johnson: . . . I got the idea that it was good to imitate the British, you know our betters, as we always say in this country, and, er, so I decided that we would have a *folie* . . . we hear the splash of water, we see the floating, dying leaves and it gives us a sort of Keatsian sense of fairy casements forlorn – I'm copying this wrong – I'm quoting this wrong, but you know what I mean . . .
>
> Susan Sontag: Very eighteenth-century –
>
> PJ: . . . an out-of-scale island away from the world and you get that feeling that a boy gets in a tree house or a girl gets with her doll house, the idea of a miniature.

Just previously in the interview, Johnson had gone to the root of his conception of morality – a conception very like that of Oscar Wilde who never stopped attacking those whose good intentions led to the ultimate sin of boredom, of obviousness.

> PJ: . . . and incidentally the English that are so good about morals and city planning and have all those London County Councils and things they are so proud of, have ruined their city in the name of morality – even worse than New York in this hopeless chaos.

Chiding those with a bloodless common sense or a pretension to social purpose has always been a constant goal of Johnson, who has the unsuppressible desire to deflate pomposity especially when it happens to be the not inconsiderable magniloquence of himself. This kind of candid self-deprecation, a particularly New York and Jewish virtue, comes out in almost all of Johnson's pronouncements on himself:

> Do we lack convictions? Do we just flit around in all directions like butterflies as we are accused of doing by the people who are still with the International Style? The English, being articulate critics, say that we are all crazy here and that the functionalist tradition of the Bauhaus, as continued by the likes of Stirling, is the only answer. Well it may be, but it certainly isn't evident in the way things are getting built . . . I copy an eighteenth-century theatre for Lincoln Center. My point is that everybody does; I am the only one who admits it.

Candid? The only one in a group of clowns, a group of court jesters, who will admit that he's joking?

Sleeping in Chartres

Philip Johnson was born in Cleveland, Ohio in 1906, the only son – he has two sisters – of a very successful corporation lawyer and a mother who taught history of art in school. His first two architectural experiences, not untypical for the wealthy young American boy on the Grand Tour of the Continent, were at the Parthenon (age

Built project.

Asia House, New York City, 1960. By the late fifties, the sleek, supercool, glass facade had become standard New York architectural practice. This design by Johnson has all the usual qualities – a high reflective surface, transparency, smoothness and very shallow relief – with the additional property of being highly articulated. The dark tinted panels on the bottom vary in size and proportion while the top four floors are treated with a consistent transparency. All the high single panes and all the small, horizontal spandrels are picked out by silver coloured frames.

Actually, this building was the third and best of three alternative proposals, shown here, that Johnson had prepared for his client. Returning to his Harvard practice of designing for different tastes, Johnson was also returning to the pluralism of Sir John Soane and his 'Alternative proposals for Commissioner's Churches'. Many deplored this seeming lack of conviction – as if any one problem had one and only one solution – but the plurality of proposals seems to be much more realistic to actual conditions which are underdetermined. Also it allowed Johnson to avoid compromising his conviction on any single project.

twenty-two) and Chartres (age thirteen). 'Catholicism was a great mystery to a young Puritan from the Midwest. There was a funeral going on. I was so moved I don't know why I wasn't dead'. In 1923 Johnson went to Harvard University where he became interested in piano playing, the Greek Classics and finally Greek philosophy. However, uncertain in his direction, he had several breakdowns and did not graduate for seven years. But then in 1928, half-way through an article on Modern architecture, the vision struck. 'The Conversion from Saul to Paul took place'. Johnson had found his Christ and seen the light. It was an article by the young Wesleyan instructor and emergent historian of the Modern Movement, Henry-Russell Hitchcock. On the spot he realised what to do. He dashed out to the nearest bookstore and treated himself to a handsome German portfolio, *Architecture in the Newest Age*. The following two summers he teamed up with Harvard classmates and Hitchcock and went on a pilgrimage to the Holy Land of Modern architecture – Germany. Mies van der Rohe said later: 'This [1930] was the year of the American Invasion.' The Americans, Hitchcock, Johnson and Barr came to Europe, discovered the International Style, took it back home and sold it in an exhibition at the Museum of Modern Art (which had just been founded by the Rockefellers, the Blisses, the Goodyears and other such families, some of whom were to become Johnson clients). In 1932, along with the exhibition, a book appeared called *The International Style: Architecture Since 1922*. It explained to Americans what the Modern Movement was all about: volume, asymmetry, flat roofs, white planes and – in spite of misguided attempts of certain pure functionalists who were then the strongest voices – aesthetics. There was a modern *style* suitable to, indeed a direct result of, the Machine Age. In 1934, Johnson produced another exhibition and book at the Museum of Modern Art – he was now Director of the Department of Architecture there – this time called *Machine Art*. Here were all the clean, clear, well-polished forms of industrial civilisation: an all-chrome cash register, an all-chrome flush valve etc. The kind of industrial products which were carefully selected for their consistent purity seemed to support Bauhaus arguments, Herbert Read arguments, Le Corbusier arguments, that the machine led directly to Plato – pure, polished, Phileban forms.

And yet Johnson had doubts and a return bout of uncertainty. Perhaps his vision was a mirage. He became involved in all the fringe groups of the thirties. 'I think the only one I didn't get mixed up with was Communism – Communists weren't very amusing even then.' His first involvement took him down south to fight the Depression at the side of Mr Huey Long, the populist demagogue and the man who did more for the under-privileged than most of the New Deal Democrats. Unfortunately Huey Long didn't quite understand the contribution of Harvard intellectuals in saving the South (Johnson was with a classmate) and they only saw him four times – so they left, depressed.

After returning home to his father's farm in Cleveland and having another unsuccessful try at populist politics, Johnson then got 'mixed up with all the right-wing fringes'. He wrote an article for the Harvard-based magazine *Hound and Horn* on Nazi architecture. It was an impassioned plea for the Nazis not to 'set the clock back' in a reactionary and racist return to the past. Johnson distinguished between three types of Nazi architecture and then pleaded for the Nazis to pick the third type – Mies van

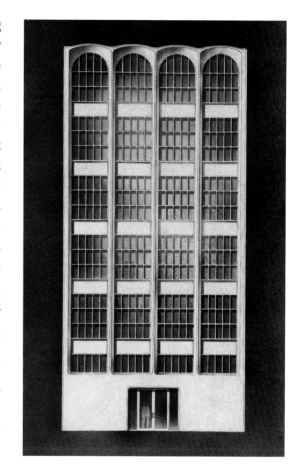

First project.

Second project.

der Rohe's purist monumentality evident in his design for Hitler's Reichsbank. After the Nazis became more clearly historicist, rejected the Modern style, and the implications of their politics became known, Johnson lost his latest-found faith, had yet another conversion and change of direction.

In 1940, at the age of thirty-four, he enrolled at Harvard's School of Architecture which was now under the directorship of the German refugee and leader of the Modern Movement – Walter Gropius. Being much older than the other students and having a penchant for luxurious expression which went way beyond the restraint of Gropius, Johnson found himself in natural conflict with the school. 'By the second year I was doing two designs for every problem – one for myself and one for the school. I still recommend that procedure today to all students.' Perhaps Johnson's conflict with Harvard was as much due to his style of life as to his design method, since he started off living in Cambridge in a luxurious hotel suite until he subsequently moved into his own private 'Court House' – which he had in fact designed and submitted as his graduating thesis in 1943. After serving his time in the academy, Johnson then served a few years in the army as a latrine orderly, Private First Class Number 31-303-426. Johnson kept out of trouble and was, uncharacteristically, part of the background.

When the war finished, Johnson returned to the limelight in his old position as Director of the Department of Architecture and Design at the Museum of Modern Art – and embarked on two projects which had a wide influence both in Europe and America. These were his book on Mies van der Rohe and his Glass House in New Canaan. Perhaps of equal influence, according to the historian Vincent Scully, were his talks at Yale University where he contrasted the functionalism of Harvard with his more formalist approach: 'I would rather sleep in the nave of Chartres Cathedral with the nearest john two blocks down the street than I would in a Harvard House [of Gropius] with back-to-back bathrooms.' Scully describes the effect of these 'pronouncements of the Devil' on him and other students in terms of their religious conversion from Saul to Paul, from building to architecture as an art. Indeed for the next twenty years Yale, with its lavishly tasteful magazine *Perspecta* and its articles on Johnson, was to lead the movement of American formalism. More particularly, Johnson's lapidary epigrams and historicist buildings were to justify it: 'Where form comes from I don't know, but it has nothing at all to do with the sociological aspects of architecture.' This summing up of his approach which occurred in *Perspecta* 1954 could be made by any number of American formalists five years later – the Harvard formalists Paul Rudolph, Ulrich Franzen, I M Pei, Victor Lundy or even Walter Gropius (by 1960) and the big name practitioners Eero Saarinen, Minoru Yamasaki, Ed Stone, Wallace Harrison etc. Indeed the formalist movement was international, sparking off such returns to the past as Neo-Liberty in Italy, Neo-Katsura in Japan and Neo-Ziggurat in Israel. However only Johnson among these historicists would admit what he was really up to and bring out the evasion of others with his laconically Camp pronouncements: 'Mies is such a genius! But I grow old! And bored! My direction is clear; eclectic tradition. This is not academic revivalism. There are no Classic orders or Gothic finials. I try to pick up what I like throughout history. We cannot not know history.'

This history which Johnson could not not know amounted first of all to Mies in his Hodgson and Boissonnas houses, to Sir John Soane and Claude Nicolas Ledoux in his

Knesis Tifereth Israel Synagogue, Port Chester, New York, 1956. That Johnson should here be influenced by the eighteenth-century 'Revolutionary' architect Claude Nicolas Ledoux is very revealing – they both share a mixture of monumental formalism combined with a sometimes reactionary politics. Here two, white, pure forms, the rectangle and oval, are separated with an uncompromising boldness. The black picture-frame of steel further emphasises the volume. This historicism and Neo-Classicism had a wide impact on the Modern Movement in the middle fifties, when they were both vehemently praised and condemned.

Port Chester Synagogue and to the German architect K F Schinkel in his museum buildings. Architectural historians have already identified historical allusions at length, but basically they break down into two types: Miesian influences up to about 1960 and Neo-Classical influences from about 1954. But this break-away from Mies, which was severely criticised at the time as the beginning of American formalism, is more apparent than real. In fact if one studies the purely architectural evidence, what is striking is the consistent classical style of the whole. All the work could be described in this terminology. Thus even the Miesian architecture has a plinth or stylobate, entablature and some kind of trabeated structure. The external columns are usually too widely spaced to speak about a true intercolumniation, but still their relation to the infill walls is conceptually like a Renaissance *palazzo*. Furthermore either the overall form is symmetrical, or a carefully balanced asymmetry which gives the classical feeling of harmony and resolution. This is further reinforced by the inclusion of cross axes and the heavy visual stops at all corners. At times Johnson produces an even more closed architecture than the classical. For instance he contrasts black and white at points of articulation to achieve the extreme visual closure that is comparable to a picture frame. His various attempts to produce an open architecture of interlocking spaces, such as the Boissonnas House, have not been followed up. Rather he has turned to the heavy arcuated rectangles of his museums or the gigantic columnar temples of his laboratories. In both cases he has chosen the emphatic visual *Gestalt* of Classicism in preference to the light, open-ended aesthetic of recent engineering.

Partially this preference must be traced to his method of design which consists of working on detailed models – working like a sculptor on a homogeneous block of material, rather than either drawing or relying on picturesque accretions due to new technologies. A television aerial or mechanical duct would be as disturbing to his unified simplicity as it is to Mies' buildings. While Johnson is admired for his professionalism, it consists in the visual perfecting of well-known motifs rather than the creating of new ones. Indeed his originality is in the refinement and obsessive elegance of the building as a whole. Few other Modern architects, except some Italians, can compete with the finesse of this sensibility. At times, such as the New York State Theater, it falls into historicist allusion and strained pomposity without the saving grace of wit or polished overstatement. Architectural historians sometimes follow Johnson into this trap, identifying influences rather than concentrating on the more relevant question of his sensibility and place in American society.

Children like a bridge to cross

When visiting New York I went over to photograph the Seagram Building (designed by Mies) and pay a call on Vincent Scully's Devil himself (who has an office on the top floor). I brought along my pocket-sized Kodak Instamatic, this superior piece of goon technology, to photograph Seagram from directly below. I wanted the vertigo shot, the dizzying, New York shot of Seagram receding into heaven like some celestial railroad track – zzzsswooooosh – parallel bronze bullets shooting up thirty-nine floors to the knife edge roof which – booooiinnggs – out like some kind of bronze Arabian scimitar. The roof line is *actually* flat, but it appears as a curve because it isn't corrected for optical distortion like a Greek Temple. Anyway, I wandered around zig-

Amon Carter Museum of Western Art, Fort Worth, Texas, 1961. This little Greek Temple of five archways was built to house the collection of the Fort Worth millionaire Amon Carter. The art consists mostly of bucking bronchos and whooping cowpunchers solidified in bronze – the 'Museum of Yippee-Yi-Yo' as *Time* magazine called it. In his quest for immortality, Johnson has claimed that his ultimate ambition is to be *L'Architect du Roi*, even if the King turns out to be a latter-day version of Horatio Alger, the self-made oil magnate.

Boissonnas House, New Canaan, 1956. A further development of the interplay between open and closed – Johnson's Glass House and his Guest House. Certainly the plan is his most masterful to date – a rich interlocking of spaces which both separates functions and unites areas where this is possible. Again the formal units are a glass and brick wall, but here a brick pier is also added on a square grid system to give a kind of intellectual ordering to the sprawling layout. By opening or closing this square bay, by using it in double height and by letting it enclose outdoor space, Johnson achieves a kind of spatial sequencing which is quite rare.

zag, drunk, with head cocked back like some baby dicky-bird in feeding, picking out the historical overtones – Phidias, Michelozzo, Schinkel, Doric columns, intercolumniation and – well, never mind. I snapped back my head into forward drive and coasted into the open and bare lobby (travertine, bronze, stainless steel etc) and thence into an express elevator to the top floors. Once on the thirty-ninth floor, the walls slid silently apart and we were debouched onto deep black marble with white veining. As I turned left, suddenly I felt this gentle hand on my shoulder – 'You must be going to my office' (I was wearing my English three-piece-Glen-Plaid-identibadge). 'You must be Philip Johnson', I said, quickly stuffing away my Kodak Instamatic. He looked across at me with that benevolent, relaxed smile, that 'we know how to handle things here' look that makes you feel warm molasses inside. He ushered me past a glass entrance, a Picasso tapestry, a few Pop paintings, Robert Indiana's *A Divorced Man Has Never Been The President* and then into his private office overlooking the East River. A large expanse of tinted Thermo-plate, a few bronze I-beam mullions, one or two potted palms, an Indian Rubber plant, a few chairs and a polished walnut table upon which was that fantastic piece of architectural literature, the colour-illustrated *Philip Johnson* (which was subsidised by Philip Johnson, composed by Philip Johnson and even, modestly, reviewed by Philip Johnson).

After I had explained the purpose of my visit – to obtain permission to quote from various articles and interviews – Johnson launched into one of his favourite subjects: the lack of a civic-minded tradition for which large, monumental public spaces could be constructed:

> Why is it the nineteenth century and even the Robber Barons had so much more public spirit than we do today? They knew how to enjoy themselves, they had the buccaneering spirit, they drained the West of its wealth – but for a purpose. To build grand spaces like Pennsylvania Station, which we just tear down, or Grand Central Station, the greatest space in New York City, which we go and ruin with all those Kodak advertisements.

I pushed my Instamatic deeper into my pocket and asked Johnson the rather delicate question of whether I could quote from his article on Nazi architecture – delicate because no other publication on Johnson had gone into his connections of the thirties. 'Sure, what did I say?' Johnson was ready to come out with the truth even before he remembered what it was. Just as I finished reminding him of his triple-decker distinction between three types of Nazi style, we were interrupted by some invisible sign on his command module that indicated clients had arrived and it was time for me to be extricated.

As I reached the door, shook hands and started to leave, in walked three Fat City New York clients all lit out in their blue Alumicron suits, Countess Mara ties (Countess Mara, the hundred dollar tie) brilliantined hair swept back over their sun-tanned creases like Hollywood moguls circa 1947. The place was literally exploding with signals, status badges, pecking-orders, classifiers. Johnson was sporting his it-had-to-be a Tripler Broadcloth shirt, shooting his cuffs through reticent grey pin-stripe, out-signalling everybody in sight – exuding so much easy-going self-confidence that you'd hand over your nest-egg in a shot. Safe keeping? The super-rich find it all but irresistible. Culture centres, museums, the four and a half million dollar Four Seasons Restaurant, private houses for the Rockefellers and the Henry Fords, the Dallas monument to JFK, the New York Pavilion for the World's Fair, all his commissions are prestige jobs in a monumental style. Johnson had written of the new Nazi Regime in 1933 an analysis which was coming true for both America and himself: '. . . architecture will be monumental. That is instead of bath-houses, Siedlungen, employment offices and the like, there will be official railroad stations, memorial museums, monuments. The present regime is more intent on leaving a visible mark of its greatness than in providing sanitary equipment for workers.'

Critics compare Lincoln Center and Johnson's New York State Theater to Mussolini's Third Rome – Noam Chomsky says that what is needed in American society at large 'is a kind of denazification'. The accusations of 'Fascism' are ricocheting around the country from New Left to New Right and nearly everyone is agreed that labels from the thirties apply. But where is the Fascist Regime, the philosophy of power, the take-over group? It doesn't exist except as some kind of covert, deep instinctual drive which even the political demagogues prefer to keep in hiding today – as opposed to the thirties when they were openly proclaiming Fascism. At that time, even the poets and architects of Futurism were openly proclaiming their aggressive commitments to war and the beauty of destruction. Filippo Tommaso Marinetti, the founder of Futurism, could find the greatest possible aesthetic delight in the Italian Colonial War against Ethiopia:

MIES VAN DER ROHE and PHILIP JOHNSON, *Seagram Building* from below entrance; unlike a Greek Temple the architecture has not been corrected for optical distortions.

> For twenty-seven years we Futurists have rebelled against the branding of war as anti-aesthetic . . . Accordingly we state . . . war is beautiful because it establishes man's dominion over the subjugated machinery by means of gas masks, terrifying megaphones, flame throwers and small tanks. War is beautiful because it initiates the dreamt-of metalisation of the human body. War is beautiful because it enriches a flowering meadow with the fiery orchids of machine guns. War is beautiful because it combines the gunfire, the cannonades, the cease fire, the scents and the stench of putrefaction into a symphony. War is beautiful because it creates new architecture, like that of the big tanks, the geometrical formation flights, the smoke spirals from burning villages, and many others . . . Poets and artists of Futurism! . . . Remember these principles of an aesthetics of war so that your struggle for a new literature and a new graphic art . . . may be illumined by them.

This is probably about as far as an aesthetics of war and enjoyment of destruction can go and when I questioned Johnson about his commitment in the thirties he was much more circumspect.

C J: Well, what was your attitude towards the Nazis there? You were connected somehow.

P J: Oh no – totally outside. I did . . . um . . . go to Berlin after the War started. Which was very, very challenging . . . in 1939 . . . for just the sheer excitement. I mean nobody got nowhere. I knew some American correspondents who hated my guts and thought I was a spy. I don't know really how they figured that one out???

Actually it was William Shirer whom Johnson met in Danzig then – who describes this meeting and the suspicions it aroused:

Four Seasons Restaurant, Seagram Building, New York City, 1959. This four-and-a-half million dollar restaurant is located on the first floor of the Seagram Building. It represents Johnson's first Camp departure for affluent New Yorkers determined to enjoy themselves on a gustatory binge (*Time* magazine: 'as hedonistic as a Caesar's court'). However, *Timemoguless* Clare Booth Luce 'can't stand the place ... because the curtain ripples make her nervous'. These are made out of thin chains of anodised aluminium which are looped across the windows and chatter and clatter when the air-conditioner is turned on. The cluster of brass rods, designed by the sculptor Richard Lippold, the thin rods of the stairway and the bubbling pool all add to the effervescent tinkle of money changing hands and food being served.

Dr Boehmer, press chief of the Propaganda Ministry in charge of this trip, insisted that I share a double room in the hotel here with Philip Johnson, an American fascist who says he represents Father Coughlin's *Social Justice*. None of us can stand the fellow and suspect he is spying on us for the Nazis. For the last hour in our room here he has been posing as anti-Nazi and trying to pump me for my attitude. I have given him no more than a few bored grunts.

PJ: Shirer's a very irresponsible journalist . . . very third-rate writer . . .

CJ: You were in Danzig then . . .

PJ: Yes, I went on one of those expeditions you'll find . . . Yes it was that night in Danzig that Shirer writes about. But uh . . . I really, I'd suppose that anyone who wasn't actively crusading was suspicious and I probably did lean over backwards . . . No I was wrong . . . I hoped something good would come out of it. No this was *before* concentration camps were started of course. But still no excuse. Speer has it right, I know. But of course I weren't no spy . . .

We had previously touched on the Modern Movement's ubiquitous compromises with all the Fascist regimes of the time and Johnson had underlined the apolitical position of Mies – which seemed somehow particularly relevant to his own pragmatic position.

PJ: . . . If the Devil himself offered Mies a job he would take it.

CJ: Yeah, quite . . . Well that's true of all the major architects . . . the Pioneers of the period. I mean Le Corbusier going to Vichy.

PJ: Corbusier going to Vichy, Neutra wishing that Hitler would give him a job.

CJ: Gropius.

PJ: I mean – semi-joking – but-uh-of course! But then – uh – a lot of people – Sibyl Moholy-Nagy can't forgive Mies. But it was going on . . .

CJ: But you even find Gropius writing a letter to Goebbels in 1934 – have you seen those?

PJ: Don't tell me!

CJ: Oh yes, saying you must not get rid of the new Modern architecture – it's 'Germanic', it's Schinkelesque, it harkens back to the Gothic period . . .

PJ: Pevsner.

CJ: What?

PJ: Sainted Sir Nikolaus . . . wanted to become an honorary Aryan and stay on . . . I forget where this is . . . but uh – Gropius???

CJ: Yes there is a book written by Barbara Miller Lane called *Architecture and Politics in Germany 1918-1945* . . . page 181 . . .

PJ: Thanks, well I probably won't read the book.

CJ: But it's surprising – all those architects were trying to make overtures. The problem I think was, among other things, that Hitler and Goebbels both came out for a 'crystal-clear functionalism' in 1932 . . .

PJ: Of course –

CJ: And you could read it either way.

PJ: You could read it *both* ways. Oh, reading Speer is one of the really exciting things. Have you read the architectural section? Oh, but read the architectural part. Because Speer was an extremely sensitive man and really a businessman

PHILIP JOHNSON and JOHN BURGEE, *Thanksgiving Square Chapel*, Dallas, 1977. A spiral ziggurat based on many historical prototypes including a ninth-century tower in Samarra. The historicism may be considered Post-Modern but its unlikely presence, as an oversimplified corkscrew in Dallas, makes it typical of Late-Modernist unintended humour. Basically a diagrammatic spiral, where the stained glass follows the twists, it is conceived as precisionist sculpture not meaningful or carefully detailed form.

Boston Public Library Extention, 1973. Heavy, indeed gargantuan, use of a stylised classical language which is meant, somehow, to harmonise with the adjacent nineteenth-century library. Such pompous formalism was characteristic of American civic centres of the sixties and criticised for falling, heavily, between classicism and Modernism.

Boston Public Library Extension, interior. Diagrammatic, flat, pristine and still classical with a typical Late-Modern doorway: ie absence of wall, no mouldings or transition. The black cantilevered stairway divides the unitary material into two different elements.

architect – he'd be good in America, a really great skyscraper architect, an organiser. But with this *mad* architect – uh – Hitler, who didn't have any intention to run the country at all – during the war. Spent the time designing – and made the drawings *himself* sometimes. Oh, you must take a glance at the book.

What the ... HITLER! An architect? *Mad* architect? Somehow it made a lot of fortuitous sense as if Johnson had suddenly illuminated a whole area of the architect's dreams, the secret desires and warped fantasies which usually cannot stand the light of day and remain hidden – even to the architect himself. But Hitler! A Thousand-Year Reich ...

The Sheldon Memorial Art Gallery, Lincoln, Nebraska. The Sheldon Museum, a clear reference back to Fascist designs of the thirties: massive, blank arcades from Mussolini's Third Rome which appear as fashion back-drops in *Vogue* magazine; Hitler and Troost's House of German Art in Munich with its Classical colonnade and Classical composition – stripped of any historicist ornament to combine Modern purity with Greek propriety – these are the roots of the Sheldon Museum. The exterior temple front, raised on a travertine stylobate, filled in by a travertine blank arcade is all surrounded by hand-carved splayed pilasters that curve up from their bases in concave swoops to merge with the entablature in an eye-ease symphony of unified, moulded travertine. It's as if a sculptor, a jeweller, took some gigantic block of homogeneous marble and went at it with a scalpel and polishing gun. All the surfaces melt into each other including the concave, four-sided, hand-carved columns – which were chosen specifically for the purpose. 'The problem, as usual, was the corner column. A concave curve at the cornice was unthinkable, so it is convex, warping toward the typical concave base.' Not only were these columns hand-carved, but they were first erected in Italy to '*test the play of shadows*'. The columns for a museum way out in the boondocks of Lincoln, Nebraska were first erected in Italy – to test the play of shadows where even *the light is different!*

The interior. Well the interior is made up of this thirty-foot high Great Hall, glazed both sides so that you can see clear through from one side to the other as you pass under a central bridge – a free-standing, gold-hued, scissor staircase which cuts up the space and leads almost *nowhere* like some Baroque stairway of Balthasar Neumann in the *corps de logis* and like that – a pure architectural *promenade* meant to display people in their latest finery and to make everybody into children. 'The point of this is it is so much fun to be on a bridge. It is like a little child. He longs for a brook with a little bridge to cross. And then he runs back and forth across the bridge. I think we are all children at heart. It is always nice to cross the bridge.'

The whole space glows with a lemon-yellow hue of gilded sunlight – honey curtains, gold carpets, golden staircase, gold-leaf lighting discs whirling above like flying saucers made out of fourteen carat bullion – Johnson has this kind of failed Midas touch – everything he touches turns to gold ... leaf.

Keepers of the architectural conscience shuddered. *Architectural Design* said: 'What commenced as a continuation of Classical tradition, now ends up as the most gargantuan piece of mannerism.' Bruno Zevi condemned the Neo-Classicism *in toto*: '. . . the dullest and most reactionary monumentalism, the most arbitrary and insignificant caprices'. Johnson had achieved another *succès de scandale*, another one of 'the

Sheldon Memorial Art Gallery, Lincoln, Nebraska, 1963. One of Johnson's masterpieces of Middle Camp of 'failed seriousness' at its best. The gigantic columnar order on the exterior contradicts the two-storey reality within. 'The essence of the exterior design, of course, is the splayed column. I don't know where I got it. But the idea of these curving columns, curving up from their bases and then into the arch itself; that is the fascination of them.' The fascination of travertine columns turning into a wall, arch, entablature and ceiling exists also on the inside which is like a homogeneous piece of marble carved away by a diamond cutter. The eye easily spills over these gently modulated surfaces until it comes to rest finally on the other objects, the stairway-bridge, the gold-leaf lighting discs and an occasional *objet d'art*.

Susan Sontag: 'Camp is the consistently aesthetic experience of the world, it incarnates a victory of "style" over "content", "aesthetics" over "morality", of irony over tragedy'.

most sincerely hated buildings in the world'. And yet, characteristically Johnson himself, with his unsuppressible perception and candour, was out in the field gently mocking his own uncertainty, his own insecurity, which would lead him to design Camp symbols to a non-existent public realm while asserting at the same time that this lack of belief was itself a possible cause of destructive potential: 'The only principle that I can conceive of believing in is the Principle of Uncertainty. It is a brave architect that can possess convictions and beliefs, and keep his tongue out of his cheek . . . I really don't know why I designed these [buildings] the way I did. Others will tell me.'

In a sense, Johnson's buildings represent this loss of belief as does so much other formalist architecture. Yet the desire to believe and produce credible monuments is still there, even if it has no acceptable outlet, even if there is no credible public realm or religion: 'What we have lost is a public passion for greatness. No cathedrals? Not even great public nuclear plants? What is our generation going vicariously to enjoy as in the old days, the palace, the church, or the Acropolis?'

It almost sounds right – but 'vicariously enjoy'? This is the Camp reading of High Culture. All Johnson's best works have this 'failed seriousness', this heroic gesture which backfires, which explodes into the grin of a sardonic clown. At best – in his self-mocking comments or his Sheldon Museum – he attains a level of candid introspection and exaggeration usually reserved as moments of truth for the court jester.

Since this piece was published, AAQ *Winter 1973, Philip Johnson has gone through another creative period, perhaps the most original of his career. As the buildings illustrated show, he is at once a protagonist of Late- and Post-Modernism, and in a loose sense, by consulting history for its examples, he has always been a Post-Modernist. Unmentioned in this essay, written in the Neo-Hysterical Style, is Johnson's personal kindness and generosity. He has been a patron of Modern artists and architects for two generations, and remains something of a power-broker in American architectural politics even today. He supports unknown, but good, emergent architects. 'Doctor Johnson', as Peter Eisenman calls him, was even generous to me after I wrote this piece, which is not a balanced assessment of his work. This will have to wait for the future. The work has, I believe, an easy and icy beauty.*

Nikolaus Pevsner has denied the innuendo above (see AAQ *vol 6, no 2, 1974, p 58). The quotes from Johnson come from two tape-recorded interviews I had with him and the numerous other published statements he has made.*

DIALOGUES WITH PHILIP JOHNSON

Modernist Morality : The Primacy of Art

– Several years ago, Philip, you admitted to being a reluctant moralist. You may have adopted an amoralist position from time to time, but like Oscar Wilde you placed art above morality and that's a kind of morality in itself – the aesthetic life.

What does interest me is the basic theme of creativity. Or is the basic human drive immortality, as Plato would have it? Is it the sex drive, or the will to power?

– You place aesthetics and creativity on a plane above both political and social morality.

Oh yes, of course.

– And that is itself a kind of restricted morality.

I like that.

– And that seems to me distinctly the Modernist position, because Modernism, the last religion of the Western intellectual, replaces both religion and work with the notion of creativity and aesthetics.

You're going back to Rimbaud?

– Yes, Rimbaud, but also Matthew Arnold and the end of the Protestant work ethic – the fact that most people today don't see work as a final goal. With the decline of the work ethic and religion, two of the most traditional underpinnings of society eroded – to be replaced by the Modernist goals of creativity and art. It's summarised as culture – you become a collector.

That's very well put.

– You would agree with this.

Of course. But you're putting words in my mouth.

– Modernism, in its heyday from 1890 to 1930, celebrated freedom, self-realisation, overcoming habits – with a belief in the perpetual revolution of the new. And it posited a kind of opposition to bourgeois life and the academic. The Salon des Refusés is the archetypal avant-garde institution. And yet with Late-Modernism (the New York School and Abstract Expressionism) and the Museum of Modern Art accepting the avant-garde – suddenly Modernism has triumphed against its traditional adversary, the bourgeoisie.

Right –

– And become its official reigning culture. So the question is 'Can Modernism survive its own triumph?' What do you feel about that? Can it be both adversary and mainstream – that seems to me your role? To be both High Church and out of the Church.

Well there's a lot of High Church threads in the Modernist religion, and that's what I would be – the continuation of High Church and anarchist.

– Yes, but I don't see anyone else in that period except Adolf Loos, who tried to be both a dandy and critic at the same time.

T S Eliot? Well the 'permanent revolution' – it's a good question. Can you go on being

PHILIP JOHNSON and JOHN BURGEE ARCHITECTS, *Transco Tower*, Houston, Texas, 1979-83. An endless grid is articulated by set-backs forming a base and crown. Johnson's predilection for the supercool sublime is evident here, an exaggeration towards anonymity and standardisation inherent in corporate life.

avant-garde after Albert Barr in the art world? What would your position be?
– *Can there be a Museum of Modern Art? If it's a 'museum' then it's to do with the past, and if it's 'Modern' then it's attacking history. That's what many philosophers and writers have said – there can't be a Museum of Modern Art.*
There can if you restrict the dates – sure.
– *But then it should be called the Museum of Contemporary Art. In other words if you accept that Modernism is an adversarial culture always breaking down habit, convention, the academy and the Establishment, then the minute it becomes the Establishment, it changes into something else – it must do. It can't be both.*
Well, the fact is that it *was* both and *did* succeed as an institution, ideologically as well as popularly – and it's still going on. We'll have to start over with the definition – the avant-garde must mean something else. The Museum of Modern Art worked as an avant-garde institution, and as far as I'm concerned, it's still working.
– *But from 1960 to recently, it's been very reactionary.*
Stodgy.
– *Backward-looking.*
I see my show on Deconstructivism as a recapitulation of the day I came in – it's history of the last eight years. When we did it before, in 1932, it was history of the previous fifteen years. But things move faster now and we've speeded it up. But it was an avant-garde statement, surely – it may not be a right or wrong one, that's not the point. It must go on and we call it the Museum of Modern Art, still. Perhaps it's a misnomer.
– *I'm arguing this contradiction is normal to Modernism: the Museum of Modern Art changed the character of Modern Art once it institutionalised the avant-garde in the 1930s. You and Barr institutionalised the International Style and thus Modernism changed its nature irreversibly. It was no longer an adversarial culture, it became the American canonisation of something that had been done.*
It succeeded.
– *This became the beginning of Establishment culture and this is why, in the 1960s, Post-Modernism started as a reaction against it – the hegemony of the Modern Movement and MoMA, and Kennedy, and American liberalism. It's clear Post-Modernism at that point is an attack on the reigning culture, it's an attempt to find a new radicalism. You clearly believe Modernism can survive its own triumph – you don't see the paradox there?*
Well there is one. You can still have paradox and fortunately go on designing anyway you like. That's the advantage of not being a 'word-person'. You can do what you like, formally. And it just happened that what came after Modernism was a disgust with the narrowness of the movement – which is fine.
– *But Philip you know words are not the problem. Your designs reflect these values and thoughts. You may be more open and say: 'I'm into every style and I always have been, and I always change what I want.'*

The Deconstructivist Contradiction

– *The Deconstructivism Show at MoMA is a paradox like all the exhibitions at MoMA – it's a canonisation of an avant-garde future/past. It brings in the same contradiction the Church would create if it brought in heretics.*
Heresy becomes the official Church doctrine – which of course the Church is pursuing

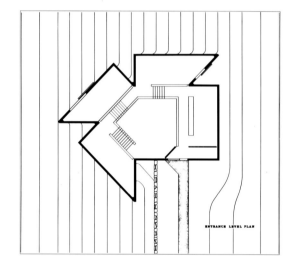

Sculpture Museum, New Canaan, Connecticut, 1970. This all white gallery, with its collection of Neo-Modern works by Frank Stella and others, has an uncanny proto-Deconstructionist quality in the way overhead beams and sliced spaces cut up the art into a lattice of black and white patterns. This assault by lighting grids and oblique angles prefigures Eisenman's deconstruction of the art museum at the Wexner Center, fifteen years later.

but a little more slowly. If Rome doesn't do that there won't be any Roman Catholic Church. In some way that's the paradox of Christianity, especially in a day like this, or else they're out of business – which they're not intending to be.

– Are you saying the Church is built on a series of heterodox positions?

Don't you think?

– And blasphemies?

The blasphemies become sacred sayings.

– That sounds like the Aquinian Heresy – proving the necessary existence of evil. I want to pursue the double-bind of the MoMA Shows, this institutionalised contradiction – to set up an orthodoxy and kill it at the same time. You find Peter Eisenman also involved in this – trying to set up an 'Academy of the Dispossessed'. Like a Woody Allen character, he's always saying: 'I'm in favour of the "out", the "rejected", the "adversarial culture"' (ie Modernism) – an Academy he leads. He refuses to admit it. So Eisenman shows the same hypocrisies and contradictions.

Sure, I think Eisenman is a perfect hypocrite, as I probably am myself. See, our interest isn't like yours in the codification of all this. If you think in terms of forms, then you don't have to bother with a lot of that – it doesn't affect the lines you make on paper.

– I believe your 'lines on paper' directly reflect these shifts and different philosophical positions, and your four periods of work. And they are endemic to Modernism and Nietzsche – and his emphasis on willpower, the Superman or man of the future, and the importance for remaining at the cutting edge of creation anticipating the future changing style – are you still reading Nietzsche?

I don't get the time to read anything. But what did he mean by 'Art is more important than truth' – or my favourite sentence 'Art is with us so we don't perish from the truth'. What the hell is he talking about?

– Art as a kind of religion.

All right.

– And that is the quintessential Modernist position.

All right, if you want to say one has a philosophy I got it straight out of Nietzsche. My position is straight from the Nietzsche-Heidegger-Derrida line.

Philip Against Post-Modernism

– I see four changes in your work: your early Modernist period, then your shift to both Late- and Post-Modernism and now I anticipate, because of the MoMA Show, a shift to Neo-Modernism.

Neo-Modernism?

– Well, first do you agree with the first three shifts?

Yes I do. What has convinced me – concerning Post-Modernism is (a) I'm not very good but (b) Post-Modernism has not shown the strength that I thought it would. I thought Graves would develop into a man who understood the techniques and everything enough, so the craft and whatever was needed would follow – and I don't believe it has. And even the pure Classicists, like Greenberg or Quinlan Terry are thinning the language down. No guts to that. And the New Baroque, which we should have, we still dislike from the Beaux-Arts period, which gets bulbous without being good. And so any return to tradition would require a much more serious approach

PHILIP JOHNSON and JOHN BURGEE ARCHITECTS, *Pittsburgh Plate Glass (PPG) Headquarters*, Pittsburgh, Pennsylvania, 1979-84. One of Johnson's Post-Modern towers which transforms, in glass, the Victorian Tower at the Houses of Parliament. The essentialisation of one idea in a different material – wooden construction in stone – was a hallmark of Classicists, so it is ironic that here Johnson should invent the process – caricaturing Gothic in glass. The absolute attitude towards transformation and the tough, sheer facade punctuated by triangular indents, give the project a certain stature. The 231 spires, with fluorescent lamps, give it a certain awesome kitsch.

than I have had. I've taken a very flippant one – not that I'm against that. So today it isn't Modernism I'm coming back to, it's a *new* type of Modernism. Words are unfortunate, but I like the word Deconstruction because it's connected to Derrida and the relativist approach to truth and objectivity. But of course what I don't know is where the form comes from, or will be coming from. But I do know it fits very glove-like into the needs of today, that kind of switch back to Modernism.

– So, for you, there is a 'crisis of Post-Modernism'; it didn't take off. You don't believe that a tradition has grown, as I argue in my book Post-Modernism – the New Classicism in Art and Architecture.

Oh yes, but I really despise the art in that book.

– Oh really?

Well, I can't digest it.

– Why?

I don't know: because you did put in a couple of my favourite painters – Salle and Fischl – but you also put in mostly what we call crap. I don't think there's disagreement on that, but you don't want them to agree with you. But let's stick to architecture – I just don't think Post-Modernism developed enough to be considered a discipline, whereas Deconstructivism, or whatever it is we are doing, is very disciplined. But that goes back to Modern.

– Really? Skews are? And fragments and decomposition are disciplined? You can't have discipline without rules.

Discipline in my sense is not about rules, but forms. The forms of Constructivism are perfectly clear, the best part of the MoMA Show – they're real. That Show is like presenting one-off little sketches in with the master paintings. In other words, Malevich could really paint.

– There is a language of Deconstructivism, just as there is of Post-Modernism, and they are equally 'disciplined'.

But I never liked the word Post-Modernism.

– But you often claimed to be a P-M.

No, I always said I wasn't.

– Now now Philip, you often said you partly were. And surely with the AT&T and Pittsburgh Plate Glass – a lot of buildings you said were P-M. And that your new direction of historicism was exonerated by P-M – after the fact.

No, I never said that, because none of us liked these words. It's like Deconstructivists. None of us are. Every single one of us screams and yells – so what. The words are very useful for categorisation; you have to use them if you're going to write articles.

Neo-Modern?

– Wait a minute. You admitted to a Modern, Late-Modern and Post-Modern period – and are you a Neo-Modernist?

Neo-Modern, I never heard till this afternoon.

– It's been around this city for years – since 1982. Ada Louise Huxtable, Douglas Davis, Paul Goldberger, even Richard Meier – they all use the term, en passant *– no one's written a book or article on it. But the word has been in the air for six years.*

All right, let's use it then.

PHILIP JOHNSON and JOHN BURGEE, *Times Square, Four Office Towers*, New York City, 1984, redesigned 1989. What were four mansarded towers with arched fronts borrowed from Palladio's Villa Poiana, have now been deconstructed into a nouveau assemblage. One mansard remains, sans finials, another mansard gets skewed and its main facades turned into very fine-grained graph paper with a few 'supersigns' – presumably in neon. The two right-hand monoliths get Neo-Constructivist treatment. All this simulation of the old Times Square 'whoopee' is preferable to the four previously proposed tombstones, but at $3 billion and 4.1 million square feet it only adds to the other megalumps next door.

158

– In New York – I assumed these people must have got it from you.

No, never heard it. Because all the time I was playing with these forms of Constructivism, I didn't think of it being Modern. But everything gets labelled: that's one thing we don't have to worry about because we have Charles Jencks.

– There's another term we could use called 'Modern Modern' – present tense Modernism, presentism. The problem with 'Neo' is that like Neo-Classicism, the Modern Movement would have had to have died completely before it could be revived consciously, and I don't see that happening.

Deconstructivism – the Small Wave

– Returning to the MoMA Show, it has the Wigley-slippery phrase 'This is not a movement'.

No, that's mine.

– That's you?

Yeah, that was my basic thought when we started.

– Well you know that we know that's the basic Freudian self-denial that means it is a movement!

Only Charles Jencks would say that.

– No, come on, everyone who says 'I am not Modernist' gives the classic confession of faith. As a historian and critic, I'm sure Deconstructivism is a Movement and a style.

Good, you're saying so.

– And your denial proves it for me!

OK.

– 'Methinks he doth protest too much'.

It could be.

– We haven't even accused it of being a Movement, and you're saying it's not.

Because everyone expects me to have a Movement, that's why I have to deny it ahead of time.

– But why bother?

Indeed, why bother.

– I mean everybody needs 'movements', it's been dry for seven years with Post-Modernism, it was desired – you wanted it.

I still don't know why it happened . . .

– It's the coming into focus of a lot of things.

But why would the Nietzschean line and Deconstruction in philosophy marry up with Constructivist forms?

– Because one of the things about a 'Not' movement, is that you can define it by what it is not, and it's definitely not Post-Modern Classicism. Deconstructivists define themselves against Post-Modernists and all that they hate out there and what is left, uncontaminated, is Constructivism.

Why?

– But, it will be contaminated in three years. I ask my students why are you doing 'little Zaha Hadids', and they say because it isn't yet corrupt. And I say, but wait, 'it's got a half-life of three years'. So it's clearly a Movement and Style and I can't understand why you and Wigley-slippery didn't define a style. I was going to do a dictionary of some formal rules and an article on 'cocktail sticks, dissociated point-grids, flying beams' and the twenty other

rhetorical terms. It's clearly a very cohesive style and has to be or it's not worth much.
Maybe it isn't worth anything. It hasn't the style or background that the International Style did when it became current – it's more like a 'manner'.
– A 'maniera'.
Yes, it isn't a movement in the sense of the Modern Movement, which had a whole philosophy behind it, very long and clear – with lines out of William Morris.
– But this has a lineage – you've gone back to Constructivism.
Constructivism reminds me more of what Hitchcock called the Viennese Secession – a thing like that, like Art Nouveau rather than the International Style. The International Style was totally basic to a *Weltanschauung* that was shared by all good people – Socialists, not quite Fascists and Fascists.
– So you still contend that the International Style was somehow different – somehow more basic.
This Deconstructivism is however still Modern. What happened in Berlin in 1919 was incredible – when Lissitzky discovered the West and the West discovered Lissitzky, the West also discovered Mondrian, it all happened in the twenties. But nobody until these Deconstructivists went back to Malevitch: this is almost a recall.
– Are you saying the International Style is somehow like the Gothic or Renaissance – one of the great periods?
Yes. And I think the reaction was perfectly understandable. The International Style lasted a long time, until after the war – 1922 to the 1950s.
– You sound like Giedion: his saying that in history there are 'constituent' and 'transitory' facts. The 1920s International Style as constituent and 1980s Deconstructivism as transitory.
I never thought that.
– But that's how you're distinguishing one from another – one's a grand epistemological shift towards the deep structure of architecture and the other one is just surface changes.
Yes, very much as Mannerism was a surface change to the Renaissance. But it was also a very serious shift with late Michelangelo and our friend up in Mantua, Giuliano Romano. It took a hundred years to shift, but today it doesn't take that long to get worn out or bored. I don't like these periods as 'words'. The International Style as written by my contemporaries Hitchcock and Barr was certainly a basic shift and it ended up in a crystallised style that could be talked about. I don't see Deconstructivism that way.
– But you can formalise it.
Oh you can formalise the Art Nouveau too with the whiplash curve.
– Exactly, and in that sense it can be just as disciplined and valid as any other movement – I don't see the distinction.
Between style and manner?
– That one is more basic than another I would dispute. For me the International Style is just one more style like any other. I don't believe there is an essential style to architecture: Choisy thought he found it, the Egyptians thought they found it, every Classicist thinks he's found it and I think they're all talking about something which – if you could formalise it in symbolic logic – then you could talk about a 'deep structure' in Chomsky's sense. They're all surface styles claiming to be universal – from Leon Krier to El-Wakil to Christopher Alexander – all claim they are designing in the eternal, 'timeless' architectural style. And all the rest is

PHILIP JOHNSON and JOHN BURGEE ARCHITECTS, *Garden Grove Community Church*, Garden Grove, California, 1977-80. On the exterior this 'crystal cathedral' looks like a behemoth from Silicon Valley, or an airplane hangar with its scaleless 'all-over' surface of reflective glass. The image is eerie, inappropriate as a church, but at the same time highly evocative and other-worldly. The scaleless sublime is continued on the interior where the sizzle of incessant space frames dazzles the eye with a vibrating white froth. At a key point in the service the Reverend Dr Robert H Schuller will press a button and the large pair of 'Cape Kennedy doors' swings open revealing the heavens – and a parking lot full of worshippers listening on their car radios. The Mechanico-Religious genre here finds its apotheosis.

superficial maniera.

I agree.

— I don't know which way you're agreeing — with me or them?

I agree with your description of everybody saying this is the ultimate style of all. The only thing you must say is that there are great ground-swells — the Gothic.

— Reigning styles — so the International Style was a reigning style, that's all you're claiming?

Yes, the International Style was a much bigger wave than this small even tiny wave. Therefore I wouldn't call it a new style. Mannerism is a small wave within the big wave of the Renaissance.

— Baroque is a big wave, Rococo is a small one, Neo-Classicism big, Neo-Egyptian small?

Big waves and little ones, that's a good way of looking at it.

— It's better than Giedion's way — which is imperialistic towards 'transitory' facts. He's just saying 'I don't want to deal with all those little waves.'

An Elite Movement And Difficulty

— Can we go back to the 'difficulty' of Deconstructivism, because it's like the 'difficulty' of Modernism — 'make it new' and unconventional, hard to decipher. And that meant making a new, élite audience, the 'chosen few', the initiates, a small mandarin group. And I come back to the problem that now the small has become everyone — the large. The Museum of Modern Art is now everywhere and Jasper Johns is the ultimate prize at auction — five, or is it now ten million dollars. One's talking about a shift to the New Church, and you've always been there Philip: that's why you have an underground Museum, that's why you collected Modern art. You've understood this from the very beginning and never flinched from it. Peter Eisenman, in our interview, put a funny one on me concerning the show. He said you were trying to make up with the old-guard Modernists who were mad at you for having left the High Church and you're trying to make your peace with them — the hard hats, the severe ones.

That I am ???

— I think that's a misreading of you.

I think so . . .

— The thing about Wigley's and Libeskind's writing is that it is opaque in a typically Modernist way. And no one reads Deconstructivist manifestos except to go to sleep.

Same with Derrida.

— You agree that 'difficulty' is a part of Deconstructivism and Modernism?

I hadn't thought of it — not in architecture.

— That's why the quintessential Modern genre is advanced music.

Which remains opaque — it's as if you had a lot of people writing Eisenmanese. As a member of the bourgeoise, I can't listen to Modern music and I'm not going to anymore.

— But I don't think you've joined the bourgeoisie — you see my point is that the bourgeoisie is Modern. Every bourgeois is split — two sides of his brain. One side rejects the bourgeoisie — the Modernist, like Karl Marx — who both celebrates the bourgeoisie and its power in The Communist Manifesto, *and attacks it. I didn't realise this was a Modernist tract until I read Marshall Berman's* All That is Solid Melts into Air *— I think one of the most important books on Modernism ever written.*

I think The Communist Manifesto *is still the greatest read — and it's not a bit opaque.*
You can have a Modernist Manifesto and not have it difficult.

The Deconstructivist Show and its Limitations

— I wanted to ask you about the difference between Deconstructivism and Deconstructionism.
Deconstructivism is a *portmanteau* word out of Lewis Carroll, taking Heidegger, Derrida and Deconstruction on the one hand and the Russian Constructivists on the other.
— In a way you're 'defanging' the Deconstructionists — as an American defanging Europeans, you're always doing it. With the International Style.
What me? I don't do anything.
— Philip, I thought you agreed with all this? To turn a 'tion' into an 'ism', to turn an action into a style, and institutionalise it in the Museum of Modern Art.
That's why people resent the Show.
— I don't.
But most of the critics do.
— It's like Appollinaire doing it for the Modern painters. You're always canonising, and freezing in a way — freeze-drying some critics might say — the great impulses of Europe. As a person who lives in Europe my only advice to them was 'if you're going to be freeze-dried then say how you differ' — but they didn't. All of the Europeans went along with it — I told you that the last time I was here in April.
I don't remember.
— And I thank you for mentioning Alvin Boyarsky in your introduction.
He's a very important man. I had a long dedication.
— But I'm sad you didn't have John Johansen in the Show. As a result of my conversation with you and Wigley I see that he now does finally refer to SITE and Matta-Clark and Fujii in his introduction — but only to push them away.
That's because he has a narrower definition.
— But, if you had five more rooms at MoMA?
I still wouldn't have put them in.
— They're part of the same movement — they really are — in a broad, critical, historian's sense. I can see the point of limitation to models and drawings — but as a historian I protest. You've got a really large movement here that includes precursors from the sixties — all of Peter Cook's work in Frankfurt, his whole school, and the AA School in the seventies.
I think you're wrong about Johansen.
—The Mummer's Theater is a seminal work of Deconstructionism — I will go to my grave insisting that it is. John Johansen is not my favourite architect, but that isn't the point. If you define the style and intentions, then the Mummer's Theater, by 1970, is the most cogently built Deconstructionist building at that time in the US.
I think any good historian, like yourself and others will be re-writing all that and properly so. Just because I didn't see it at the time — think what I missed in my catalogue in 1932 about precursors. And the ideological differences with James Wines and SITE are very interesting. Like some of your work, we were perhaps a little fast.
— But is it because it was 'a little fast', or was there an intention to be High Church? Certainly

Wines is Low Church.

I think you may be right there too – my preciosity, or desire for it, comes out.

– Couldn't Fujii have gotten in your Church?

Fujii could not have – but he was close. I remember discussing Archigram and the whole Japanese thing. It didn't really add up. And to make a High Church you have to have dogmas, or forms in my case that were close together. But leaving out Mackintosh in the story of Art Nouveau – although he doesn't use the whiplash – would narrow it down terribly.

– Exactly. That's why I want a broader Church.

All right, but I wanted a narrower one.

– What's the response been – any good or bad criticism?

No good or bad, just uninformed – the stupidest was the first one.

– By Sorkin?

No, Sorkin is a good man – most helpful, a bright man – we don't get along, shall I say. Goldberger was the only thoughtful one. It was the ex-*Times* man – Hilton Kramer – who wrote in the New York *Observer*, 'A Twirpy Show'. An ill-informed, personal attack about me. There was no good critical evaluation. Last year, Joe Giovannini and Aaron Betsky set my mind turning around – you need a bit of grit to make a pearl. I talked with these two men within a week and they brought up Coop Himmelblau, who I didn't know very well, and Betsky knew all those other Californians I also left out.

– Morphosis?

That was very deliberate, after making a study of them, and of course there are the other Californians.

– I think you ought to open your church doors at both ends – really!

There can be other shows.

– There's not even a mention of Derrida in your catalogue – how can you have Deconstruction without Derrida? Actually that absence is refreshing.

Wigley has written his doctoral thesis on Derrida and Architecture.

– But he's not mentioned in the catalogue.

I don't know why, I thought he was. I think Wigley wants to be Derrida's connection to architecture – Derrida doesn't know anything about architecture.

– Actually Derrida's written three or four articles on Tschumi and Eisenman and other architects. He said, at our conference in London, on video-tape, that at first he was very sceptical, but now he thinks there is a Deconstructionist Architecture.

Modernism: The Perpetual Transvaluation of Values

– I think the contradictions of your successive positions are very modern – to keep moving and cancelling your previous positions. Ultimately, as Marx makes out in The Communist Manifesto, *it is the power of the bourgeoisie to destroy all the traditions that it creates in its past, even the 'Tradition of the New'. In other words, the quintessential aspect of Modernism is to tear itself up, like Robert Moses rebuilding New York City – that's the ending of* All That is Solid Melts into Air. *The 'transvaluation of all values' – New York is melting into air – the quintessential Nietzschean quote is what Modernism is about. And this transvaluation now is made through the belief in art and culture, while in the nineteenth century it was made in factories and in Modernisation.*

Yeah.

– Modernism depended on Modernisation, the two were really interlinked, but no one went to the heart of it. Today we live in Post-Modernisation – information is what it's about, factories are in the Third World and Brazil. So the curious thing is that we live in the First World, where only twelve per cent of the population works in factories and 'does' Modernisation, and Modernisation really is in Japan and South Korea. So if you want to be Modern, Philip, you should go to South Korea. Modernism is the Catholic orthodoxy left over from the reality which has long ago disappeared, and therefore this kind of love/hate or contradiction which I've been talking about which your position shows – is very much like David Salle or Eric Fischl's paintings (except they are Post-Modern). I think you're ultimately a Nietzschean Modernist.

That's a good feeling, probably better than anything I could say. I wouldn't know, but I agree with you it's the perpetual 'transvaluation of values' – I'm still a Modernist in the long term.

– Yes, but whereas Fischl shows that kind of fear and Salle that kind of loathing for the bourgeois, it seems to me you're much more like the dandy of Apollinaire and Adolf Loos, or Konstantin Melnikov, the peasant in spats who danced through the Revolution, the great Modernist. Neo-Modern, Modern Modern, or Still Modern, it's people like you who are keen to come back into the fold.

The one exception to my categories is Frank Gehry who is simply an individual that doesn't fit anyone's framework.

– Oh Frank is a Late-Modernist although he's hard to categorise. But Bruce Goff doesn't fit easily, either. Yet he's not too far away from the 'Organic Modern' of Wright. And certainly Frank Gehry comes out of Late-Modernism, Abstract Expressionism, Larry Bell, Ron Davis and all that art. Frank makes no denials. At the end of the day you are a Modernist.

But the word 'Modernism' is a curse word because it was connected with the International Style and that badly needed shaking up. But the 'Modern Movement' – how can you get out of it?

– My argument is that you – as the last living Nietzschean – are always transforming what you did before.

Sure.

– And that's very Modernist.

Okay, in your definition I'm a Modernist.

– It's a Marxist definition too.

Yeah, I'm delighted – I haven't read enough Marx.   (August 1988)

Modernism and the Speed of Change

– Ten years ago you talked about having twelve styles – and recently about your 'relativist' approach to truth and objectivity. One of the things that philosophers such as Derrida and Lyotard are talking about is the difficulty of finding legitimate foundations for any field and the 'end of meta-narratives' – holistic world explanations. These ideas relate directly to your relativism and constant shift in styles – which approaches the condition of fashion. You have a social and contextual justification for the use of each style but there's no deep foundation for it. You, like these philosophers, would also say there's no direction to history.

History doesn't have a teleology.

PETER EISENMAN, *Social Housing*, IBA, Berlin, 1982-7.

JOHN BURGEE ARCHITECTS with PHILIP JOHNSON, *Canadian Broadcasting Corporation*, Toronto, Canada 1988-1992. *Elevator core* juts into the atrium and skylight, setting up a secondary diagonal structural grid. Note the columns dying into the piers and red balconies giving 'snap and sparkle'.

CBC Building. The south-east corner entrance is defined by a silver cylinder which interrupts the white metal 'meta-grid.' A secondary red grid defines the floor lines, while an angled blue curtain wall – extending to the eighth floor – indicates one of the top television studios; red another one. In this way the architects have dramatised the main feature of broadcasting. Micro-wave dishes and cooling towers are also accentuated. Thus a Modernist functional expression is articulated by a series of modest juxtapositions.

– And it may not, for you, even have a meaning.
It has no overall 'meaning'; but it has its own meaning. That is why I hate Plato so much and his idea of objective truth – with the Idea – capital I – having objective existence.
– The Modernist's position, that of Le Corbusier and the 'religion of Modernism,' did have *a direction,* did *have a social agenda.*
That's right.
– You are in a very curious position, because you are like a Nineteenth-Century Modernist. I don't want to call you (as you did Frank Lloyd Wright) 'the greatest architect of the Nineteenth Century'.
I *am* a Nineteenth Century architect!
– The other day I called Bob Stern the 'greatest architect of the Edwardian period', as he has followed Norman Shaw's development from Queen Anne Revival to the Edwardian Baroque in a somewhat revivalist manner. You have said that you were never really a Post-Modernist, you never liked that label.
Yes, I'm still a Modernist in my approach to function.
– In a deeper sense, you are a person who does believe in continual change. It is like Peter Eisenman's argument that Modernism in all the fields except architecture had a Nietzschean, anti-humanist twist. Whereas architecture had a social direction.
It never did for us who rejected the political and social myths of those such as Hannes Meyer – Mies and I never shared this.
– There is a reason for social idealism: architects, by profession, must have an ideology of social amelioration and progress.
But *we* don't believe in progress.
– People like Margaret Thatcher and Norman Foster say they do – there's still that left-over ideology.
Absolutely, 'liberalism' in the English sense of the word.
– Whereas your kind of Modernism is much more Nietzschean.
Nineteenth Century.
– Let us return to Marshall Berman's book, All That is Solid Melts into Air, *and its idea that Modernism is the cultural expression of modernisation. You are one of the most pure believers in that because of your relativity, your constant embracing of change, your putting creativity at the top of the agenda and your belief that that's all there is. You've come straight out of Kant, and the Enlightenment version of Modernism as pure aesthetics.*
Hegel is better.
– I want to find out about your changing relationship to Post-Modernism – even though you can see it turn into an architectural style of nostalgia.
We have been asked by clients even to repeat previous buildings – like the La Salle Tower in Chicago – it's all part of the nostalgia business.
– But then you suddenly embrace Deconstruction, in this CBC building in Toronto; you certainly take on elements of Eisenman's version of Deconstruction – at least his Berlin Housing. But you use the different coloured grids and intersections as signs of different use rather than – as he did – as signs of the past and 'anti-memory'. This transformation of his vocabulary shows your constant embracing of any style regardless of its background as long as you can be creative with it. A rather heroic stance – except it cuts style off from semantics, locale and cultural continuity and leads to the relativity of all styles. When aesthetics are

166

prioritised to such a degree they become the *ultimate value.*

From which other values can be derived.

— You can argue, as Post-Modernists have, that aesthetics has been the legitimiser of uprooting people and destruction. Look at the flip-side of this, what Nietzsche already announced as the 'Destructor-Creator' — Superman. He melts things into air as does the cycle of modernisation. It has destroyed all previous cultures, and the only thing that has saved the West is that it was the first to modernise. There is a wonderful book by Theodore von Laue, a German who settled in America, called The World Revolution of Westernisation. *He says what escaped everybody: that modernisation is basically Westernisation, because the West took four hundred years to modernise, slowly, and could absorb it; all cultures that are non-western are being destroyed by trying to be western.*

But they're going to destroy us very quickly — they'll out-produce us and out-reproduce us.

Fashion Devouring its Young

— What has happened since our talk on the Decon Show and its effects?

The effects were as I prophesied: everybody denied the word and the concept; but then architects like Peter Pran, designer of one of the largest firms in America, creates these buildings with everything flying around everywhere.

— But that's the Modernist problem. Modernism is directly related to fast-changing fashions, and stylistic shifts. No sooner do you have a 'live' movement than it is turned into a fashion, to make way for the next one. This is where there is a hidden anti-creativity within the fashion industry.

I don't think that is avoidable with the present communications. What we need is a Mies van der Rohe or Le Corbusier coming up.

— But they can't come because the system moves too fast and precludes it. Fashion didn't smother the twenties, did it?

Why didn't it?

— Because the speed of production was slower. You said that Michael Graves didn't grow into a major Post-Modernist because of over-production. And why is Deconstruction deconstructing? It's the process of quick speed which makes everything still-born, and that's what pushes everybody on.

Except Classicism, which would be a Rock of Gibraltar in the swirling, changing world.

— There's a very Modernist thing here — 'Don't look back, someone may be gaining.'

But that's to do with communication — with you and reporting.

— By reporting you turn up the heat. But I'm trying to describe your relation to this. In the sixties you were the first person to say, 'It's all change,' and you admitted boredom — 'ennui' — the great nineteenth-century word of the Modernists like Baudelaire. And you articulated the problem which no one else would face. And since the sixties the situation has only deepened. You were saying, 'It's all changing, it's all fun . . .'

'No rules.'

— You were celebrating that Nietzschean, Dionysian aspect of creativity and fashion. And you were facing its nihilistic overtones —

Society is eating its own children every morning for breakfast.

— It's time for lunch, Philip, so I suggest we stop.   *(April 1989)*

JOHN BURGEE ARCHITECTS with PHILIP JOHNSON, *CBC Building, west entrance corridor towards atrium.* Like Koolhaas and the early Modernists, the architects have used coloured abstract forms to define functions and break up the mass in a relaxed, jazzy way.

CBC Building, atrium floor pattern in terrazzo. The layered grids of the facade are here given their shadows, and they make explicit the thirty foot structural bay. TV studios, which are shifted off axis, are represented in yellow while the circulation tower juts into the space.

WOLF BITES WOLFE

Cedric Price, terror of the bourgeoisie, steps to the microphone. The audience at the RIBA is hushed and individuals sink deeper into their seats hiding from a possible Price-harangue, well known to chase innocent bystanders right outside the door. He leans forward on the podium, jaw jutting out like Vladimir Ilyich Lenin . . . silence, long silence. A cigar shoots into the mouth at an angle, a hand clasps the brandy glass – pause. Starched white cuffs clipped on to his black striped shirt, starched white colour ('it's functional, these clip-ons get dirty at different rates from the shirt') – the clip-on starch holds the round head in place. Aristocratic features gaze out over the cowering but blood-thirsty audience: they are here to see a mob-up at the Annual Conference on 'Frontiers of Design'. Pause (he's forgotten his lines?). Vladimir Ilyich crossed with Oscar Wilde drops a sarcastic glance to let his followers know he's waiting for the proper contempt to well up from his desert boots. He sips the brandy, puffs the cigar, shuffles the idiot cards; some of the delegates are wondering whether it's a sudden case of aphasia, or maybe the title 'Frontiers of Design', or its subject (micro-chips), or 'what the hell is Cedric going to do with Wolfe's opening address?', or he's brought the wrong notes . . .

'YOUNG WOLFE!' he suddenly snaps out and the audience responds with relief. 'Young Tom' – and he starts landing body punches and a few nasty elbows. It's billed as an architectural punch-up, Young Price (way over his mid-life crisis) meeting Young Wolfe (just pushing fifty) and the crowd is relishing the spectre of an Anglo-American slug-fest. Condescension is in the air, the anti-MacEnroe, anti-Super-Brat condescension is out in force. Thump, thump, thump, Price lands stunning barbs, his followers roll about holding their waistcoats and knitted pullovers looking around for Young Wolfe's red face, wondering 'how's he going to trump *this*!' They know the opening blow 'Young' has him straight in that 'sternum' he's always banging on about: that'll teach the fifty-year-old adolescent in the body-hugging white suits; that'll show smart-ass 'Young Tom' with his supercilious grin leering out of every back cover, *Young* . . .

But where is he? Where is the Man in the White Suit? Has he skulked out of the ring – fled? Here is Vladimir Ilyich, terror of the bourgeoisie, producing the kind of vintage mauling he used to do twenty-five years ago in his prime – and the object of all this withering, English, kill-the-Super-Brat is . . . where? I don't believe it. He's upstairs in some private suite at the Royal Institute of *British* Architects oblivious to the whole thing, getting interviewed by the national press!!! It's hard to believe. You set up one of the epochal battles of the century – Fischer/Karpov – in front of four hundred professionals in the lecture-hall basement, and this 'Young' white-clothed hairdresser is receiving literary bouquets on the top floor.

Once again the Man in the White Suit has outflanked an attack with his fancy

GORDON BUNSHAFT and SOM, *W R Grace Building*, New York, 1974. New York skyscrapers and glass boxes - what Wolfe sees as worker housing pitched up fifty storeys', can also be seen as ultimate pillars of powers and prestige.

footwork, by changing the frame of reference – yes. Price the professional is no match for Wolfe the national performer, they are in different leagues with different rules and umpires. One the mere King of a provincial tribe, the other a white-smocked anthropologist reporting on this near-extinct species to the national press (on their top floor!); one drawing an audience of four million, the other four hundred. No match.

The Wolfe's profession is invading other professions. He starts as an anthropologist might (he even gets honorary awards from that profession) by looking at such small bodies as if they were in-breeding clans. Where there's a profession, there's a coterie, and where there's a coterie, there's a conspiracy – and a story to tell. It's simple: start with the conspiratorial conclusion and work backwards. If it's the Modern Art Clan, then the amazing con-trick pulled on the public is that paintings are produced to aid theories, critics and The Clan: 'Not "seeing is believing", you ninny, but "believing is seeing", for Modern Art has become completely literary: the paintings and other works exist only to illustrate the text.'[1]

What a nice idea, what an amusing theory, what a funny text Wolfe produces after the height (1975) of Textual, that is Conceptual, Art. Being a hypertextual man himself he can change the frame of reference of these mere art-scribes with his crazy open field running, his DOUBLE REVERSE, that takes the verbal ball down the wrong side of the astro-turf and outflanks all these heavyweight tackles like Clement Greenberg and Leo Steinberg waiting for him to make mistakes. Mistakes!!! My God, how the man can make mistakes . . . Don't they understand in what genre he's writing, haven't they read IA Richards' *How to Read a Page*? Can you make a mistake in parable? Can you get a fact wrong in the Structural Analysis of Myth? If it's done to send up the critics and write a bigger, zanier THEORIE than they could dream up on one of their advanced seminars on Surrealism, then . . . it works. The anthropologist knows what status-nerves to tweak, he has a keen eye for the Tribal Rank and can tell you who's in, and what's taboo.

The taboo for the literary culture, the 'Neo-Fabulists' – John Barth, Borges, John Gardner, James Purdy – is social realism, all the anthropological-scatological data which can be dug up and turned into a kind of sparkling Word Painting. For Wolfe 'The New Journalism', which he promotes, is a kind of Post-Modern fabulism. 'Balzac prided himself on being "the secretary of French society". Most serious American novelists would rather cut their wrists than be known as "the secretary of American society", and not merely because of ideological considerations. With fable, myth and the sacred office to think about who wants such a menial role.'[2] Our Man in the White Suit, that's who.

Remember that movie of the fifties with Alec Guinness, a diffident scientist, the absent-minded boffin, who bounces around his laboratory tubes until he stumbles on the perfect *white* material that never gets dirty. That's right, the ultimate weapon of the rag trade, a synthetic fabric which sheds gunge, never wears out and magically mends itself when cut. Alec Guinness goes about his business in a disinterested way, elevated above the rest of the rag-trade mob because of the purity of his heart, his THEORIE, trying to offer his super-synthetic to the industry, while they (ultimate conspirators) are always trying to buy him off, corrupt and black-mail him (as if they were some inbred mafia), compromise him with heavy-breathing-my-voice-is-lower-than-Lauren-Bacall . . . Glynis Johns. The Clan must destroy him because he threatens to bankrupt the entire industry. But the damnable boffin, with his heart of pure theory, always steps aside just when he's going to be done in. He's saved by his own gullibility, he levitates clear out of trouble, being on another plane of existence. Yes! The number of journalists, critics, High-Minded Editors, Abstract Expressionists, Serious Neo-Fabulists who want to get our Man in the White Suit; the number of limousine liberals who want to run him down after his piece on Lenny Bernsteen and the Black Panthers; the number of tribal High-Priests who would like to take his thinning Southern sandy hair and pull it out *with* the scalp! But our escape artist is never around when the scalping party gets going, he's on the top floor being wafted by literary, perfumed nosegays, on another plane of reference, being 'the menial secretary of American Society', a Yankee-Balzac. ARCHITECTURE!

Peter Eisenman, New York's pugilistic answer to Young Price, Young Eisenman (also pushing fifty) dons his white suit, pulls out his supply of aromatic *Flor de Lancha* (aged in Jamaica teak) and sets off for a *Skyline* interview (*Skyline*, the by-line of New York's head Compound, *'The* Institute', IAUS) – an interview to trap the slippery anthropologist. Wolfe counters this sartorial ploy by turning up in Cedric's detachable collar and black-striped socks. A black-edged handkerchif juts out of his pocket as perky and suave as his Southern Comfort smile, the down-home grin aged to near perfection in Richmond, Virginia.

Eisenman, undeterred by so much charm, makes the opening 'thump' supposed to level Wolfe through its sheer, magical unlikeliness.

Eisenman: 'Your earlier books seem to have been an attempt to terrorise the reader by exposing him to anarchy and alienation, and saying, "Look, this is what is in your society." I had thought you would introduce the same nihilistic approach to the architectural "compounds" you discuss in your book.'

Wolfe: (Grinning down his double-breasted 'off-whites', taking about $\frac{1}{32}$ of a second to defuse Eisenman's booby-trapped compliment) – *'Nihilism? Terror? I only wanted to discover new slices of life and bring them alive in print . . .'* (Me, Honorary Fellow of the Society of Anthropologists, an Anarchist??? I just want to get on with the job of reporting the courtship patterns of *genus architecturalis,* and they always keep throwing these labels at me. *Alienation, Anarchism, Nihilism!*[3]

The interview winds down after this unpromising beginning to what one would expect of two equally matched gamesmen: a draw, a stalemate, followed by the disappearance of Eisenman in the second interview – he didn't have time to correct the new questions to Wolfe's new answers to the old questions. However, a nice clarification of the obscurity emerges.

Wolfe: *'For a start, there* is *no bourgeoisie in America* . . . (but architects, silly guppies, believe there is, which is very helpful to me) . . . *look at the way Venturi, Graves and Moore combine Classical motifs – bourgeois – with cardboard walls – non-bourgeois'.* (There, that contradiction will take care of Eisenman's attack for a few minutes. In case it doesn't, I shall repeat it in a new key.) *'In America the "bourgeoisie" or "middle class" wants nothing, intends nothing, and takes no action, because it has no existence other than as the modern intellectual word for what used to be called "the mob" . . . Without a nobility, or the tradition of one, the notion of a bourgeoisie loses all meaning.'* (Convenient bug-word this 'bourgeoisie', it still makes those cryptic Marxists like Eisenman, those Institute Leftists, bolt straight up on their coccyges. Great to luck-out on 'bourgeois'. What a theory, what an architectural cattle-prod.)

In the second non-interview, we have the absent, disembodied voice of Eisenman (offstage correcting his questions) accusing Wolfe of being 'anti-intellectual, anti-ideological and a populist'. And how does he answer these withering Kill-the-Superbrats? Sink in a trace of apologies – recant? Suicide? Change his clothes? You guessed it, by changing the frame of reference.

Wolfe: 'As for being a "populist" – I think the word being sought is "philistine"'. (There you under-done eggheads, try fooling around with a Yale PhD in American Studies – go ahead if you want to play this game, no problem. Accuse me of being a populist, and I'll up the ante, and give you an education into the bargain.) 'I was often called that after The Painted Word came out. Very few people who use that epithet are aware of its origins. It was coined by Matthew Arnold . . . to represent those members of the middle classes who did not worship culture – who were not in the compound as it were. That's what it means. So, in that sense, I certainly am a philistine. My whole viewpoint is one established outside the compound, whether in painting or architecture. That's what the word "philistine" means: outside the monastery wall. I honestly think it's the duty of the historian or the critic to stand outside the walls . . .'[4] (Pity to have to take this message inside the walls to Skyline, but then the anthropologist has to talk to the ethnics now and then on their own turf.

From Bauhaus to Our House starts off in high gear in its very title, ripping forward like some express train of history (one of Wolfe's favourite aphorisms), like the scholarly-sounding 'From Renaissance to Baroque', Von Ledoux bis Le Corbusier (with all the German credentials of Kunstwissenschaft . . . PLUS international rhythm, assonance, and meaning). Their Haus = Our House! A slightly sinister thing this German takeover; the Nazis, Commies and the like, but America loves a conspiracy theory just as much as the next nation. The good, old Nationalist Anthem rings out in the first sentence – 'O beautiful, for spacious skies, for amber waves of grain, has there ever been another place on earth where so many people of wealth and power have paid for and put up with so much architecture they detested as within thy blessed borders today?' (There twits, anyone who doesn't realise that the next 143 pages will be a resounding 'NO' should try How to Read a Page.) The anti-American conspiracy builds as Calvinist architects chuck out 'cosiness and colour', as they rebuild New York skyscrapers, 'worker housing pitched up fifty storeys high', as they proffer revisionist conspiracies such as Post-Modernism (which don't change anything except the tightening grip of The Compound'). By page six we are so sure soulless aparatchiks are subverting the national style that we're ready to phone The House Subcommittee on Un-American Activities, except . . . that it's probably also located in some damn German workers beehive, and they've also been cowed into modernism. 'I find the relation of the architect to the client in America today wonderfully eccentric, bordering on the perverse.' In the past the clients called the tune – at least Napoleon I, Napoleon III and Lord Palmerston did, and Alva Vanderbilt – 'hired the most famous American architect of the day, Richard Morris Hunt, to design her a replica of the Petit Trianon . . .' PETIT what ??? Hold on there, Mr Yale Survey Course of Americana, your Secondary Sources are beginning to show – Richard Morris Hunt designed The Breakers which was a replica of two or three Vignola

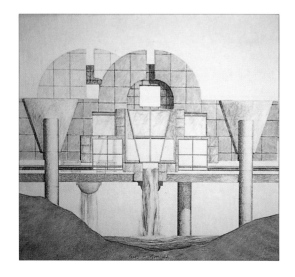

MICHAEL GRAVES, Fargo-Moorhead Cultural Center Bridge, Minnesota, 1977-8

villas thrown together, and William K Vanderbilt asked for Azay-le-Rideau in New York not the Château de Blois, and ... Just as a bit of scholarly tut-tutting is about to take off, just as Professor Primary Source is about to slice up the arguments into thin little errors of fact, an idea begins to make its way through the cranial layers of cross-reference cards that we've got something kind of new here, a new type of history, and our anthropologist knows his Vanderbilts who built so many *château* replicas that he might be ... And he's cross-quoting, and what the hell it's *'history without footnotes'*, history without acknowledgements, sources, index, or any of the scholarly paraphernalia that slows down the old type of history writing ... it's Wolfe-Man History! It's not history at all (read *How to Read a Page*) and better for that. Real history never has a single-line story, a one-liner driven by a conspiracy, so it never makes as much sense, and amusement, as the fictionalised version.

There you PhD shufflers, there you Avery Library Drones, any fool must know by the end of Wolfe's introduction (by the tone, let's spell it out for all you blue-stockings, Addled Louise Flexible, Robert Hugely Obvious) ... it's clear to any journalist that we're in for a parable which may tell us more than the truth (and very much less). Wolfe: *'But just think of people like Ada Louise Huxtable, or Robert Hughes, or Douglas Davis, or any of the rest of them. Just ask yourself: which of them has ever done a piece of original research – or enunciated a provocative theory ...'*[5] Theory, a provocative theory and parable – that the plutocrats of America have bought German workers' housing for their office – their CORPORATE PALACES and you want to know why? For sado-masochistic reasons: *'that bracing slap across the mouth, that reprimand for the fat on one's bourgeois soul, known as Modern architecture'.*[6]

Here *is* a new idea, a new theory, a new angle on the old story of what went wrong with Modernism. Young Wolfe is riding home one wet New York evening on the uptown Madison Avenue bus looking at all those sad, drenched skyscrapers slide past, thinking of all those po-faced Captains of Industry cowed into their grid-pens – when he has this THEORIE. What if these Commanders of Millions whose expense accounts are larger than some Gross National Products, are *frightened because they feel guilty about being bourgeois.* Aha! What else could explain this prole-junk, why else would they accept this anti-bourgeois style? Guilt, that's it. And all the variations on Modernism – all the 'Posts' and 'Lates' and 'Neos' and 'Sub-Mods' are putting out versions of the same prole-cult to assuage the guilt of the capitalists. The architecture may look superficially different but it's still basically sack-cloth-and-ashes. The architects may appear new, but deep down inside, deep in their Compounds, all of them are anti-bourgeois even if, like Venturi, Moore or Stern, they pretend to use bourgeois motifs.

The climax of the story, *The Conspiracy of the Compounds*, occurs when Wolfe has to explain this seeming paradox. *'Studied closely'*, our anthropologist says, fine-tuning his Structuralist model, *'Venturi's treatise turns out to be not apostasy at all but rather an agile and brilliant skip along the top of the wall of the compound ... He sends out that signal at the very outset: "I like complexity and contradiction in architecture. I do not like the incoherence or arbitrariness of incompetent architecture nor the precious intricacies of picturesqueness or expressionism". Translation: I, like you, am against the bourgeois (picturesque, precious, intricate, arbitrary, incoherent and incompetent)'.*[7]

This is a translation of bourgeois? Of Venturi? Our translator-anthropologist goes

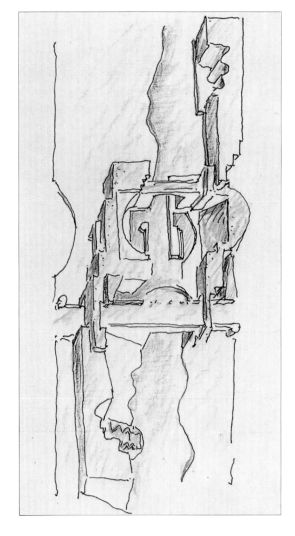

Fargo-Moorhead. Preliminary site plan study.

on to make another one with much the same conclusion. He has Venturi say: "'I am going to show you how to make architecture that will amuse, delight, enthral other architects." This, then, was the genius of Venturi. He brought Modernism into its Scholastic age. Scholasticism in the Dark Ages was theology to test the subtlety of other theologians. Scholasticism in the twentieth century was architecture to test the subtlety of other architects. Venturi became the Roscellinus of modern architecture . . . Venturi's strategy was to violate the taboo – without violating it. He used red brick (bourgeois) on the upper part of the facade of the Guild House – but it turned out to be a dark red brick especially chosen to match the "smog-smudged" brick of the run-down working-class housing around it (non-bourgeois). He placed a huge column (bourgeois) at the entrance – but it turned out to be undecorated (non-bourgeois), with no capital (non-bourgeois) and no pediment (non-bourgeois) . . . O complexity! O contradiction! To violate the taboo – without violating it! Such virtuosity! Venturi had his detractors, but no-one in the compounds could help but be impressed. Here was a man skipping, screaming, turning cartwheels on the very edge of the monastery wall – without once slipping or falling . . . He was keeping the non-bourgeois faith.'[8] The Compound was impressed by this description of the contradictions within Complexity and Contradiction and interested in some new 'I-was-there' gossip. Insiders began to ask: 'Who is Wolfe's Deep Throat? Graves, Jencks, or some first year drop-out from "The Institute"' (the Vatican of Compounds). Wolfe's impressive accomplishment was to reduce the whole Modern Movement (and its scholastic offshoots) to gossip, elevated gossip, the parable of Walter Gropius as The Silver Prince, and the conspiratorial way he, along with other European Übermenschen, corrupted the youth and plutocrats of America.

'Our story begins in Germany just after the First World War. Young American architects . . .'[9] He's off – with his theory – and soon Walter Gropius appears, 'the Silver Prince, the White God Number One' who quickly hypnotises the young American intelligent-sia with his spiritual compound known as the Bauhaus and 'with his thick black hair combed straight back, irresistibly handsome to women . . .'[10] Yes, 'irresistibly handsome to women' – have you got it? The momentous act of twentieth-century architecture? Where everybody was converted? It's not Vers une architecture, it's not the new materials like steel and glass, it's not . . . Cleopatra's nose that changes history, but Gropius' 'thick black hair'! Have you got it – black hair swerves the express train of history onto a different track! Of course, how stupid of us not to have recognised it all along: the black hair – thick. And Paul Klee called him the Silver Prince not so much because of his ultra-fine sensibility, not just because he was throwing out the old bourgeois detritus and leading the new war-torn Europe 'like a Prince' – but, maybe, perhaps, because some of that Young Black Hair had just begun to acquire a little silver fleck. Wise silver streaks just-so along the temple? Do you doubt me? You know those whisky ads with Mr Moghul Wiseman greying his sideburns, sending out those signals of utter competence. And you think a young American architect straight out of Harvard could resist?

By turning Gropius into a Utopian-Socialist (which he was for five minutes at the end of 1918), by putting anti-bourgeois slogans and 'translations' into his mouth and by equating the whole of Modern architecture with workers' housing of the twenties, Wolfe constructs his anthropological Structural Machine, his sublime theorie. From

VENTURI and RAUCH, Brant House, Bermuda, 1975-8.

MOORE, RUBLE and YUDELL, Rodes House, Los Angeles, 1976-9.

then on it's as easy skating over thin ice. All Modern architecture becomes anti-bourgeois housing turned on its side, or up-ended. And the attraction of the theory is that it can also be played for laughs: since it is a badly kept secret that workers of all countries hate workers' housing, there must be a conspiratorial group involved in putting them there. Can one guess who?

The Museum of Modern Art, head propaganda unit of the European Compound, Fifth Column of The *Internationale* (style) . . . was founded in John D Rockefeller's Jr's living-room by you-know-what kind of bank accounts. The irony of *that* complexity and contradiction doesn't escape the Structuralist Machine. '*Our visionary avant-gardists! Rockefellers, Goodyears, Sullivans and Blisses! O oil men, lumbermen, dry-goods jobbers, and wives! It was marvellous. It was like the plot of Gilbert and Sullivan's opera* Utopia Limited . . .'[11]

'*All at once, in 1937, the Silver Prince himself was here, in America . . . Other stars of the fabled Bauhaus arrived at about the same time: Breuer, Albers, Moholy-Nagy . . . The reception of Gropius and his* confrères *was like a certain stock scene from the jungle movies of that period. Bruce Cabot and Myrna Loy make a crash landing in the jungle and crawl out of the wreckage in their Abercrombie and Fitch white safari blouses and tan gabardine jodhpurs and stagger into a clearing. They are surrounded by savages with bones through their noses – who immediately bow down and prostrate themselves and commence a strange moaning chant.*

The White Gods!

Come from the skies at last!

Gropius was made head of the school of architecture at Harvard . . .'[12]

But of course, with his thick black-silver hair how could these poor American undercooked savages resist the White Gods, the White International Style, the White Workers' housing. Yes, all American culture was being colonialised by European refugees ('Every time Hitler shakes the tree NYU picks up the apples' was the way Panofsky reported it) – Freudians in psychology, Schoenbergians in music and all the little continental 'isms' in every other art. The universities were taken over by these little white men – Yale, Harvard, Princeton – the rest followed the Ivy League stampede into the arid land of prolecult. The ultimate irony, ultimate conspiracy, had happened in the Land of the Free, the Home of the Brave and John D Rockefeller Jr: '*In short, the reigning architectural style in this, the very Babylon of capitalism, became worker housing.*'[13] The capitalist bows down to the architectural Compound, every time, and takes his anti-bourgeois medicine because it's a castor-oil good for his guilt-ridden soul. After Wolfe lifts factoids liberally from my factoids (Pruitt-Igoe was blown up in *April*, not July 1972, but every Secondary Sourcerer from Peter Blake on down has ripped off this untruth) he raises the tempo until he reaches the not surprising crescendo of his concluding words: in America '*The bourgeoisie was still baffled. The light of the Silver Prince still shone here in the Radiant City. And the client still took it like a man.*'[14]

And you can guess what finely-cut mince the critics made of *that* – those little white men that Wolfe calls '*messenger boys . . . worshipful couriers of other people's tastes and opinions*' – you can hear them protest: 'But Modern Architecture is *not* workers' housing written large; if anything it's hospitals, warehouses, bridges, factories and airplane hangars . . .' (The protests mount and so do Wolfe's sales.) You can hear them scream 'Modern Architecture *is* American – invented in Chicago AMERICA 1880 and Mayor Daly said so seven times.' (That put-down was worth 10,000 more copies.) You can hear Russians and Leftists and left-of-centre-SDPs contesting that Post-Modernism *is* bourgeois, *petit-bourgeois,* petty-bourgeois. ('The more they complain, the more they're playing my game.')

You can read Robert Hughes dealing the death-blow in *Time;* ' . . . he brings nothing new to the argument except, perhaps, a kind of supercilious rancour . . . The late bird has got half the worm . . . Mainly the glass box won because it was cheap to build.' (That cut-down was worth 50,000, and now Wolfe's on the Best Seller list, first time for an architectural book.) You can imagine the architectural faculty at Columbia, Assistant Professor Fidler on the Flat Roof, respectable historians Frampton and Scully, minor Section Men in Fine Arts 13, flanks of lumpen-pedants, whole departments of history . . .screaming 'Get it right!'. Future PhD students proving their theses – 'New York Plutocrats and Their Architectural Tastes – 1956-59' – that these moghuls bought their aluminium cages *not* because they were workers' housing, oh no, but because they were rational, upstanding, luxurious totems . . . *polished* aluminium symbols of corporate power. 'Yes they're vertical Rolls Royce radiators, turned up Lincoln Continental grills – all the way down Sixth Avenue – black tinted glass and Rolls rads, do-you-hear-me?'

With every stunning blow the sales mount inexorably, with every definitive censure, every Eisenman uppercut, every high-Price jab – up, up, up, from 100,000 to 200,000 and still climbing. Another tribal assault? Another invite on The Today Show. Sixty Minutes. William Buckley. Johnny Carson. Every last rebuke is a plug for the book. Wolfe-Man has done it! He's found a way of turning scholarly disasters into literary triumphs, of parables into 'truths', of non-bourgeois into bourgeois into . . . and he consigns the whole category of bourgeois to the scrap-heap of history. *'For a start, there is no bourgeois in America . . .'* All that castor-oil guilt was in vain. He turns *thick* black hair into epochal history, attacks on his character into copy for his flyleaf; he turns an insignificant quarrel in a wee-little compound into a BIG ORGANISED MEDIA EVENT. Four million versus 400 – no match. Nothing can hurt him, nothing can reach him, each blast puts him further out of touch because he's on another plane of reference.

And what precisely, exactly, is this far-out realm, this literary magic carpet, this escape clause, this GENRE that Wolfe has invented? *'Le Style est l'homme même'*. Yes, but what is it? *'There Goes (Varoom! Varoom!) That Kandy-Kolored (Thphhhhhh!) Tangerine-Flake Streamline Baby (Ragghhh!) Around the Bend (Brummmmmmmmmm) . . .'* Seventeen mmmm's, it's easy to misquote. Critics knock it as Para-journalism, a bastard form which is half literary and half pseudo-truth factoids, gossip calumny on an epochal scale. Wolfe defends it as old time reporting *plus* the novelist's arsenal. *'It was the discovery that it was possible in non-fiction, in journalism, to use any literary device, from traditional dialogisms of the essay to stream-of-consciousness, and to use many different kinds simultaneously, or within a relatively short space . . . to excite the reader both intellectually and emotionally'.*[15] The critics are right and Wolfe is right, the genre fluctuates back and forth between bastardised psycho-history of the maudlin sort ('I was inside Hitler's brain when . . .') to the Supra-factual, Hyper-realistic, Over-excited,

Neo-Hysterical, Tele-grammatic, I-am-more-truthful-than-truth conjectures of Wolfe. At his best in *'There Goes (Varoom! Varoom!) . . . etcetera'*, or *'Las Vegas (What?) . . . etcetera'*, or *'Radical Chic & Mau-Mauing the . . . etcetera'* his unique style has discovered truths that others couldn't reach.

'The style is the man himself', as George-Louis de Buffon wrote, and to discover a literary style is to invent a tool for digging up part of a buried reality. Wolfe's particular aerated form of the Neo-Hysterical Manner is good at getting behind pretension, social custom and half-articulated feelings. If it's 'The Last American Hero', Junior Johnson the famous stock car racing driver, he can get us into an élite world which few others could crack (and a kind of subject which very, very few other litterateurs would investigate). By constantly shifting viewpoints and literary devices, with his ultra-realism he has invented an equivalent of Salvador Dali's 'Paranoid Critical Method'. 'The spontaneous method of irrational knowledge based on the critical and systematic objectification of delirious associations and interpretations . . .' Yes, delirious association based on facts and systematised to reveal unsuspected patterns. Like a Surrealist painting the more real Wolfe's description and reported conversation get, the more powerful reality becomes as an adjunct of parable. This Hyper-realistic Parablism, to give it a name that will never be used again, is better than reality to the extent that it illuminates the drama and unspoken feelings which drive events.

It's a November evening in New York. Young Tom has just come from Farrar, Straus Giroux where he's been watching sales curves vortexing straight up, and he's wondering if there's ever been a book that just continued to climb. Vertical. He's smiling that Southern Comfort JR smile at the silly thought. 'But it just might happen.' He leaves his wife Sheila in their East side sixties apartment and steps into a Checker cab heading down-town for the big evening. This is it, the moment of truth, and young Wolfe is dressed in black. Yes black tie, tuxedo, After Eight, that sort of thing, because he's been invited into the very heart of The Compound.

Downtown he goes to the forties, just a block or two north of 'The Institute', within libel distance of the *Skyline* by-line. He gets out of the cab (non-bourgeois) in his black tie (bourgeois) and steps on to the pavement (non-bourgeois) with his patent-leather pumps (bourgeois). Oh what the hell – he walks straight into the Century Club, invited as one of the bi-monthly speakers to give his inmost thoughts on architecture and to listen to them rebound around the élite and off the dark pilasters. Young Peter is there to greet him with his smile and his *Flor de Lancha* plugged into his mouth. Young Michael is there and Bob and Jack and Ted and Alice. And Young Philip, but of course, is hosting the whole thing as he always does. And just after he settles down to a little Southern Comfort they start going at him, swinging away, cutting him up –

'Where's your white suit?'

'Where is your *white* suit?'

'You're not wearing your white suit!!!'

That's the most they say against him.

'NO WHITE SUIT', Peter is saying with that satisfied look, as if he's just discovered *House 13*.

'But it's a black-tie evening', Wolfe answers, 'as usual.'

Young Philip says 'I haven't read your book, but I'm not sure about the ending. I won't

Charles Jencks and *Tom Wolfe,* photo collage.

comment because I haven't read your book. I read the first page and the last page and the middle page, which is what I always do, but I haven't read the book. No comment.'

It's a warm November evening, academic and warm, with brandy and *Flor de Lanchas,* lots of amusing shop-talk, and the Clan sits back to enjoy itself theorising. Only this time the tribe is passing around the peace-pipe with the anthropologist, and he's saying – 'If only the painters treated me this way; if only the astronauts had me into their club . . .'

It's a friendly November night, just before Christmas, when all through the club not a creature is stirring . . .

And Our Man in The White Suit is not in a White Suit,

And he's got into The Compound, without being in The Compound,

And he's the first man to get into *all* of the Compounds, without getting into The Compounds, since Anthony Blunt, another architectural historian.

This review of Tom Wolfe's From Bauhaus to Our House *appeared in 1981. His notion of the bourgeois/non-bourgeois motives of Modernism was interesting if not entirely original, and indeed his populist rhetoric was quite unusual for the time. Some of his ideas were lifted from my own* The Language of Post-Modern Architecture. *Prince Charles, latterly, lifted some of his rhetoric, but lost the humour.*

SYMBOLISM
AND BLASPHEMESIS

In 1928 Hannes Meyer proclaimed proudly 'My League of Nations Building symbolises nothing.' This tough-minded Marxist, who had just taken over the Bauhaus, wanted his architecture to function, just to work like a machine, not *mean* anything. Writers at the same time decided 'a poem should not mean, but be'. Le Corbusier termed a house 'a machine for living', Ozenfant said 'a painting is a machine for moving us', Eisenstein that 'the theatre is a machine for acting' and I A Richards opened his *Principles of Literary Criticism* with 'a book is a machine to think with'.

The letters on this page are a machine for making us understand how silly all of this is. Of course architecture, like a machine-gun, works or misfires as the case may be, but it also always means something, even if only the minimal idea of its own utility. Hannes Meyer's scheme symbolised the high technology and socialism of its time, just as today the buildings of Norman Foster symbolise the high technology and capitalism of ours. Like one's unconscious, symbolism is inescapable and all one can do about this is suppress it, or deal with it positively. Unfortunately most architects would prefer to repress their symbolic unconscious and this leads to the three current architectural neuroses: malaproptosis, archiamnesia and blasphemesis. As a building medic I have spent the last fifteen years diagnosing the first two ailments, prescribing cures and trying to stamp out the viral strains, but like a growing epidemic they have resisted most therapy. Buildings still, unintentionally, look like stacked coffins or TV sets on the blink, and the blank, dumb amnesiacal boxes, misnamed 'skyscrapers', spread through our downtowns like chickenpox, even if they now come with funny protrusions and skin tones.

It looked as if I M Pei was almost cured. After I diagnosed several of his malaprops – the phallic symbol seen from the air in Boston etc – he changed his ways at the Hotel in the Fragrant Hills, Peking, where he set out to symbolise a new Chinese architecture, and succeeded. But there's been a relapse of a most alarming kind caused, as it usually is, by that virus to which all architects are prone: megalomania. It is well known that Boullée and Le Corbusier suffered from this, occasionally; for Hitler and Speer the disease was chronic. It is also known the ego is most likely to be infected near the centre of great cities, such as Paris. So when Mr Pei went to talk to Mr Mitterrand about adding a few new entrances to the Louvre one could guess the dreaded disease might strike again.

Basically he was asked to widen a *porte-cochère* here and open up a waiting space there, modest refurbishments that would have kept the courtyards and facades intact. But like Le Corbusier who, when asked to design a fountain for Paris produced a new city for three million, I Am could not resist, as they say 'expanding the brief'. At first, apparently, he said to President Mitterrand with becoming modesty that he might not

View of the pyramids, fountains, Cour Napoleon and pavilions by Lefuel. Is that *The Victory of Samothrace* about to do a half-gainer where the pharoah would be buried? What does a pyramidal form have to do with an entrance, both functionally and semantically? As one can see, the physical entrance is a truncated pyramidal void twelve feet high – so the remaining twenty-eight feet are all symbolic. Of what? Pei and Mitterrand.

take the commission for he might not have that stroke of genius which every great Architect should suffer. However he would like to go away for three months just to think about it. Ponder it in peace. Thinking and thinking back in the quiet alleys of New York City, he came to the amazing thought that – 'Yes!' – he did have the genius required and so he quite rightly sank the needed space clear out of sight, underground. And then he thought some more and – presto – the oldest form of self-proclaiming immortality rose straight up (but where is its pyramidion?).

The virus had struck again: *blasphemesis horribilitis.*

Now this bacillus is a new, virulent strain of malaproptosis which affects the nerve endings, particularly of statesmen or elder statesmen, to make them go very uptight. Rigid, dumb platitudes are bound to flow from the mouth or drawing pen, followed by such puffery from the jaw as Pei was heard to emit: 'No foreign architect has ever left his mark on the Louvre'.

But these are symptoms, what of the disease itself? Dr Siegfried Giedion spent a chapter of *Mechanisation Takes Command* analysing a strain of the parasite – 'Napoleon III and the Devaluation of Symbols'. Blasphemesis occurs most often when one takes a potent historical form – the Christian cross – and misuses it in another potent context – on the top of an airport control tower. Chairman Mao suffered this ailment when his mausoleum was built as a Classical temple right on the axis of the Forbidden City (an axis on which it had heretofore been forbidden to build temples to oneself, especially Greekesque ones).

Now Pei and Mitterrand have succumbed to the same virus, and for much the same reason: they want a memorial to their memory which no-one can avoid. Thus they are building an Egyptian pyramid sixty feet tall in high-tech glass right on the sacred axis which even Louis XIV, in all his humility, would not occupy. (It's true he couldn't resist a little Sun-God portrait of himself over the doors, but that's a forgivable allusion.) Not just one, but three more Egyptian pyramids will be built – Cheops, Chefren and Mycerinus might have been allusions, if they'd stopped to think about it. These are at the foci of the pavilions that Lefuel put up in the 1850s, blocking out all views, disturbing all unities of meaning and history, just asking to be regarded themselves. In terms of material, contrast and placement these jewels will always catch the eye (by blocking it) and be the very centre-piece of the surrounding broach. No doubt they will be aesthetically appealing, even delightful in their sparkling, brazen whiteness: blasphemesis always is a beautiful disease which is why so many people try to catch it. But for the greater meaning of French architecture, Egyptian architecture and even Chinese and American architecture, the mania cannot be termed healthy.

It's certainly no use trying to stop the infection with the usual methods of aesthetic control and negative zoning: architects don't suddenly gain a respect for history and symbols by being told what to avoid. No, the only known remedy is an applied and sustained ointment of satire, so that whenever the patient starts to puff up with self-importance, the pustule of ego-mania is quickly deflated by a sharp guffaw.

It is true that some architectural doctors, of a Modern agnostic persuasion, will say that blasphemesis is impossible today because people have long ago stopped believing in anything: Egyptian pyramids, Christian spires, heavenly domes, or whatever form you care to name. Even the Constructivist diagonal and the purist language of Le Corbusier

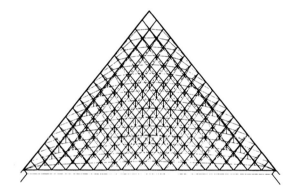

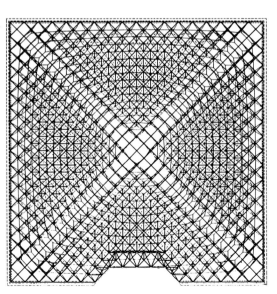

Elevation and roof plan.

have been abused if not altogether devalued in the last ten years. How can there be blasphemesis when there are no ideals or idols to blaspheme? This question has its point and a very simple answer, a human one. As the atheist knows, even his non-beliefs require constant sharpening and respect: all symbols are the transient nourishment of life, built up through social usage. One may change the meaning of forms, indeed their health depends on a slow, consistent change, but the change must acknowledge both the new and old contexts or else it is virulent to both.

This article was written when the Pyramid design was first shown in 1984, the following article on completion in 1989. Reaction to the design was mixed and polemicised. Defenders of Modernism took it to be a political coup for their side; traditionalists as a stab in the back from Mitterrand. As often in history a minor piece of architecture becomes the site of a major ideological battle for quite fortuitous reasons. This amplification of a molehill into a pyramid could be called 'The Prince Charles Effect' and it has struck at many minor (but sensitive) sites.

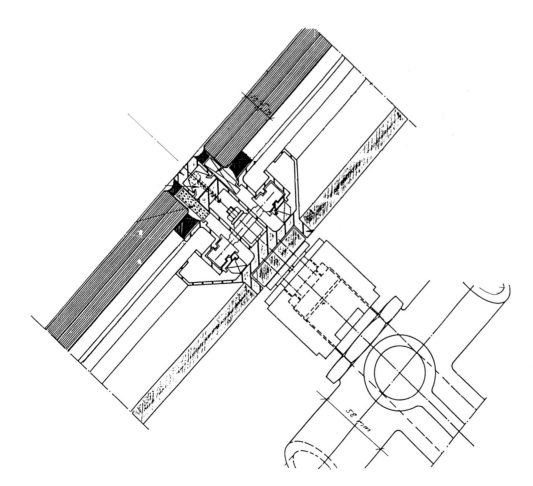

Detail of the glass and steel joint.

PEI'S GREENHOUSE EFFECT

I expected it to be more beautiful on completion. Pei's buildings normally have a pristine resolution, a consummate ease, with the only fault of being entirely predictable. But for reasons which will become apparent this facility has suddenly vanished in the heart of Paris. Take the most characteristic view of the pyramid – from mid-distance to close up – where the dull, flat glass fights it out with all that block and tackle known as High-Tech.

Blankness is set against a scratchy filigree of metal struts which don't even create a nice tension. Rather the impression is nervous, as if Pei, summoned to the Court of Napoleon IV, were so anxious to please he could only produce one note on his violin – *spicatto furioso*. All those itchy cicadas buzzing away, crawling and rubbing their legs together – projected onto the facade of Lefuel's nineteenth-century frame. Why don't these bugs leave it alone? How can Pei have miscalculated his background building so completely?

The answer, of course, is that he hasn't. From the start, like any first-year architectural student, he knew perfectly well that a glass wall seen from the outside is almost never transparent – especially not two sheets of it, such as now come between you and the old buildings. From almost every angle, for ninety-nine percent of the day, it will be more or less a mirror reflecting the sky overhead. Photographs don't completely lie, and as you can see, Lefuel's buildings become grey hulks obscured by the two planes of four reflective surfaces and all these scratchy spiders crawling about inside to hold them up.

None of this would matter a bit had Pei not claimed his specially made thin glass – created by St Gobains, the French glassmakers – would be transparent and allow the Louvre to be visible through it. He mounted such a media campaign, and made so much of the *thinness*, that the press looked clear through the layers and forgot to notice all those creepy arachnids chewing away. Amazing – the panache, the chutzpah, the sheer gall of claiming transparency ... when every first year student *knows* it won't work.

Parisians, in the year 1989, love it – and so do the media. Here is the grand revolutionary gesture, shades of Ledoux and Boullée and their pyramids, a *grand projet* which brings grandeur back to France in a modern guise. No-one wants to be told they can't see through the structure – for them it is totally transparent, an 'absent presence', a kind of glass suit without the Emperor. The ideology of the French Revolution, as the first Modernist *événement*, is now completed by the triumph of the New Modernism right in the heart of historic Paris. For if there is one place which can serve as a national symbolic heart it is not the Opéra, Bastille or Nôtre Dame, but the Louvre, the centre of the artistic and cultural worlds, a function which is today the equivalent of religion.

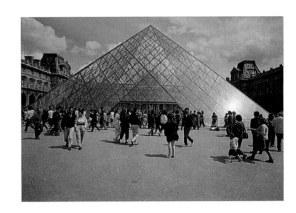

Glass entrance to the Louvre, Paris, 1984-9. Reflections create a solid plane unless the background objects are brightly lit – a rule every architectural student knows. The visual impenetrability was actually increased by the very attempt to decrease the thickness of glass – by using a filigree of metal tension members. In spite of these two visual facts, Pei claimed transparency – and the critics followed the party line.

Small and large pyramids together. As Ledoux, Boullée and every architecture student knows, you enter a pyramid visually either by 1) a front porch, 2) a centralised shaft set perpendicular to a plane, or 3) underground. Here a fourth method – the voided trapezoid – violates the purity of the pyramid. How do you *clean* a pyramid? Once a month – by mountain climber!

In this sense the form of a pyramid is appropriate, because it marks what we find holy, transcendental and worthy of excess expenditure. The only problem is that here it merely marks an entrance. It's no more than a *porte-cochère* revealing the function of transition. And this is a devastating problem (but more of that later).

What I find surprising is the lack of the aesthetic sublime in a pyramidal form. Compare the reality to photos of the model and you will see that the sheerness of the wall plane has been lost to the buzz of those incessant insects. If Pei had not been forced, by his specious argument of transparency, into these webs of internal structure he could have adopted a much more convincing solution by tripling the thickness of the glass, allowing it to span much larger areas, and then placing it flush on the surface – joined edge to edge. This would have given a truly dazzling one-liner, instead of the bungled one-liner we have, and have really been a Modern equivalent to Cheops' original glowing white monument. But for ideological reasons (Modernists can't admit historicist allusions even when they're undeniable) he was forced to swerve away from the reference and provide that typical obfuscation of function and technology – that is 'transparency' and 'High-Tech'. Journalists, the profession and the people of Paris – for the moment – appear to have swallowed the bait. Perhaps, in the year 1990, they will look again.

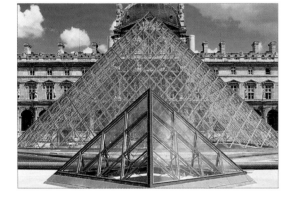

The smaller pyramids are surprisingly out of rhythm with the large one – and have no filigree of tensile members. They also block the cross axes.

But let me say something nice – I'm trying very hard to think of something. On the inside, looking at the Beaux-Arts pavilions and white ornamented stone, the lozenge grid of structure *does* provide a very effective frame and contrast. Here the 'tensions and juxtapositions', the rhetorical tropes of Modernism, really do work. The dark metal lines divide up Lefuel's endless surfaces like a perspective grid laid on a Renaissance townscape, giving it measure and rhythm. Also, when you look straight up from the centre of the pyramid, the sky is gridded in a wonderful lacework of tensile members. Indeed, in one of the few refinements of the building, the central cross of the four glass planes has been given less webbing – allowing more light and focus – and the tensile chords (horizontal to the ground) dance in a slight curve around the central apex.

The heavens are very nicely cut up into black diamonds and the scratchy creatures which weave delicate webs in gentle circles around the apex.

This brilliant technical and formal device almost makes one forgive Pei the other infelicities. But not quite. There are too many. The three surrounding pyramids are dinky, fussy and unaccountably out of rhythm in their glass proportions; the entrance void is a ham-fisted, truncated pyramid – more a guillotine or missing wall than welcoming door; the climax to the whole arrival, the central column that was meant to carry a one-liner fitting to the exterior, now has nothing on top because the French could not quite bring themselves to the double blasphemy which they had contemplated – putting the Winged Victory of Samothrace in that position. Oh probity, decorum, *bienséance* – oh appropriateness and suitability – is it not a little late for your arrival? Is this not, rather, timidity and cowardice? If you're going to turn a sacred pyramid into a passage for tourists, why not turn the Winged Victory into a logo?

The Egyptians, it is jokingly said, are annoyed by Pei's blasphemy. To get even, they will surround the pyramids of Cheops, Chephren and Mycerinus with a glass version of the Louvre, designed by Kenzo Tange. It will overheat, as this one does, and they will have the last laugh as Pei's 'greenhouse effect' reduces everyone to the toxic giggles induced by too much carbon dioxide and afflatus.

This reaction is the typical response to blasphemesis. When the State swells up in a boil of pride, the people are bound to prick it. A favourite sobriquet of Parisians for their revered leader is *Mitterramesses I* – and caricatures of his stony face often appear in profile like some megalomaniac pharoah.

Replace the pyramid with a series of Metro entrances, updated from Hector Guimard and suitably hidden within French topiary, and you'd have a very good solution to the museum's problems. Actually, the underground layout of Pei's design is sensible and it does make a dramatic sequence for discovering the medieval remains which have been excavated. One now wanders through a labyrinth of subterranean passages to come upon fragments of sculpture and huge corner turrets all framed, quite appropriately by a white-grey background. A billion dollars will be spent, by 1993, to make this hidden Louvre into one of the largest museums in the world. One might deplore this overcentralisation, as do many Parisians, but at least it is good, minimal, background megalomania.

One can't say the same of the foreground. This will prove an eternal problem to those who want to change the Louvre, or add further buildings on the sacred axis. Pei has effectively closed down the game of six centuries, made the final move on the chessboard of urbanism, and from now on the axes and pavilions will focus on his jewel. It will terminate all views, like a glistening diamond set in a golden ring, and it will trump all subsequent symbolic moves. For what can be more potent than a sparkling pyramid? Perhaps a dome or obelisk, or some Deconstructivist gesture? It's hard to imagine anything which can upstage this shape – in symbolic form or position – and so from here to eternity the most important idea you will contemplate when you go to the Louvre is 'here lies the front door and the ego of I Am'.

French press reaction to *Mitterramesses I*

From inside the glass *is* transparent and Lefuel benefits by Pei's grid.

FRANK GEHRY, *Edgemar Farms Conversion*, Santa Monica, 1987-9

SECTION III
NEO-MODERNIST PRACTICE

FRANK GEHRY – THE FIRST DECONSTRUCTIONIST

'Just call me Daniel Boone', Frank Gehry said to me after I had called him that and everything else I thought appropriate: the Industrial *Adhocist*, the Father of the Botched Joint, the Son of Bruce Goff, the Noble Savage of Santa Monica, the Leonardo of Galvanised Sheet-Metal, the Malevich of Lighting and Rodchenko of the Non-Sequitur (most influences are Constructivist), the Charlie Chaplin of Chain Link (he can look rather wistful disappearing into one of his industrial buildings, like Chaplin sauntering off into the horizon), the Over-Psychoanalysed Jewish Master-Builder, the Zen Priest of the Unfinished Finish, the Martin Escher of Reverse Perspective and Impossible Space, the First Deconstructionist Architect (still ahead of Peter Eisenman) and so on and on. The problem with Frank (soon to star in a film with Claes Oldenburg as 'Frankie Toronto') is that too many labels work. He is, like many architects I have tried to pin down in *Bizarre Architecture*, almost unclassifiable. This is part of his strategy, like that of the clever Yankee backwoodsman; to escape detection by moving fast and shooting from behind trees. As Harold Rosenberg has written, the all-American art fighter like Jackson Pollock can outflank the European avant-garde by adopting more informal and pragmatic tactics. Instead of conducting his campaign according to orthodox military procedure – like the Impressionists or Surrealists moving through the salons in rational formations – Daniel Boone blends into his environment, uses whatever is at hand and picks off the ordered Redcoats one by one.

Frankie Toronto is telling me how he beat the over-psychoanalysed Peter Eisenman at his own game. 'About 1979 I gave a dinner for Michael Graves to introduce him to Max Palevsky, who wanted a multi-million dollar house.' At the time Peter was trying to hold the party line of Modernism against the counter-attack of Post-Modernism and was losing on all fronts. One after another the troops were deserting and going to the other side which increased his paranoia. So Peter tried to kill off Post-Modernism and wrote *The Graves of Modernism* to show what a turn-coat Michael was. 'Because of my dinner-party he gave me an angry call: "Frankie", he said in his New York mafia voice, "I'm afraid you gotta lose a finger for that." And he lopped one off, or at least sabotaged a special issue of *A & U* on my work by telling Gandelsonas not to write the article. So when Peter came to LA for a visit I took him to an Italian restaurant where I know real mafioso – who owe me some favours. After dinner I arranged for Clarkie to sit down next to Peter and put in the knife: "I hear you been messing around wit my friend Frangouch. The boys don't like suckers who fink on their buddies, understand? I'm afraid you gotta lose more than a finger Mr Egg-head." The blood drained from the East-Coaster's face.' Daniel Boone broke into a big grin and hearty laugh; once again he had used his ready-made piece of industrial realism, his acquaintance with the netherworld, to beat the Big City Conspirator at his own game.

State of California Aerospace Museum, Santa Monica, 1982-4. Interior view.

Let 'Em Eat Fish

As a young boy in the Canadian suburb of Timmons, Ontario, Gehry had learned to play tough with the majority. Raised as the only Jewish boy in a Catholic neighbourhood, he learned the role of the professional outcast at a young age. His grandmother used to bring home carp, which she would keep in the bathtub for several days, to prepare as gefilte fish for the Jewish Sabbath. The rumour of these bathtub fish spread, and the boys would chase Frank home from school calling him a 'fish eater'. This lesson was not entirely lost on Gehry. Fifty years later he was asked, along with several other leading architects, to design furniture or objects for the Formica product called Colorcore. Unable to come up with something interesting – the material has a pristine finish opposite to a Gehry unfinish – he threw the plastic laminate to the ground in desperation. Luckily it broke and shattered into shards with very jagged edges. The rip joint, the imperfect fractures, inspired Gehry to create a fish-scale surface and from there a series of translucent fish lamps. With the same 'destroyed' plastic he created coiled rattlesnake lights about two feet in diameter. The line of fish and snakes now sell quite well for over $20,000 each. Once again the creative outcast had turned a mistake to his own advantage. The moral? If you're going to be chased home by a mob of prejudiced fish-haters . . . make them pay for it.

Architectural critics and others have speculated on Gehry's fascination with fish; his fish columns, lights and buildings. Naturally both Christian and Freudian interpretations are offered and Gehry, who has been in analysis for some years, does not discourage them. Like many other Californians, he regards psychoanalysis as a normal mental exercise; he also uses it as an aid to his thinking, and as a tactic to sharpen his perception of symbolic ambiguity, and assist him in outmanoeuvring the avant-garde. Thus it may actually be a mistake to think that Gehry's fish means, or reveals, anything profound. It may simply be a convenient symbol, an enigmatic sign that he knows to be potent and whose volume is, luckily, very practical. Like the elephant and dinosaur, which have also played roles in architectural history, the fish is most significant because it encloses a lot of space.

Not Pliny's Villa

Gehry often proceeds by creative negation. He takes an existing prototype and reverses it, allowing the new rule of architecture to emerge after his negation. This process, related to critical analysis and the recent French philosophers' practice of Deconstruction, has even been practised by architectural critics such as Demetri Porphyrios in his *Classicism is not a Style*. The negative definition may not tell us anything positive, but nevertheless, it acts as an allusion to the positive. Thus 'Classicism is not a style' really means that 'Classicism is a set of values' (as well, of course, as a style to which it alludes by negation). Several years ago Leon Krier met Gehry in a debate in Miami and proceeded to treat him with the same (dis)respect that his former schoolmates had shown. Krier, the archetypal European, was then breaking up cities into small village units, redistributing the income symbolically and decentralising the city figuratively. Gehry was also beginning to do the same thing although in an entirely different style (or non-style). Krier was soon to re-create the European city as a reconstruction of Pliny's Villa – a set of small Classical pavilions enclosing positive urban

Low White Fish Lamp, 1984.

space. Gehry did likewise but where Krier adopted the 'Classicism is not a Style' style, Gehry used plywood, sheet-metal, the dumb stucco box and raw concrete to create his answer; the 'Not Pliny's Villa' style.

This model is used in what is undoubtedly his most successful urban ensemble, the Loyola Law School. Laid out as a (non)palazzo and three (non)temples, it is a very effective collage of volumetric urban forms, recalling, in fact, the theory that had influenced Krier, *Collage City*. The anti-palace sets up a steady rhythm of windows, like a building by Adolf Loos, with the dark voids becoming their own new form of ornament. A (too) small glass temple breaks the centre while the side wings of the palace have eruptive staircases where there would have been corner towers. The street side of the (non) piazza is partly closed by a dark red chapel – easily the most beautiful Gehry creation here. It is made of 'Finply', a plywood which has been chemically treated to withstand weathering and resembles, appropriately, that *ad hoc* invention by Bruce Goff, plywood plus mahogany shoe polish. It is very well detailed both externally and internally, and were it not for the *démodé* materials, one might think it positively harmonious and Classical. It is, rather, a stone Romanesque chapel built of the wrong material.

In any case, the (non)Classicism is quite an obvious response to the client's desire for a cool, rational style that recalls Roman law. It can be seen in the many (non)columns and the concrete pillars, minus their capitals and feet, which decorate each temple. It can be seen in the Acropolis planning, the tilted axes, the porticos, and the rhythmical window wall. And the law students respond to it in an appropriate way. They walk around and pose in the piazza, mixing informal and formal clothes; one student I saw was wearing a white formal jacket over a bathing suit. They converse on the stairways which swing out over open space, they eat on the temple steps and lean against the colonnade as if at a cocktail party. Perhaps only in the Californian climate, or in the Mediterranean, can such an urban ensemble be used so effectively to create the public realm. Here the *res publica* really does exist again, and it is the very (non)image of Pliny's Villa. Its tough materials are the vernacular of the surrounding neighbourhood, one of the poorest and roughest in LA. It borrows this skin, in the same way a chameleon borrows its colour, for protection, but also to pull in the surrounding landscape and make a new (negating, but not negative) comment on this old urbane ideal of the public realm.

The Borrowed Landscape

Thus Gehry's work has to be seen as a series of current strategies turned on their heads. This is the dialectical method of Duchamp, Dada and some Pop artists such as Oldenburg, whom Gehry knows and admires. It is also the method of the *bricoleur*, or French handyman, who makes old tools do new tricks. Unlike the scientist or Classicist who tries to re-create the whole situation and its parts, the *bricoleur* tinkers and manipulates ready-made materials. The results are not high art, or science, in the accepted sense; the handyman does not try to create a jet engine. In part his is a conservative and reactive strategy in that it entails a response to a pre-existing situation. But Gehry does not aspire to be a Michael Graves. In the TV film *Beyond Utopia*, Gehry questioned the conservative tendencies displayed in the Portland

Loyola Law School, Los Angeles, 1981-4.

Building, referring to it as the architecture of Ronald Reagan. Not long after, the unamused Graves, still the friend of Gehry, went off to the White House for dinner, perhaps determined to prove Frank wrong in some as yet unfathomable way. While Gehry one day may be invited into the Establishment, he will not, like Graves, be asked to build its temples. Or if he is, they will explode in unlikely ways.

His most eruptive temple is the California Aerospace Museum, a construction reminiscent of Duchamp's 'explosion in a shingle factory'. Like a Chinese garden it borrows the adjacent landscape by mimicking and enframing its parts. Odd disjointed shapes, leaning polygons and interrupted rectangles, recall the demi-forms of the nearby Exposition Park. An equation is thus made between the designed object and the *objet trouvé* so that they both become part of a larger whole. The environment near downtown Los Angeles is, like many American urban areas, a crazy patchwork of collaged forms all competing for attention. There is no European 'wholeness', no urban identity beyond a cacophonous rhythm of forms, no harmony of differences as in Amsterdam. There is no urban 'heart', or finished centre: the American city is, for the most part, a permanent building yard, and about as noisy.

The Aerospace Museum is an analogue of this city as well as of flight. Made from galvanised sheet-metal and other factory materials, it resembles the surface of an aeroplane hangar. A Lockhead F 104 Starfighter takes off on the side, like some aggressive rocket about to unleash its payload. And this plan announces the function of these distorted boxes like a giant Constructivist billboard. The welter of conflicting shapes conveys the mad, glorious dash of flying. It also suggests the contradictory aims of the aerospace defence policy, where billion-dollar weaponry is built and destroyed for no other purpose than that of symbolism (which of course is quite enough).

Gehry has used the Constructivist method of compilation rather than composition. The individual rooms that were pulled apart in Loyola's freestanding temples have been conjoined at dissonant angles: a septagon looms out at a skew to the main seventy-foot space which is symbolised by the black box and window below. But oddly, the internal space is not divided in quite the way it appears from the outside, and this 'lie' prepares us for the last Gehry paradox.

Reverse Representation

In a Greek temple stone represents the facts of construction, and ever since the Egyptians invented stone architecture it has had this representational function. Fundamentally, architecture seeks to make the transitory aspects of life both monumental and permanent. In a sense, with his (non)architecture, Gehry reverses this role and, as with the Romanesque temple at Loyola, transforms permanent material into ephemeral plywood. Most of Gehry's work, since designing his own house in Santa Monica, has been involved in this reversal process. It deconstructs, peels back and reveals, like archaeology, the botched and bungled inner layers which are hidden in any normal work. Like psychoanalysis, a favoured *métier* of the Deconstructionists, the result may be a patchwork of disconnected elements in search of a story. Analysis, whether critical or psychoanalytic, is not necessarily synthetic or meaningful. It does not unite by idea, theme or aesthetic, nor does it try to change the world for the better. It simply shows the working parts in their semi-autonomous state.

State of California Aerospace Museum, Santa Monica, 1982-4.

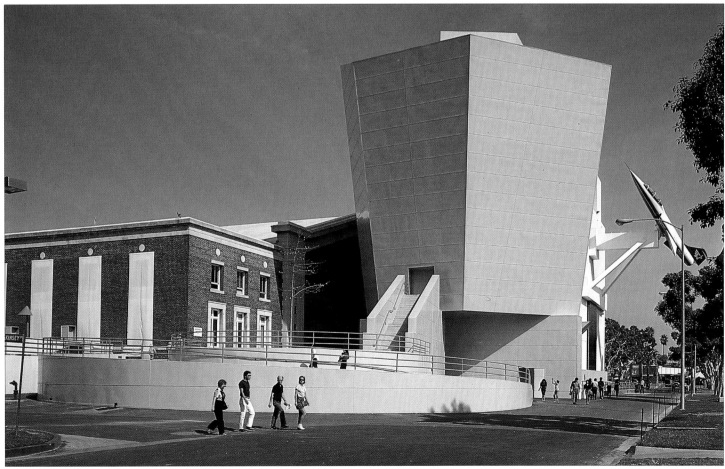

As a process of design, however, this method results in an aggregation that is experienced as meaningful. Gehry is currently deconstructing three or four multi-million dollar houses, ripping away their Classical pediments, driving odd-shaped rectangles at a skew to their grids; generally destroying their equilibrium. The fact that some of these houses are ersatz Classical partly explains this critical destruction, but another motive is positive: to provide contrast, smaller scale and the delight of incongruity. Whereas appropriateness and wholeness were the Classical virtues, oddness and disharmony are the expressionist virtues employed by Gehry. However, the opposite qualities of this dialectic have to be seen as necessarily linked, for no Gehry deconstruction is complete without its antithesis: a pre-existing, finished 'perfection'.

This can be seen in the Wosk House addition, which has been placed on the top of a decapitated apartment building in Beverly Hills. The pre-existing type, a five-storey stuccoed rectangle that is common in this area, still exists as a pristine, pink cube, its International Style surfaces and ribbon windows much as before. But set in juxtaposition to these simple harmonies is the arched window of the owner, Miriam Wosk, and her own little 'Not Pliny's Villa' on the roof. What planning authorities will make of this is an interesting point. It clearly violates every aesthetic norm in the book, and enjoys doing so. Like Antonio Gaudí and Bruce Goff, who also got away with unlikely additions, Gehry openly subverts conventional building codes. But is the Wosk House subversive architecture? As a generalised proposition no doubt it is. What if our cities returned to the medieval jumble implied by this *ad hoc* roofscape? The result might even be like Venice, Siena, or the back streets of Dubrovnik. It is well known, however, that planning legislation is determined not to let these mistakes of history recur. But Gehry proposes that they should, and so 'mistakes' are written into his deconstructions.

The north and south facades of the Wosk Roof Villa are broken up into seven and five discernible sections, respectively. These parts do not correspond exactly to interior articulations – in fact the space flows, surprisingly, from the artist's studio on one side to her living-room on the other. But, as if to break even this rule of non-correspondence, *some* shapes do hold discrete functions. For instance the spherical *Domus Aurea* of Nero (sic), now a blue not golden dome, contains the kitchen. This collides with the greenhouse/dining room and the pink volume of the elevator shaft. Collision City, that paradigm of seventies *adhocism*, continues to jumble its way around the penthouse/duplex, with green tile smashed into Cadillac-golden ziggurat (the industrial car paint was used) and overlaid by a hairy pattern of blue tile shingles. According to Gehry these were meant to bring out the front corner. Above the stairway, skylights separate a black marble aedicule from the bowed roof studio. Thus, from the north side one can see ten volumes and eleven colours collide in humorous cacophony. They were originally meant, it turns out, to recall temples on the Acropolis!

The disorganisation of this is more apparent than real, for actually the penthouse functions quite sensibly. A perimeter walkway and balcony provide light, space and access to the rooftop, one of the most unlikely spaces in Los Angeles. From here, one can not only step outside at any point, but also clamber over the flat tops of these collaged temples and survey the mountains, or a dramatic sunset through the towers

Wosk House, Extension, Beverly Hills, 1982-4. Interior.

of Century City. In nearly every way the arbitrary forms find an attractive function, and Daniel Boone disarms his critics once again.

When one analyses this deconstruction it turns out to be yet another example of reverse representation. If it's an acropolis, Gehry's first conception, then its brilliant industrial tile and glass have to be seen as anti-stone. The flat roofs are anti-pitch, the polychromy anti-white, the collisions anti-space, the cacophony anti-unity, and the balcony walk an anti-temenos. The point about these 'antis' is that they recall their antithetical 'pros' and in this involuted way the building can be considered strangely canonic. It is certainly pleasant and functional, and with Miriam Wosk's interior tiling and painting could even be considered as a 'finished' work of art. That Gehry should achieve such resolution of his deconstruction process is due in part to the existing building, used as a podium and foil, and in part to the tenacity of the client. De-architecture, such as his own house, is most successful when there is pre-existing material to operate on and a person, such as his wife Berta, to spur him on to the completion of his unfinished work.

This essay was written in 1985 well before the current rush to deconstruct and in anticipation of Peter Eisenman's desire to be known as the first Deconstructionist.

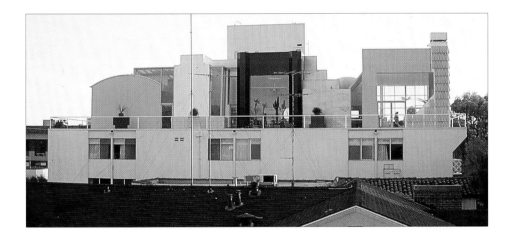

Wosk House Extension, Beverly Hills, 1982-4. Exterior and interior.

© Dennis Crompton &
Architectural Design
London MCMLXXX

DECONSTRUCTION
THE SOUND OF ONE MIND
LAUGHING
(OR THE SOLIPSIST'S DELIGHT)

What is Deconstruction? Almost everyone has an overdeveloped idea since this concept has been in the air since 1971 and has been a major focus of French and American literary theory for ten years. Indeed we are aware of the central paradox that Deconstruction has become an academic orthodoxy in some departments of literature, art and architecture, in American universities. This presents a problem to its practitioners such as Peter Eisenman, professional dissenters, who will have to deconstruct themselves (or self-destruct) in order to remain at once a focus of orthodoxy and a subversive agent.

Deconstruction is Post-Structuralism – at first a reaction to the Structuralist theories and practice of Claude Lévi-Strauss, Noam Chomsky and all those who found meaning, wholeness and explanation in the relationships between things, in structured oppositions. But 'Post-Structuralism' doesn't have the provocative overtones of 'De-Construction' – the somewhat revolutionary and subversive *frisson* associated with a process of dislocation, de-composing and de-coding. There are international conferences, not to hear a neutral academic debate on the relative merits of Life After Structuralism, but rather to experience something we hope is radical – the breaking of taboos, the attack on hierarchy, the dis-establishment of the Establishment.

In short, to indulge in the word-play and etymological associations and alliterations of Nietzsche and Derrida, we should hear all the de's and dis's embedded in Deconstruction. It decentres, decomposes and detaches whole structures into parts; it debunks, derides and deprecates all values and goals which are held with a single-minded fervour, and shows how they are self-contradictory with fractures and slippages; it demeans, debauches and deludes those looking for a unitary system; it dehumanises humanism, desacralises religion, dethrones monarchs, decentres the city and it deflates those who still believe in evolutionary progress with a theory of decline, desolation, degradation – or simply devolution. Finally, for those who propose social harmony and buildings which can actually stand up there is devastation, demolition and destruction.

But on one reading this is 'affirmative' action – Derrida doesn't want to de-press you. Does Deconstruction equal destruction? Not completely, according to Derrida and Tschumi: there is 'affirmative deconstruction', or 'Deconstruction/Reconstruction' – a twin, an opposition, a dialectic. Like Bakunin and Nietzsche in the nineteenth century, Deconstructionists play up the creative side, perhaps because they have been accused once too often of being nihilists. Now that Deconstructionists like Bernard Tschumi are building a *grand projet* for President Mitterrand and he has accepted the *légion d'honneur* and the Deanship of Columbia University's School of Architecture, it is clear that the 'De-' will be slightly defused leaving 'Construction' as the major focus.

DENNIS CROMPTON, *Under the Shadow of Serlio (The missing fourth scene from the Strada Novissima)*, Venice, 1980

Here is the paradox: Deconstruction is a laughing matter. It should always be humorous, ironic, playful, sceptical, irreverent about itself, or else it is an imposture, a misunderstanding of its own agenda, a betrayal of the non-faith. Scepticism, curiosity and laughter are its fundamental modes – the liberating dissection of the existing constructions, hierarchies and orthodoxies. As Nietzsche put it in the canonic Deconstructionist text, *Thus Spake Zarathustra;*

> He who must be a creator in good and evil – verily, he must first be a destroyer, and break values into pieces.

> I love those who do not know how to live except in perishing, for they are those going beyond.

> I love the great despisers because they are the great adorers, they are arrows of longing for the other shore.

Anyone who has watched a child take a radio apart or play a practical joke on an adult will know that Deconstruction is one of the most basic and amusing instincts which needn't find any further justification than its own pleasure. It's also closely related to the comic instinct, the long tradition of laughing where we cannot afford to cry. Deconstruction, perhaps in all fields, is an essential part of the comic tradition, but it is especially so in architecture where there has been a long history of showing buildings in an unfinished state, of conventionalising 'mistakes' in grammar, of using rough and unfinished materials. In short, of attacking conventions with codified unconventionality. Rustication is one case in point, the 'primitive hut' another.

The most established convention of unconventionality however is the formula for the Comic Scene. A typical example comes from the cubiculum of a Roman House from Boscoreale, now in the Metropolitan Museum in New York. Here we find the Comic Scene set apart from the Tragic and Satyric murals showing a typical Deconstructionist architecture: fragmented, asymmetrical, disjointed, *ad hoc,* skewed and full of unexpected discontinuities. The perspectival space is contradictory, buildings tilt away from each other, some look unusable and the entire scene is pervaded with a sense of instability. This is canonic 'deconstruction from within', a slippery, wiggly architecture that uses the Classical language in order to subvert it, an in-between architecture that is both Classical and anti-Classical.

Vitruvius, among other Roman writers, codified such rule-breaking conventions and they were taken up by Renaissance designers and theorists such as Sebastiano Serlio to become major formulae for actual theatrical stage sets. Serlio in one Comic Scene of Deconstruction shows the town hall going to seed, literally sprouting bushes, and surrounded with a mixture of building types of heterogeneous style. The brothel in the front right is in the Gothic style, a wry comment on what some sixteenth-century Italians thought of that manner. But the essentially humorous and Deconstructive aspect is in the medley of motifs, their juxtaposition and lack of order and finish.

Post-Modernists, the target for Deconstructionist contempt, adopted the same heterogeneity for their purposes and one portrayal of the *Strada Novissima* at the Venice Biennale, 1980, borrows Serlio's Tragic, not Comic, Scene to show this *mélange.* Here is a joke on a joke and one that becomes more ironic when one notes how much deconstructionists try to separate themselves from Post-Modernists, especially Post-Modern Classicists. The spectre of this latter movement seems to have

SEBASTIANO SERLIO, *Comic Scene,* 1537

frightened them into action, united them against a common enemy, in spite of the fact that both movements are subversive to canonic Classicism. At any rate the deconstructionists are momentarily a united movement – the disclaimers at the Museum of Modern Art exhibition suggest this point – and they share aspects of a common style, although its practitioners claim different goals. What are the main differences, in a movement which supposedly celebrates *différence*? There are basically four divergent tendencies.

First is the fragmentation and *discontinuity* of Frank Gehry – breaking up the whole into dissociated parts and juxtaposing them with an artful informality. The beauty of dissociated parts is that of the medieval village, an all-too-human botched and bungled pot-pourri that would have displeased Nietzsche, but one that is far superior in scale to the organised chaos of the industrial city, or the typical skyscraper cities of today.

Second is the Neo-Constructivism of Rem Koolhaas and OMA – the rotational inversions of big slabs into colourful distorted, perspectival de-compositions. Or his five superimposed layers of strips, confetti, grids, circulation elements for the Parc de la Villette, the competition Tschumi ultimately won. In the Neo-Constructivist repertoire Zaha Hadid has perfected the 'flying beam' and 'cocktail stick', and the anamorphic projection which makes Deconstruction so beautifully decentred, dislocated and – in her words and Leonidov's – anti-gravitational'. This Neo-Constructivism is populist, optimistic and realistic about mass-culture. It seeks the promise hidden within modernism of a hedonistic play with social and technical forces.

Third are the follies – *folies* of Bernard Tschumi – a cross between Late-Constructivism of Chernikhov, the aesthetics of Kandinsky and the current French Deconstructions of Foucault and Derrida. These are well-known and considered the heart of the movement, but some of the same ideas and forms are synthesised and taken to an extreme by Daniel Libeskind. He has absorbed notions from several sources – Gehry's fragmentation, Koolhaas' 'flying beams and cocktail sticks', and Eisenman's hermetic representation – and combined them in a frenetic and intense language which is both very personal and 'anti-architectural' (although with the aid of the engineer Peter Rice it is structural).

Fourth is Peter Eisenman's position, a *positive nihilism,* which finds in representation itself the final goal of architecture. It is true Eisenman is concerned with the loss of centre, the alienation inherent in Modernism, the uprooted masses, the end of ethnic identity – but these themes always take second place to his rhetorical figures and are sublimated in a set of changing tropes: 'catachresis', 'arabesques', 'grotesques', or in the past 'scaling', 'self-similarity' and 'transformation'. For the most part his architecture is very abstract (although a few conventional representations are now entering it) and consistent. It represents the process of design and formal choice with a fair degree of rigour, as long as one understands his intentions and knows the generative rules. Most people do not have access to this knowledge, nor is it provided in a supplementary symbolic system attached to the architecture. The only way one can fully appreciate Eisenman's work is by reading about it and looking, and for this reason it is primarily solipsistic and aesthetic, quite beautiful and moving, but private.

So we have here four different positions which are grouped together in the Deconstructivist show that Mark Wigley and Philip Johnson have mounted at the

ZAHA HADID, *IBA Housing, Block 2*, West Berlin, 1985. View from the east.

205

Museum of Modern Art. The question is: will these *differences* be allowed to surface, will the designers be allowed to deconstruct from each other in public, or will a homogeneous veil be drawn – as usual in art politics – over their heterogeneity?

And then what about the missing Deconstructionists, those who should be in the Pantheon but are likely to be left out? What about Richard Meier and John Hejduk, Alvin Boyarsky's students at the AA, or Peter Cook's in Frankfurt? What about the radical *adhocism* of John Johansen, or the carefully cut emptiness of Hiromi Fujii?

Indeed, if Deconstruction has another non-centre, apart from London, it is Tokyo, and the presence of the absence of the Japanese is ethnocentric to say the least. My list of the *Salons des Refusés,* or rather self-refuses since some have turned down the opportunity to exhibit, could be extended. But the point will be granted before it is even pressed: the MoMA Show is simply a selection coloured by an international movement and the taste of two or three individuals. The absences only matter if we believe historical justice is being done to a movement – which it is not.

That there is a world movement no-one but a curator at MoMA, can deny. First is the shared style and set of formal motifs – the cocktail sticks and excavated buildings which Emilio Ambasz and Eisenman have been designing for several years. Second is the call to a 'New Spirit', the *L'Esprit Nouveau* of Le Corbusier subtracted of his geometry, reason and white and black aesthetics. Third is the unity against Post-Modern and other Classicisms – a pervasive boredom with everything presently dominating the scene. Fourth, there are the divergent views of these architects – their *différence* which comes from a peculiar exploration of an idiosyncratic, even anti-social hermeticism. And lastly, something we could wish was more powerful in a movement that tends to take itself too seriously, there is the latent humour of unravelling everything we spend our lives tying up: the 'de-architecture' of SITE and others which makes a modest art of the present and past. If Deconstruction is not amusing it doesn't exist.

This summary was given as a paper, before the MoMA show on Deconstructivism, at the First International Conference on Deconstructivist Art and Architecture, March 1988, Tate Gallery

JOHN JOHANSEN, *Oklahoma Theater Center,* Oklahoma City, 1970

HIROMI FUJII, *Miyata Residence,* Japan, 1986

DIALOGUES WITH PETER EISENMAN

Psychoanalysis and Excavation

– In theorising about yourself, Peter, you've always pointed to a 1978 shift which is a kind of compound shift as I understand it. It's when you started undergoing psychoanalysis in an extended way and it's at the time that you produced House X and the Cannaregio project and became conscious of Deconstruction, and decentring in particular. Would you agree with that?

I think I would almost agree. You have the sequence wrong. House X was the end of a certain phase. I started psychoanalysis when I went to Venice to do Cannaregio – instead of building House X. The clients wanted to start that summer and I said 'No, I want to do Cannaregio' and when I came back the house had been abandoned. It is then that I felt I needed to go into therapy. I was really upset, having spent so much time on a house and then not having it built. It was when I started to go into my unconscious in my analysis that I became less oriented to the head. This caused a shift in my architecture: it went into the ground. I mean House IIa, House El Even Odd, Fin d'Ou T Hou S, all of those projects were in the ground in a sense, they were digging into the unconscious, as were the projects for Cannaregio and Berlin. They were all grounded projects. Before, none of my houses had any grounding; they were all in the air. Yes, the shift came in '78, when I started analysis. It came at the same time as the split from the Institute. I needed to establish another identity for myself. I think the identity for me as the Institute-man, as not myself, was something I found very problematic in my analysis. It took a few years, but certainly by 1980 it was clear to me that I would not continue at the Institute.

– All of your life has been very much a conscious moving from position to position and in a sense a perpetuation of crises, maybe unconsciously, and then consciously confirmed and seen straightforwardly. In other words you don't shy away from naming them and then acting them out in a completely honest and straightforward way. If we can shift to the crisis in the Institute, that occurred in around 1982?

The crisis occurred before that, during the tenth anniversary of the Institute in '77. The high period of the Institute was '76, '77, '78 – that's when Rossi, Tafuri, Scolari, Tschumi, Koolhaas and Fujii were there. And then my practice, as it was then constituted, started to go downhill and I knew by 1980 that I really wanted to get out. The crisis came in '82. First of all, nobody believed that I wanted to leave and that I would walk away. I kept telling everybody that I was going. It was very clear to me that I was going, I do not think anybody was prepared for that. It was this that many people resented.

– Did you lose a lot of friends in this period? In a sense, to put an overly cryptic interpretation on it, you 'Deconstructed' the Institute and a lot of friends at that time, didn't you?

I would say that inadvertently that was probably true.

Cannaregio, Venice, 1980, overall view of model

Bio-Centrum, Frankfurt-am-Main, 1987-9, view of model

– Did your psychoanalysis allow you to do that without too much heart-rending pain?
My psychoanalysis was very important for me to become myself. Before the analysis, I was always a political animal reacting to public pressure. After analysis for the first time I was really able to deal with myself, not as the public wanted me to be, but as I needed to be. Therefore it really did not matter what other people thought. I knew what I had to do for myself. I never thought very much about what it was doing to other people because it was more important to work out my own problems.

The Jew and Outsider in Us

– In the Krier interview you say 'as a Jew and an outsider I have never felt part of that classical world, I feel that Modernism was the result of an alienated culture with no roots'. So your definition of Modernism as alienation is first of all, as you have already admitted, only really possible outside architecture, it isn't true of architecture.
It has not been true of architecture, but I think it should be. I think it's more difficult in architecture because, as I have said on many other occasions, architecture is so rooted in presence and in seeing itself as shelter and institution, house and home. It is the guardian of reality. It is the last bastion of location. I think this is the real problem. Architecture represses dislocation because of the paradoxical position it maintains. You don't have that problem with theology or philosophy or science.
– It seems to me that you're trying all the time to reconcile people to alienation and to present being a Jewish outsider as a universal state. You're trying to take the homeless Jewish intellectual as Kant's imperative and say that everybody should be, or is, a homeless Jewish intellectual, either openly admitting it like yourself, or inadvertently.
I do not think it is inadvertent, but rather subconscious. I do not think that you have to be a Jewish intellectual to be desperately lonely, an island of the unconscious. Architecture has repressed the individual unconscious by dealing only with conscious ness in the physical environment that is the supposedly happy home. I think it is exactly in the home where the unhomely is, where the terror is alive – in the repression of the unconscious. What I am trying to suggest is that the alienated house makes us realise that we cannot only be conscious of the physical world, but rather also our own unconscious. Psychoanalysis is talking about this. Psychoanalysis is partly a Jewish phenomenon, understandably for a people who need to be in touch with their own psychological being. I would argue that we all have a bit of a Jew in us; that the Jew is in our unconscious; that's why there is anti-Semitism, because we do not want to face our unconscious, we do not want to face our shadow; the Jew stands for that shadow. We do not want to face the issue of rootlessness. I am from New York but I do not necessarily feel more at home here than in many other places. However, I do not feel any more alienated here than I would in any other place. But this is not necessarily a Jewish problem, but rather one of Modern man in general.
– Well, I would agree that to be in New York is to feel alienated and alone, and at the same time to be a Jew in New York is to feel everybody is alienated and alone, so that it's a kind of universal New York experience. I think a certain amount of irony should creep into your view of yourself in that light. I mean you get a lot of Woody Allen films made on precisely that subject. In a way, it's a fact of being in New York and you can be considered canonic,

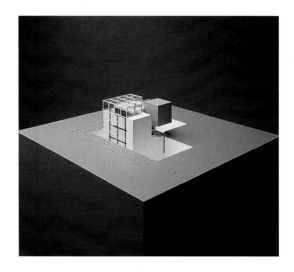

Fin d'Out T Hou S, view of model

you are actually acting exactly as Harold Rosenberg claimed — 'a herd of independent minds' — you are very independent, but you are still part of a culture which is, at least seen from the outside, so strong that it's overpowering.

I think that New York is the one place where the subconscious and the lack of a collective is very much on the prowl. I would not say 'universalised' because I do not think we can ever universalise. There are some people who will never see the haunted beings in their houses, the ghosts that inhabit all of our homes.

— Don't you think there's a danger that by emphasising alienation and the Holocaust and the Second World War and the atom bomb and all of the things that are, if you like, dis-locating and disorienting, your position becomes a kind of terrorist tactic that forces a closure of discussion; that in its own way is just as repressive of the true otherness of Pluralism as Classicism?

I think we ought to be careful about Pluralism. I do not believe that Pluralism is at issue here. Although I certainly believe in 'the other', I do not believe in the dismissal of Classicism.

— You don't dismiss Classicism? You've changed again then, when did you stop being anti-classical?

Where my position has slightly changed is in the fact that repression of any kind comes to haunt us. For example, if you are interested in catachresis you do not throw away metaphor but rather you try to find the catachresis repressed in metaphor. If you are against Classicism you do not throw it away, you try to find the hidden other that has been repressed in Classicism. In other words, it is what I call the anaconda strategy: you squeeze Classicism, suffocate it as it were until you squeeze out of it what was repressed. I believe that this is a big difference, I am no longer talking about alienation because I believe that politically it is a loaded word, that kind of terrorism is exactly what I found in Krier's position and I agree with you that the kind of demagogic condition that I accused him of is exactly what I had to be careful of myself. The way to another architecture is not to suppress the classical but in fact to cut into it, to use the previous metaphor: to be a surgeon in Tafuri's terms rather than a magician. Not to repress but to surgically open up the classical, the modern, and to find what is repressed. I think that is really an account of Deconstruction if you want. It is about multivalency.

— I agree, I think that is canonic to Derrida too.

Derrida and others say 'Let's not throw these things away, let's find out why we want to throw them away.'

— Which is a way of hanging on to them too.

Post-Functionalism and Post-Modernism

— In your article 'Post-Functionalism' of 1976 it was a kind of Not-Post-Modernism. It was your answer to Robert Stern and me and ever since then you've slid in and out of Post-Modernism. As you know, in our debates over the last twelve years, I've always thought of Post-Functionalism as a kind of ultra-Modernism or Late-Modernism, and I'm aware you declared Post-Modernism dead and appalling three or four times, particularly in 1981 when you were interviewed by Stephen Gardiner in the Observer *over here. You announced its death at least a year before the British did.*

House X, 1980, axonometric model

The death of what you would have called Post-Modernism.

—Well it's not just me, Peter.

I mean the Post-Modernism of eclecticism and Neo-Classicism, of people like Robert Stern, Michael Graves, Charles Moore, and I still believe that that will not be seen by history to be Post-Modernism. I think that what we are talking about now is another Post-Modernism.

— That goes back to a much bigger debate as you well know, back to the origins of Post-Modernism and its essence or if you like, its idea, its agenda and of course the court is still out on what that agenda really is, whether it's what you and the Deconstructionists do. By the way, of course, you are very aware that the Post-Structuralists don't want to be called Post-Modern by and large.

It's an occupied term in architecture. I have been for several years telling you that I thought I was a Post-Modernist.

— In the sense of someone like Ihab Hassan, yes. You have consistently been a Hassanian-Post-Modernist although you've slipped in and out, even about that you've shown great scepticism.

Being slippery by the way is the trait of a Post-Modernist.

— Not my kind of Post-Modernist. I value consistency and you value slippage, what greater word is there in Deconstruction than slippage? The phrase 'slippery' is used by Mark Wigley à propos Deconstructivist architecture.

That's right. I agree that your kind of Post-Modernism is not at issue in this interview. You asked me to define my position and that is what I'm saying. For me when you're saying there's been slippage, I would say that being slippery is part of the discourse.

— Well you know the famous remarks of Karl Popper and others: 'from contradiction in philosophy anything follows'. There are no rules of the game, if you start slipping, if you can claim to be both a Post-Functionalist and a Post-Modernist, align them at some times, distinguish them at others and operate in an ad hoc way. I find that kind of slippage anti-philosophical and just pure opportunist pop-gun politics.

Well if that was the case I would agree with you, but that's not quite what I've done.

— You insist on certain positions on Post-Modernism one day and then others another day and you aren't quite clear. It struck me when I read your work Architecture and the Problem of the Rhetorical Figure *(1987) that it was perhaps influenced by, God help us both, my* Rhetoric and Architecture *(1972) and* Current Architecture *(1982) – a lot of rhetorical terms appear, like oxymoron, anastrophe and chiasmus – not catachresis – was there any influence?*

Well Charles I read a lot and I am not saying I do not read you. I don't think I dredged these things up from you however. I also read Derrida and Kipnis and Vidler and Wigley and Nietzsche. It's not clear to me how much is consciously or unconsciously present. To me the question of who wrote it first is of little value. It does not matter to me if Philip Johnson says Frank Gehry originated the Deconstructionist movement, because I know that Frank Gehry did not 'originate' it.

— I'm not trying to claim priority, I'm just trying to clarify the overlapping funny dialectic. Let me put another case to you, to go back to Post-Modernism; all of a sudden in your reminiscences of the Armoury at Ohio and the ramparts and the abattoir in the Paris garden project, are they not my kind of Post-Modernism?

House III, Lakeville, Connecticut, 1969-71, exterior view

I think that they are not trying to be. Your historical imagery returns architecture to itself. Mine tries to move architecture away from itself – to be disjunctive with its past. It tries to move architecture to what I call 'between', between its old past and a repressed present.

– You can say between simulation and dissimulation, but they are very much like the ghost buildings of Venturi, and Jim Stirling at Stuttgart. In other words they are very much in the Post-Modern tradition, whether you intend them to be something else is your affair, but they are very much like Post-Modern ghosted signs which allude to the past.

They allude to a past without nostalgia or the necessary continuity proposed by both Venturi and Stirling.

– Well nostalgia's probably in the eye of the beholder.

I think that all continuity and tradition deals with a nostalgia for a tradition that is no longer possible.

– Well what's this fear of nostalgia?

Not fear, because I think nostalgia leads to what can be called 'the aestheticisation of the banal' which is what Post-Modernism is also about.

– Nostalgia can be perfectly healthy or perfectly radical. In the case of the French Revolution, Roman dress and recalling Republican virtues was positive radical nostalgia. In the case of someone recalling his parents, or his background, or his race, or his Jewishness, or his position, or his memory, it's perceived as a very functional and real thing, it's talking about having a feeling about something that was and isn't now. How can memory not be involved with an element of nostalgia, why repress it?

I am not against memory as a tissue of forgetting. There is a difference between this kind of memory and the sentimentalising of memory which is nostalgia.

– The word nostalgia is so corrupt for you, but a lot of people, even tough-minded people, have a place for nostalgia, as long as it's recognised as a part of memory.

Well, I guess Charles, my new position would be (as opposed to the way I would have answered you six months ago) that you're right; what one must do is find out why one is so much against nostalgia, ie thematise the problem of nostalgia which is what I am trying to do in my work. Six months ago I would have said 'no, I'm against nostalgia' – that's a very tough-minded attitude. I think I'm more tough-minded now in saying 'I want to find out why I'm against nostalgia' – 'What is it in nostalgia that threatens me? Why does it make me so anxious?' If you said Deconstructionism it doesn't make me anxious, but when you say nostalgia you push a button. Another button that you push is to say banal; I want to find out why I get so upset about banality.

– I find you backing into my kind of Post-Modernism stage by stage as you get into thematics, representation, signification, communication, memory – a whole lot of rhetorical tropes which Post-Modernists of my kind rather than the Hassanian kind have been making. Most important, of course, ornament and arabesque are precisely the areas that Post-Modernists have been exploring. I think you're a closet Post-Modernist of my kind!

Let's talk about the difference; let's accept that all the things you say have entered into my vocabulary, into my work, but I have been trying to dislocate them in order to find out what they repress, not using them straight. The difference is that whereas Robert Stern uses them straight, I use them in a different way in an attempt to dislocate.

– So does Stirling. Don't make everybody into Bob Stern. I would say that Jim Stirling and

House VI, Cornwall, Connecticut, 1972-6, view of west elevation

Venturi and Umberto Eco and the kind of Post-Modernism that I've been defending – I'm not defending an accommodating Post-Modernism, but the ironically displaced or dislocated Post-Modernism – acknowledge the historical, so there's a way in which I have no trouble with dislocation at all. In fact I would argue it's canonic to Stirling and Venturi. Which is the irony in your position, where does the difference hold?

They all still assume the naturalness of the architectural language. I am not against representation, as long as representation uncovers what the natural language of architecture represses. You do not need to use the natural language of architecture to represent the ironic. There may be a value to the ironic but not if it means maintaining the language of architecture intact.

– OK. Well I can see that's a valid distinction from your angle.

I am not trying to put forward what my angle is, but rather what their use of irony really is.

Derrida and the Choral Works

– OK. In the Chora Works, or Choral Works – I want to call them Choral Works because I've seen them called that half the time . . .

They are called Choral Works.

– So there's a chorus, and the chorus is you and Derrida presumably? – singing away.

There are also other people in the chorus, they just may not be identified – Plato, Tschumi, they're all people in that chorus.

– A choral work is something slightly religious, cantatory and rhythmical: it's a musical chant sung in unison.

It's also done with a group of people, there's no one single voice; they sing in different parts. Derrida's contribution was a musical instrument, a lyre, you will probably want to spell it liar, but that would be all right with him.

– It seems to me that in the design you have completely dominated Derrida. You even said something to that effect in an interview in SD. Is it true that you're disappointed he hasn't taken a greater part?

In some way that is true.

– What exactly has he contributed?

The failure of the work in a certain way was that I was not contained, that I was not played out of my position into some new position. Jacques contributed an unfinished text that he was working on from Plato's *Timaeus*. We took this as the programme. We then worked with the idea of chora as the programme. Jacques would criticise it until we got to a point where he was more comfortable with what we were doing; I think really more comfortable with architecture than any particular part of the work. I was probably and not coincidentally doing chora before I read his text. I think it is a collaboration that will happen some day; it has not happened yet. We finally forced Jacques to draw something. He then drew the lyre which became both the figure and the frame for the site.

– I see, I couldn't decipher those strange bumps in the middle, the kind of a wall that isn't the ramparts . . .

That other wall comes right out of the site of my Cannaregio project, in Italy.

– Let me ask you some factual questions: the Corten steel, is that part of a tilted plane?

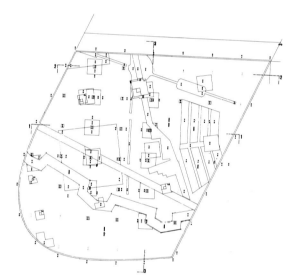

Choral Works, 1986, Garden for Parc de la Villette, plan

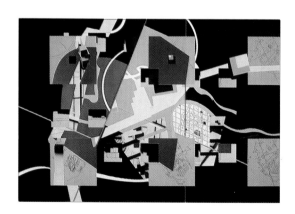

La Villette collage

Contextual object for *Cannaregio* project, Venice, 1980

That *is* a tilted plane.
— *What are the lines? Are the lines etched into the steel?*
The lines are acid-etched into the steel.
— *And when will it be built?*
That is a good question. From what I gather the Director of the La Villette project, a very decent man by the name of Goldberg very much wants to build it. As soon as they have their budget for next year they will begin construction. Everything is ready to go so that it's going to be open by the time we have the show in London.
— *How big across is it? About thirty feet?*
No, it's about seventy by ninety feet. You realise that the whole thing was this idea of no authority. In other words, there were two sites, one in Paris, the abattoir site, one in Venice which was also an abattoir site, a coincidence. A Swiss-French architect, Le Corbusier, comes to Venice and puts down a grid. An American architect picked up that grid and elongated it to the Cannaregio from the abattoir. Then another Swiss-French architect comes to Paris and puts down on the abattoir site another grid like Le Corbusier's, an abstract grid. Then he invites the same American architect to put a grid on top of his grid. So naturally I put my Cannaregio grid on top of La Villette. What this attempts to do is to undercut the notion of originality and authority, in other words that no one can take authority or credit for it or for who came first.
— *Well it does to those people who have an Eisenman text in their hand, or like me have slaved away reading and looking.*
I think you will realise it's a text if you look at the thing.
— *Well yes, there's a bit of representation, I can recognise a rampart when I see it.*
Can you?
— *Just barely.*
Well that's what I mean by 'between'. It is a between image that is both rampart at one moment and a piece of river in another. You can read them as several things.
— *Well you're slightly missing my irony, but ... Peter, just on the anti-business of Deconstruction — decentring, disorienting.*

Deconstruction, Nihilism and Laughter
Charles, you miss the irony of your newly found interest in Deconstruction. You should know that Deconstruction is a *positive* activity, not an anti-activity.
— *You don't have to testify to the House Committee on Un-American Activities.*
I just want to establish the ground rules.
— *Even Derrida believes in affirmative Deconstruction, like some kind of feminist you know; affirmative action, and so does Tschumi. They all have obviously faced this question too many times, so they have to go on record as saying they're positive. Let's just go back to the negative part of it for a minute, the nihilism, because it seems to me that the emphasis on alienation and decentring and anti-Classicism and negation, dialectical negation if one calls it that, or being anti-memory or anti-thing, in a sense putting forward and, I would argue, universalising the notion of the Empty Man, the man contemplating the void, the nihil with pleasure and/or fear, I wonder is that true?*
I'm talking about a man who is fulfilling himself through his unconscious, realising that the emptiness is *in* man and that the alienation lies between the conscious and

unconscious individual.

– *But when your Empty Man contemplates the void?*

That is not the unconscious.

– *Well also the void, if you like, of a superior existence or the metaphysics of alienation, does he contemplate it with pleasure? Do you smile to yourself and a warm glow comes over you? Or with fear?*

With anxiety, with a lot of stress, that's certain.

– *Is that why you use puns all the time to show the kind of breakdown . . .*

That kind of humour you know covers some kind of anxiety. When somebody laughs at those kind of things, there's anxiety there and what one is trying to do is uncover what that laughter is repressing.

– *Is that laughter a kind of belly laugh or nervous laughter?*

It's a nervous laugh.

– *But don't you enjoy it, Peter?*

I wouldn't do it if I didn't enjoy it.

– *I'm trying to prove the kind of latent humour behind your intellectual position.*

I do not think there's anything latent about it.

– *No, but some people have a kind of mad laughter, other people have a belly laugh and yours seems to be somewhere between constrained and mordant – a kind of black humour.*

No it's not black humour. I love playing, I am one of the most playful people you know, I don't think there's anything else in life but to play. What my work does is to show how play very much animates and activates, for instance, the seriousness of what we do. For me play is a very serious activity. I do not play to win. That is why people do not understand my machinations, they think I am a political power player. But I do not love power as an end.

MoMA Exhibition and the New Academicism

– *What about the exhibition at MoMA, there are three rooms and who's in them exactly?*

I don't know, from what I understand there are now only two rooms, in the first there are the Constructivist precursors, I don't know who they have in that room.

– *They must be Leonidov, Malevich, Lissitzky and Chernikhov.*

Mark Wigley can tell you all of that. I can tell you who I think is in the show – Frank Gehry, Bernard Tschumi, Rem Koolhaas, Zaha Hadid, Daniel Libeskind, Coop Himmelblau and myself. Like many other people I proposed names to Philip. My original list had eleven names. I have fought for those eleven names but have lost quite a number.

– *What is the name of the working title at the moment?*

I think it is called *Deconstructivist Architecture*.

– *Wasn't it* Violated Perfection *before? When did they come to Deconstructivist?*

The Museum wouldn't let them use the title *Violated Perfection*. They didn't like it, they thought it was an off-putting title.

– *So Deconstructivist means it's slightly Constructivist?*

Well Philip believes firmly that all of this work is picking up from the long-dead Constructivists. I would have called it *Violated Perfection* and therefore I would have had John Hejduk and Raimund Abraham and people like that, who are not necessarily

Constructivists at all. Constructivism is giving it stylistic overtones. It seems to me it should not be about Constructivists, but about Deconstruction.

— Well I would call this a very slippery slippage in the use of the word. I call it Deconstructionism rather than Deconstructivism for precisely the reasons that you were wanting to call it Violated Perfection.

You're right, it is not Deconstructionist, it is not deconstructing in the theoretical sense of the word.

— There is a big wedge you can drive between a Deconstructivist and a Deconstructionist. If that is what you want to do, then you can call me a Deconstructionist and there are Deconstructivists in the show. For myself I have never been either. There is no question that my work is animated by the spirit of Deconstruction.

— Why isn't someone like SITE in the show?

I do not think Jim Wines' work has anything to do with the show.

— Well in his 'De-architecture', wouldn't you say that he has a lot more to do with Deconstruction than the Neo-Constructivists?

I guess he would, but if you look at his work you have to make another assessment.

— European critics have seen him and Frank Gehry as Deconstructionist because they literally tear down, break through and violate.

I would say that tearing things down is one-liner stuff. It is a form of illustration, not a theoretical position.

— It may or may not be one-liner but we're not talking about quality, we're talking about categories. Is there not something contradictory between a joint exhibition and Deconstructionism which should be anti-hierarchy? Are you not setting up a new academy? Is that not a betrayal of Deconstructionism?

If it does set up a new academy I will be the first one to be against it.

— I see, still you were instrumental in setting up that other academy.

If the Institute was an academy it did not have a Deconstructionist overtone in it at the time, even though my work might have displayed a spirit and tendencies in that direction.

— Oh come on — its magazine was called Oppositions. *It certainly had a very strong academic bent that was taken up by many of the East Coast academies and then Harvard, Columbia, to a certain extent Yale, and all the magazines that came out as little* Opposition *books. You became the new academy, I think this is just a confirmation of that neo-academic trend.*

Philip gets very upset at anybody thinking that I am doing the show. But in reality I was not the one who said 'Hey Philip, let's have a museum show'. I think it's a very exciting thing because it's going to rocket things around a bit.

— It certainly is, but it's also going to solidify them in an academic way. They are in any case in that way now, they are already present in all those schools — the little Zaha Hadids, the little Gehrys and . . .

You have not said little Eisenmans.

— There have been little Eisenmans now for twenty years.

I have never seen those guys. I see little Hadids and little Gehrys and little Libeskinds all over the place and it's boring.

— Well there are little 'excavators' too.

What is interesting is that new things are going to open up. I think there are other possibilities for architecture. That is what I have always been interested in. I think we are going to start to enrich architectural language.

— Enrich it, now you sound even more Post-Modern, good heavens!

I am Post-Modern but not in the transcendental sense that you speak of. Enrich for me is not to give something new value, but to uncover what has been repressed by old values. I think the difference between my Frankfurt project and Richard Meier's work, for example, is that my Bio-Centrum project in Frankfurt is about the multivalent nature of text and I do not think Richard's work is about multivalency. The difference between what I'm doing and the other people in the show is that my work is about textual multivalence or *betweenness*.

— Or rather, 'inter-textuality'. But you have to, as you admitted in London, know the other texts, the written text about it relating to DNA and all of those other things. Is your work, insofar as it is a text, a Mandarin text demanding a reader's guide?

I don't think so, I used to believe that we needed a new reader. I believe that my texts are available not as information but as text. They have merely been repressed by the traditional texts of architecture.

— You don't think that they are so self-referential: your Choral Work is referring to Corbusier and to Cannaregio and to abattoirs that no longer exist . . .

When Venturi does it you do not seem to mind.

— But Venturi uses a popular code. The only popular codes you use are the ramparts, and maybe a little bit of the abattoir. The ramparts are I admit understandable and popular — you have one popular sign but even the abattoir needs a code. You are really creeping into Post-Modernism, not jumping in.

My codes may not be as accessible as Venturi's, but they remain repressed by your so-called popular codes.

— I'd say you are a Mandarin. You're an élitist and absolutist, why not a Mandarin too?

I'm neither élitist, absolutist nor a Mandarin. I believe I'm a centrist. It takes an enormous effort for someone comfortable on the edge, on the periphery, to attempt to occupy the centre. In an age where there are no new frontiers, the edge may just be the centre, the centre of the periphery.

— I'm not trying to marginate you but you're about to be in yet another 'academy of the new' at the Museum of Modern Art. You ought to be the ultimate character in a Woody Allen film, always trying to occupy the centre of otherness.

I am that character in a Woody Allen film.

— OK you shouldn't be resisting my interpretation, alienation as the 'here comes everybody'. My problem, as a pluralist, is that even if you go to your gardens in Parc de la Villette, you look around and see all the people who are going to be building gardens there, like John Hejduk, Chemetov, Price, Nouvel and so forth. Most of them are Late-Modernists within an abstract style and most of them come out of the same Deconstructionist stable or share a lot of stylistic, ideological and valuative positions — in other words, I would argue that it's going to be a kind of Disneyworld of Deconstruction and instead of having real différance or otherness or pluralism it's going to be very integrated, very canonic, very much like a new academy. What do you say to that? Why haven't you invited Michael Graves or Quinlan Terry or a traditionalist?

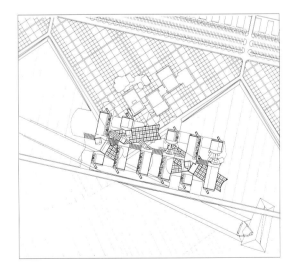

Bio-Centrum, site plan

They never invite me. Why should they play in my sandbox if they don't want me to play in theirs? It's that simple. I am a team player and a groupie. If I were doing the exhibition I would have a different group of people there in my team, because I like playing in a sandbox. Philip hates this idea of a team.

— *What do you think it is then that motivates Philip? Why does he not want a team, what is behind his Deconstructivism?*

Well I think Philip has interestingly enough always been a dislocator. Look at the International Style show: he has always been jumping before anybody else and I think he wants to go out, firstly with another jump, and secondly with a jump that puts him back in favour with the left, or what is thought to be left intellectually, in other words so he's not seen as someone of the right or the establishment but has academic and intellectual respectability. He probably would not articulate it that way, he has always been worried about the left and this is one time where maybe he is co-opting the left.

— *Oh you think so do you?*

Well if you were to take Tschumi, Koolhaas, Eisenman and Libeskind as representing a certain left in architecture.

— *They certainly aren't left-wing.*

Not politically left-wing, left architecturally. They are the darlings of the left in the art world.

— *Well that's an interesting substitute for avant-garde semantically. But you know Philip always jumps after the ground has been prepared so he lands safely. You say he jumped before anybody else but that's simply not true — he jumped into Post-Modernism in 1978 after maybe twelve years of carefully patting the ground so that he would bounce. In the same way with Deconstruction. You and others have been preparing the ground since 1978 if not before — I think you mustn't give him too much credit. By the same token you mustn't think that's going to heal the breach with what you call the left and I call the avant-garde. It's still going to regard him with suspicion and they could regard it as his final kiss of death- life to the movement. This could kill off Deconstruction the same way he killed off Post-Modernism; when he embraced Post-Modernism, the Yale students came running up to me in 1978 and said, 'Is Post-Modernism dead because of the AT&T?'*

I was called a 'Philip Johnson loyalist' by Michael Sorkin, and Michael Heizer said to me, 'You know, Peter, you ought to be proud of that, because that takes real guts.' He said 'I'm a Philip Johnson loyalist, all the artists are Philip Johnson loyalists, he has been a patron to all the best artists in the world and we are all loyalists'. So why the hell should architects not risk being in the centre?

— *I wasn't questioning your loyalty.*

Some people cannot understand why I have been loyal to Philip. But he is one of the few architects one can talk to about ideas. Do you know anyone else who pretends to be anti-intellectual who reads Nietzsche in German?

— *But when he embraces Deconstruction, if that's what he's doing, this could have the same effect as when he embraced Post-Modernism, what do you say to that?*

I cannot really answer that because I don't think he was responsible for the problems of Post-Modernism.

— *But when it went public at that scale for the largest multi-national in the world.*

I think it is interesting if Deconstruction can go public. It says something about the possibilities for theoretical activity in the centre.

– It is going public at Parc de la Villette, Mitterrand came along and launched Bernard Tschumi's Folies.

I would not agree with you. That is a form of Deconstruction. I don't think Bernard Tschumi is about Deconstruction.

– He certainly thinks he is.

My sense is this: I believe that Deconstruction is not ultimately visible. It is about building unbuildable ideas. I do not think any multi-national corporation is going to build Deconstruction just as they do not build any other ideology.

– You just have to wait Peter, I bet that a multi-national builds a large Deconstructionist building, a headquarters in four years, a major building in two.

And do you say one of the people in the show will do it?

– No that's another question. It will be Kohn Pedersen Fox who will do it.

Perhaps.

– Philip is always in that camp as well, don't forget that – he plays in both sandboxes. He might admit it himself, he wouldn't mind because he's a nihilist, Nietzsche is his favourite character.

You have to be careful about Nietzsche. You can read him two ways, pro- or con-.

– Of course, I'm a great Nietzsche fan too. Here comes everyone, like Woody Allen.

(*December 1987*)

Reactions to Decon: The Media Event

– I would like your reaction to the Decon Exhibition and its follow-up.

First of all I have an enormous complicity with that show, but it did nothing to help my own situation. You can argue that I have been doing Deconstructivism before it became an architectural term. There is no question that Philip and I discussed this thing. There is no question that Philip was very interested in jumping, moving again as he always has. If you go back and look at his Kline Tower at Yale you find a jump to Post-Modernism. Philip was really interested in moving things, shaking things up. Also getting on the right side of the intellectual left in an interesting way, to position himself where no one could fault him for being corrupt, supporting something that was supposedly ideological. He made a very good choice of taking Mark Wigley on as co-curator. He is an ideologue with a Deconstructionist background, and a PhD thesis on Derrida. I was the reader of that thesis and had an effect on it. Mark had been hanging around me since I'd been teaching at Harvard. He had flown in and out from New Zealand and floated into my office and I introduced him to Philip. Therefore I had some investment in the exhibition. A lot of people said to me 'Why did you have to invent the cast of assorted characters, why did you not have your own show?'. I've never understood why I do things like that. There is no question that it didn't help me in terms of having a one-man show at MoMA, etc. It was like inventing the Five Architects, like inventing the Institute, like another one of these smoke-screens on my own work. But basically other than Bernard Tschumi there is no one who might fall into that label of Deconstructionism in that exhibition.

– Libeskind?

Libeskind, true. I think that the title of the original show was called 'Violated Perfection'.

— So 'Violated Perfection' comes from you?

Yes, but the Museum objected to this name and also 'Deconstruction'. The original name of 'Violated Perfection' was not necessarily mine, but I introduced two students of mine in Chicago to these ideas. Wierzbowski and Florian had a studio on Deconstruction with me. They got the idea of an exhibition and the whole thing was deflected by Aaron Betzky from Yale, the fellow that worked for Frank Gehry, who turned it into a young architects show. He approached Philip who asked me about it. I said that I did not think that it was such a great idea, to get involved with Betsky, as I didn't think that he knew what he was doing. I shouldn't have got into it myself, but I gave Philip a list of eleven names, including John Hejduk, Morphosis and a lot of people who weren't finally chosen. Ultimately, Philip and Wigley picked the thing and changed the name to 'Deconstructivism' which, if you are talking about Deconstruction, is a truly Deconstructive name because it is duplicitous and slippery. You could, of course, defend it for slipperiness. Naturally nobody likes to be called a 'Decon artist', and I never used to use the term.

— To be a 'Decon' is like being a 'PoMo'.

I have tried to avoid the label. What hurt me was that they would not let me exhibit my Ohio State as a finished building.

— But you weren't really hurt by the show?

No, but I didn't gain anything.

— Come on, you are part of the wave — this is your moment.

I never was part of the wave, I don't see myself as part of the wave.

— I've always seen you as the High Priest of Decon. Anyway, I am not trying to get at your contribution, but at the way it was perceived: the way Peter Pran and large firms are suddenly going Decon; its message and co-option by the media.

The over-reaction by the media is an interesting signal in itself. There was an *enormous* over-reaction both pro and con which has to be analysed.

— But that was contemplated at the time. You cannot tell me that it wasn't planned as a media event.

Not by me certainly. Once Wigley got into Johnson's camp I wasn't involved at all. If you go round the schools in the United States, they were all doing this stuff before the show. It was already in the air, in Princeton, Florida, Kentucky and it came from Zaha Hadid, Morphosis, Libeskind — and it became a *style*. I went down to Florida and excoriated these people for doing this *style*: because I said it is no different than Post-Modernism. It has no depth, no ideology, no intellection, no theory. So what hurt me was it further crowded a position where I could establish my own work, because the style was corrupted. I never did Stick Style like Coop Himmelblau; I would never do a thing like that. Now there is less space for me: I felt very much constricted and claustrophobic by that Show.

— You certainly wanted to paint yourself in a corner. I have never seen a person surround himself with so many brushstrokes. You have to claim primary culpability for setting up this media event and New Academy and so you cannot now claim that you feel angry or betrayed or claustrophobic.

The last project that you saw last night, 'The Columbus Convention Center', represents me trying to jump out of that box. It is a project that I don't think is like Hadid

Wexner Center for the Visual Arts, Ohio State University, Columbus, Ohio, 1985-9. Symbolic and real structure in different size and tone. Grids of 12, 24 and 48 feet are dramatised at the entry. One hanging column looms overhead (symbolic of the 48-foot grid) while another bisects the stairway (indicating the 24-foot system) — and the skewed angles refer to the grid of the city, Columbus, Ohio, and the campus.

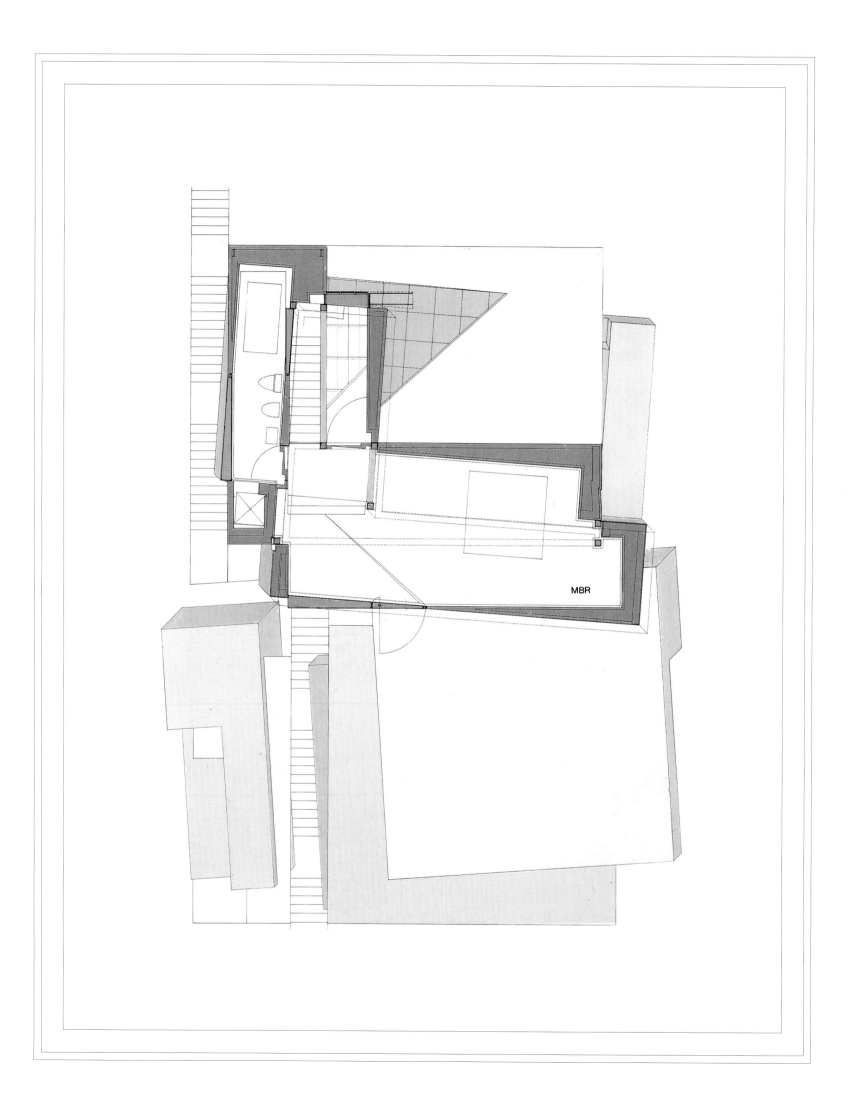

MBR

or Himmelblau, or Libeskind. It is a project all to itself.

Subjectivity and Tyranny of 'The Theory'

– In your article 'Post-Functionalism' written in 1976 and published in 1977, you follow Michel Foucault in his basic épistémè that the modern world is a rupture with Humanism: that it has displaced the author and the author's relation to artefacts. It has gotten rid of the subject. This might lead us to expect a new modesty and restraint, a new impersonality and self-effacement among 'non-humanists'. But what it seems to produce is the very reverse, a new egomania. The 'end of the subject' has paradoxically increased subjectivity, the 'end of the human' has increased humanism. The end of anthropomorphism has increased the anthropomorph. It seems to me that in place of the subject and the author has come 'the theory' and 'the idea'. So my question, in the form of an answer, is that according to Duchamp 'the idea is a machine for producing art'. What has happened in your work, more than any other architect alive, is that 'the idea' or 'the theory' is the machine that makes your architecture work. It has tyrannised your projects, it has tyrannised your client in the Guardiola House who isn't allowed windows looking over the ocean because you said the theory didn't allow it and placed them in the floor.

It is not as simple as that. There is something from the earliest projects about my unease with the 'creative subject' as the central condition – my notion of numbering the houses from one to eleven, my notion that they were transformational projects. There is a whole process of trying to talk about their rationality and they certainly have never been concerned with subjective aesthetics. That is 'I like the look of this, maybe I should move this here or there'. They are not concerned with self-expression; they are concerned with 'the loss of the subject', or the 'creative subject'. I am not going to say this is true for others. The fact that these other guys have gone crazy, they do not understand 'the loss of the subject'. They are not interested in the idea; they wouldn't know what it is. As for the ideas which generate my work: first of all they used to be far more compulsive. I no longer believe in a mechanistic process, in a kind of rationality – that there is a kind of deep structure, that there is a kind of ontology or typology. All of these beliefs, even the belief in beliefs, have weakened in my thoughts.

– Weakened but not disappeared. You were protesting last night that your theory hadn't caught up with your practice. Nevertheless, you justified on a theoretical level every move that you made.

That is my style. But it is not as tyrannical as you might think. What I am looking for is to uncover those things which I admit to myself. You have to read the essay in *Houses of Cards*, the long kind of *mea culpa* essay where I say that a lot of what I did was a theoretical smokescreen for another real kind of investigation that I was unwilling to admit to, that is an investigation into those things which I *myself* was repressing. What I am more open about now is that the work is very much more about the *repressions* of any architect. For example I never used natural forms before the Columbus Convention Center and the Cincinnati Architectural Project. What I am saying is that there are no more 'nevers' anymore. I am trying to open up my own repressive mechanisms in the essay in *Houses of Cards*.

– When you were asked last night about people in your buildings you got defensive. You have heard the humanist attack on your buildings so many times over the last twenty years

Guardiola House, Santa Maria del Mar, Spain, 1988, upper level plan that you are probably sick to death of it?

I think my buildings are very exciting to people.

– But the clients still can't look at the ocean.

What I resented about that kind of question is that I have made perfectly clear that I am interested in buildings that function and shelter and which work superbly well, but do not necessarily *represent*, or symbolise, function. I definitely am against representation of function.

– But there is still a contradiction. You've always said that if there is a hole between two beds and people fall into the living room, 'I don't care'; if they have a child, 'I don't care'; if there is a pier that comes out of the dinning room table, 'I don't care'; if they can't look at the ocean, 'I don't care '. The building is only allowed glass on the floor because this is all 'the idea' allows. Here again is the tyranny of the theory. You can't have it both ways. You care about carrying out an idea consistently. You said of the Wexner building, that the brick isn't right, the colour isn't right, the tilt isn't right, the slope isn't right – that you hadn't realised your idea, your theory. You place those values above functional and humanistic issues.

Wexner Center of Art of the Twenty-first Century

Let's look at this museum. I maintain that it is a very interesting functional idea to make it *difficult* to show paintings in a decontextualised way. You may have to force the artist to recontextualise his or her work because of the environment in which it is going to be put. Here is a new kind of object which says 'it is a context'. It is not just the initial container, saying 'here are these lovely neutral walls'. The spaces of Ohio State are not neutral containers.

– But how do you show a painting against a wall of light; you get glare.

Maybe you don't have paintings.

– But what if you do?

Maybe they go to the nearby Columbus Museum; what about that! What about sculpture? Maybe you should change your paintings.

– Now your idea, or theory, is tyrannical because it will not allow what everybody recognises is the function of a museum: to hang paintings on a wall. It is just a convention.

That is a convention which I find repressive. I am against conventions that seem to me do not open up other possibilities.

– Why must architects open up Art possibilities?

Because that is what architecture is all about; I really do feel that.

– You are a wonderful Modernist, Peter, that's what I love about you. As the quintessential Modernist you are provoking artists to produce something in response to your building. You are trying to change the situation.

Yes, I am trying to recontextualise art, force artists to become upfront, because they want it both ways too – like Richard Serra. I am tired of being some kind of background for art. Let's see another kind of architecture. There's going to be a big stir over Ohio State. I don't believe it is against humanism, or function, or tyrannical; it is merely against the tyranny of the conventional acceptance of the artist having it both ways. Basta! If you want you can call that Modernism, and if that helps fine. I am being very clear with you. You can't say that to open up other avenues for discourse between architecture and art with a frame, and a wall is tyrannical.

Peter Eisenman and Jeffrey Kipnis holding a painting of 'before and after Armoury' by Robin Bell.

Wexner Center for the Visual Arts, Columbus, Ohio, 1985-9. Gridded lighting and skylight to the main gallery space.

Wexner Center, view of armoury

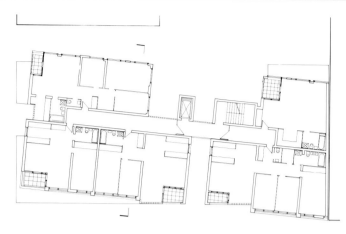

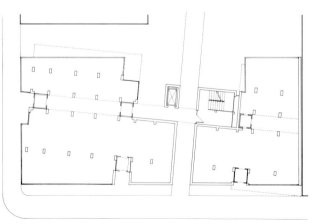

– Yes it is, because it closes down the habitual and customary relationships. You are closing down the way most artists and the public perceive art.

Yes, I am closing that down to a certain extent, sure.

– You don't have walls that you can hang paintings on. You just have glass full of glare. That is a direct attack on the way art has been collected for the last five thousand years.

The Museum was seventeenth-century.

– There was a museum on the Acropolis, the Greeks started collecting art: read your Joseph Alsop. Great art collecting goes back to the first forgeries under the Greeks and that is when they start museums, private collections, start distinguishing pedigrees and the relationship between good and bad art and hanging art from the walls and decontextualising it. The Romans were also great decontextualisers. They would throw any number of statues all over the place, like a used car lot. Look at the Acropolis itself: they had a thousand and one stellae from all over the Greek colonies. They didn't mean anything beyond a chauvinist presence. And you say you are the first to decontextualise art!

I don't want to overrule your objection, but to go back in the discussion. To be against habit cannot be seen to be tyrannical; but rather tyrannical to habit.

– I accept that. You talk about the Wexner Center of Art in the twenty-first century – everything 'being in fragments', everything 'being tilted' , 'no ends, no beginnings'. Those are the phrases you use. That obviously is a kind of symbol to you of the Art in the twenty-first century. As well as something that goes back to your 1977 article on Post-Functionalism. You used fragments then, and you also used the word 'decomposition'.

I am not against a style of fragments. I am against the notion that it is a style. Because when you talk about fragments, you see them as wholes. I don't see them as fragments when I look at those things. I see them as the breakdown of two things: the notion of the metaphysic of enclosure as the dominant one, and the notion of the metaphysic of shelter, that architecture shelters art in this particular case, the dominant metaphysic of our time. Again what I am against is the habitual notion that architecture shelters and encloses, and that architecture is an object that sits on a landscape – essentially a Palazzo type. Even our shopping centres are Palazzos sitting in parking lots. Where there is a frame, there is an edge and a distinction between inside and the outside – all that I question.

– Is this the first excavation you have done?

No, the Berlin housing, where I broke down these distinctions.

– This landscape approach, with no beginning, no end, no frame, no up, no down, no ground plane. The level of disorientation and dissidence goes further than any other building?

Yes, this goes furthest because of the scale, and the landscape. The attack on the upright human standing on the ground is very strong; and the attack on the vertebrae of the building which is broken. There is a very strong attack on what is the ground; who occupies that plane; where is the ground level, etc. It also deals a lot with the Indian Mounds; the grid is symbolic of the Indian Mounds.

– Indian Mounds?

Forty miles south of the site – it came from visiting these Indian Mounds.

– How are they represented?

You can see the way the earth is pushed up into huge earth mounds.

– Why is there a tilt in the outside auditorium?

Wexner Center for the Visual Arts, Columbus, Ohio, 1985-9. The 'north arrow' grid in white is the background focus for the prairie grass over a representation of Indian mounds.

Social Housing, IBA, with typical floor plan and ground floor plan

Well, to use an exedra, which is a classical form of grabbing a line: you don't want this line to get confused with the diagonal axis that you put in. There is this axis which you blunt; with a classical form. There is a curve at the end. You want to twist it, and not quite stop it.

— But you had in mind people sitting on a tilt. Was the angle wrong? Did they construct it wrong?

They sit at an angle, the angle is not wrong. The drawings were right. If you are an inch out and you are placing pre-cast pieces, they didn't fit together — that was wrong.

— You said that Vincent Scully had a great aesthetic experience implying that old enemies have become friends, and opposites are meeting. But perhaps Scully is just showing his Modernist prioritising of aesthetic experience over social and political issues. One of the great recurrent images of Modernism is aesthetic. Since Kant, since 1800, aesthetics has triumphed over the social, the real and the habitual. Your work is metaphysics as aesthetics. You aestheticise a metaphysical position, that is what you are always doing.

I formalise metaphysics not aestheticise it. I also think it's anti-Hegelian. I think it is important to go back to Kant because I don't think you can otherwise understand Modernism.

The Guardiola House and The Carnegie Mellon Research Institute

— With the Guardiola House you talked about using your signature forms plus 'Chora'. I am interested that you use signature forms, because part of your argument is that you have 'a weak formal system'. From Le Corbusier to Aldo Rossi to Michael Graves, all of the Modernists have had signature tunes which everybody recognises. This is an important part of how they are perceived and consumed. And Eisenman has, since 1960, had his own signature form. How do you think about this signature?

There was a time when I used to repress the idea. I didn't want to admit it. But they are easy for me to work with; they have meaning for me, and they are ideological. They are destabilised forms: the L-shape in three dimensions is destabilised. It is an incomplete form. It is also topologically symmetrical, and yet unsymmetrical. It forces many issues. When Robert Morris was using those giant 'L's' in the Paula Cooper Gallery, in 1974/75, they were really important to me. They started talking about a different kind of space, and the relationship of the object to the subject, to the space, to the context was very interesting. 'Chora' is a new thing for me to start working with — the whole concept of another 'Topos' or 'Paratopos'. I went to an old thing that I knew how to deal with — the L-shapes.

— You talk about 'Chora' having two parts. The first is a trace, the second an imprint. You say with these how difficult it was to produce working drawings — with all these tilts and things that go off the two-dimensional page. You also say, which is a very Modernist remark, that the spaces will be interesting and sensual. Two terms that come up again and again, against the habitual. You are an un-regenerate Modernist.

Yes. I am an un-reconstructed Modernist, but so are people like Jacques Derrida. You cannot be a Deconstructionist and not be a Modernist.

— I am glad you said it rather than me. For the Carnegie Mellon Research Institute, the client asked for a twenty-first-century representation of science: as the struggle of man against information, or knowledge. Why is the Boolean cube of n-dimensions a representation of

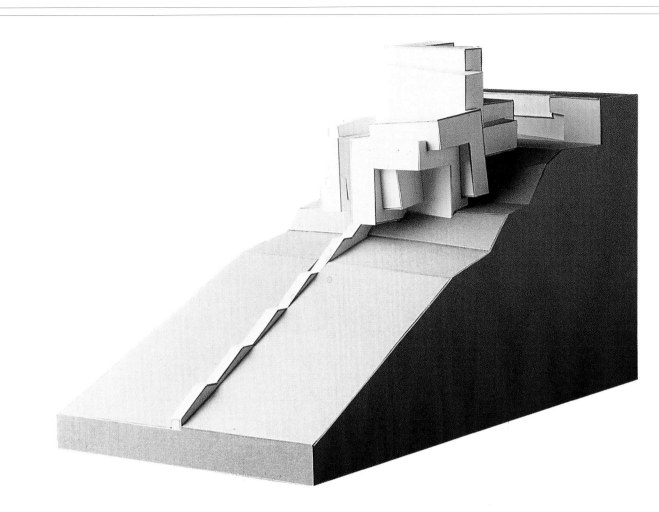

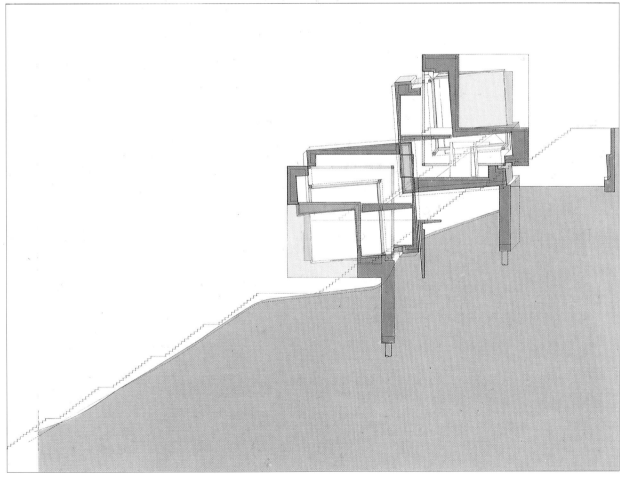

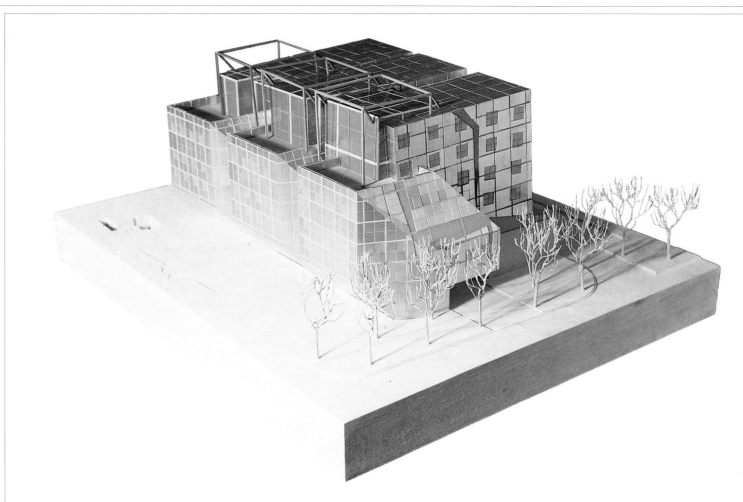

knowledge or information?

That is basically the logo form of how a computer works. I asked what would be the shape symbolic of information, and was told it is the Boolean cube.

– So you unpacked it. It looks wonderful – the way it confuses the ground plane and tilts. I think it is one of the most exciting things to come out of that project. I have to give you this: there is a new formal idea to each scheme. You have kept young and creative, because your 'idea machine' usually churns out one new idea per project. Even if it is quite abstract, at least you are not repeating yourself, or getting stale.

People love my projects on a sensual level.

– That's because, like you, they're Modernist aestheticians.

Bananas and Pilasters and Public Ornament

Look at my perspective of *Carnegie Mellon* with Mies in it. It focuses on that intersection of elements I call a 'banana' – that's a wild drawing. You say: 'I haven't seen one of those before'. What I like about my work is that I haven't seen one. That is always interesting to me. You have never seen that space in the Guardiola House. My work is not derivative.

– Il faut être absolument moderne. Can you describe some of these 'bananas' which are positive voids representing intersections?

The Boolean cube is when you take a 5n and a 6n cube. You have to understand that it is so difficult to conceptualise and build. We were trying to get both 'traces' and 'imprints'. It is easy to take this one form and push it into another and get an 'imprint'. Then you leave a trace of the imprinting mechanism. Those 'bananas' are the trace of the thing that was imprinted, a new element in my work.

– What are they used for? What is going to happen inside the 'bananas', and what is going to happen in the towers that are memories in the Wexner building?

People use those as offices.

– Even though they have no windows?

They have cuts as windows. But in these 'bananas' nothing happens.

– Now, Mr Eisenman, I am going to tell you that's extremely decadent.

What about your house? We can put 'bananas' in all these useless spaces and you say that is fine. A 'banana' is no more opulent than a pilaster, a capital. That is what is so funny with you guys: you don't mind a capital or a pilaster.

– But what makes them non-decadent is that they are habitual and representational; people understand their meaning and relationship to other forms.

That is precisely what makes them decadent.

– If you say: 'I am going to spend excess money on pilasters and capitals' and it is in the budget and agreed then everyone finds it OK. But if you are going to take the tax-payer's or client's money and spend it on some 'banana' , you are doing what Frank Gehry does with his 'fish'. Your 'banana' and his fish are your guilty conscience, because you are putting ornament on a completely gratuitous level that no one can understand: that no one can relate to, that has no semantic and that is just there as pure gratuity, that only you understand.

It is there for aesthetic reasons, for theoretical reasons. It is an attempt to show a new topos. Basta.

Carnegie Mellon Research Institute, interior perspective

Carnegie Mellon Research Institute, view from northwest and conceptual model

– You say 'basta'. But you know that the scientists at Carnegie Mellon, who want it, are consuming it as an ornamental 'banana'. The scientists are paying for you as a gratuitous architect, and they don't want you as a Functionalist. That is why you have Mies scratching his head, and wondering what has happened to Modernism, and rationality. The 'banana' is hanging there saying: 'To hell with functionalism, I am a Neo-Modernist'. You also say it is not a question of the way it looks.

I tell you Charles, we don't sit down, and sketch these 'bananas': they just happen to come out that way.

– How do you tell the difference then between a good or bad, or well-proportioned, 'banana'?

There isn't. The client knows how he wants to spend his money. And another one has come along who wants to do the same thing. And he has influenced yet another guy who says 'yes I want a "banana"' etc, too.

– That is no reason, that is fashion and populism.

I love it. I have been trying to move towards the center for a long time: that is where I am heading!

– Well, you're succeeding.

The Columbus Convention Center

– Your Columbus Convention Center design which you say is a populist building, you also describe as the public building type of the twenty-first century which might replace the museum. Why the Convention Center?

Because of the way people do business today in a Capitalist Society; people going around as travelling salesmen or whatever. What happens today is that people go to these Convention Centres/Trade Shows and they do all their business there. I understand that ninety per cent of their business is done at Trade Shows. These Trade Shows move from city to city like the old farmers used to – the Trade Show will be in Columbus one week, Lousiana the next week, etc. People interested in farm machinery will go to the Trade Shows and make all the sales. The economic structure of the country is such that the people who run the Convention Centres meet and show off their products, in this case: dairy machines, dairy farm equipment, whatever. At these meetings their products are sold, we are talking here about Agri-business.

It is a new Agora, the Agora of the twentieth century. The building type which I find very interesting is the new Agora and I think every city has to have one. Columbus, Ohio has got to have one that is bigger than the one in Indianapolis. We were doing a hall that was going to be 216,000 square metres and they said they needed one at 300,000 square metres because Indianapolis has 268,000 square metres. They are into Agoras, but they are like Shopping Malls, no one has worked out the scale nor the context in terms of organisation – we try to do this. We say 'Let's look at New Urbanism, another kind of urban form', that is something that I hit on in that project.

– You and Koolhaas are both looking for new urban forms. You have said the curves or 'vermiforms', which are a new idea, come from reading Baudrillard's America *and that they relate to the new freeways?*

What he says concerns a 'weak image', a multiplicity of meaning and a different kind of time. Baudrillard says that the difference between the structure of American

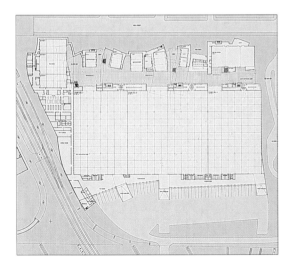

Columbus Convention Center, Ohio, 1989, level 750 floor plan

234

transportation and movement is the difference between one of axial movement which is European and one of the swirling network-like curving forms which are American. He says these forms are usually thought of as the boundaries of the cities. But no one has used these forms as the primitive forms of a new kind of urbanism. He says that America is potentially the primitive culture of the twenty-first century of this age of information, because it has the possibility of forms that not only are like through-ways but also like fibre optic cables, they twist and turn. There is a symbolism of the fibre-optic, the railroad and movement – a country of light and movement, etc. So what I try to do is to capture in freeze frame a point of time, a piece of movement.

– I understand that one of the reasons you won this competition was that six hundred people voted for you. They were divided into constituencies, and you won by a two to one margin against Michael Graves. You said that they found Michael's work patronising – why? Because they thought it looked like Disneyworld. And they didn't think a major urban monument of the twenty-first century should look like a theme park.

– Why should it look like optic cables and curving forms? You said, because they wanted to be frightened.

People I think want to have a little *frisson*. In today's world they want to take little risks.

– This is the typical *Modernist position, the 'shock of the New', a little* frisson, *something different: 'the new, improved detergent'. That is on a consumerist level, but on a cultural level people have always looked for something that is frightening. This is decadent in the same way as Adolf Loos is being conceived by historians and critics today as being decadent. Not in a negative way, like the Marquis de Sade who said 'there is nothing so exciting as a shock to the nervous system'.*

Let's take the *range* of interpretation of this project you described as decadent in a way. But it is also an attempt to look at a monument and the notion of space and time in a different way. To look at what is monumental form and urban form in a different way.

– Like Adolf Loos' work it is both progressive and *decadent. When I heard about this vote and that you had reversed positions with Michael Graves that reminded me of your essay in defense of Richard Meier written in* Architectural Design, *1972, in answer to an attack on Meier's work for being popular. You said Le Corbusier actually was preaching to the man in the street, and that he said he wanted to reach the populace of mass culture. And you wrote that Richard Meier had actually done it. Now you have broken this barrier!*

I am getting there.

– It is nice that one can now read that previous essay about yourself. It is interesting that this was done with a so-called 'weak image'. A weak image which has to be supplemented with images of railway tracks, freeways, laser beams and optic cables. It does tell you one thing, like your 'bananas' or Frank Gehry's 'fish'. It suggests that for a weak image to work and be powerful it needs associations.

But Frank Gehry's fish is not a weak image.

– No, it is a strong image. But for abstract images to be popular you need to supply the code: the slide show helps a lot.

It did help a lot, I agree.

– That is a fascinating theoretical step beyond the weak image, because it suggests that weak images have to be made associational to be strong.

They do not *need* to be made strong, they need to be made palatable. We are saying that

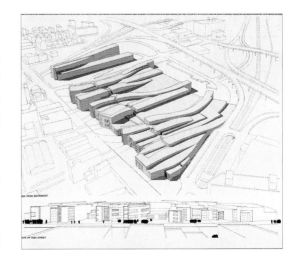

Columbus Convention Center, Ohio, 1989, birdseye perspective

the image should be multivalent, and have a lot of possibilities, but not look like a logo. We are trying to give the possibility of openness for imagining what it might be.

The Cincinnati Architecture School

— With the Cincinnati Architecure School, you mentioned ornament as structure, that is an anti-Puginian position. He said 'you should decorate your structure not construct your decoration'. That is a very Late-Modernist thing, exactly what Richard Rogers and Norman Foster do. They make giant ornaments out of their structure.

They make a giant aesthetic object, but not ornament. Ornament is the stuff of what is usually seen as the banding, the edge; it is not the object itself. What I am trying to do is take the chevrons and the arced bands and arabesques together, which we are also studying, as Sullivan did when he did sixteen plates in his last book on the theory of ornament. The Chicago Art Institute has asked me to do sixteen plates on Eisenman's theory of ornament. I am interested not in ornamenting but in the *concept* of ornament.

— Again you are moving towards my kind of Post-Modernism. I have been writing for the past ten years on the necessity of looking at Owen Jones and Gombrich's writings; they show ornament as having a symphonic form, as information theory has illuminated it.

I have been looking at Richard Wagner in that way. I am fascinated with Wagner's *Gesamtkunstwerk.*

— You accept now that you are becoming a Post-Modernist in my sense who is interested in ornament as music? As a structured play of information for itself?

I accept that.

— You talk about the chevrons and 'vermiforms' eating into each other, hooking into each other, tilting away and being like vertebrate forms. But not like any animal we know?

They have vertebrate qualities.

— Again you reveal your Modernist position by not wanting them to resemble anything. It seems as though you hated, like a Modernist, to be caught with any explanation that anyone knew of beforehand.

I am against habit. I am against repression and habit is about repression. A repression of habit is something which I can be accused of.

— In twenty years of knowing you and your work I have always been impressed by both its consistent development and freshness. Perhaps you more than any other Modernist have 'made it new', but also kept it within a clearly growing pattern. Congratulations for staying young and continuously interesting, at a time when so many of your peers have become famous and old. (May 1989)

DAAP University of Cincinnati, Ohio, 1988, plan and model

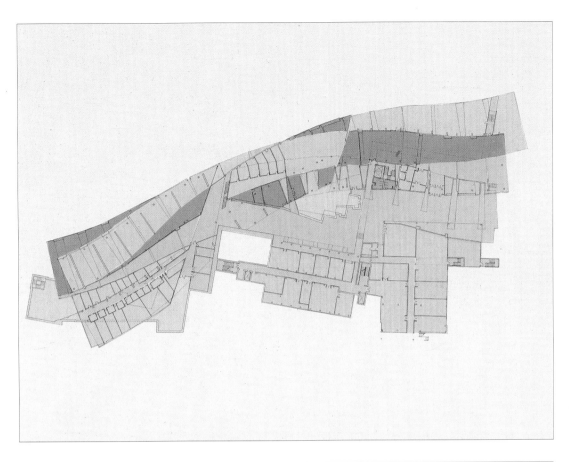

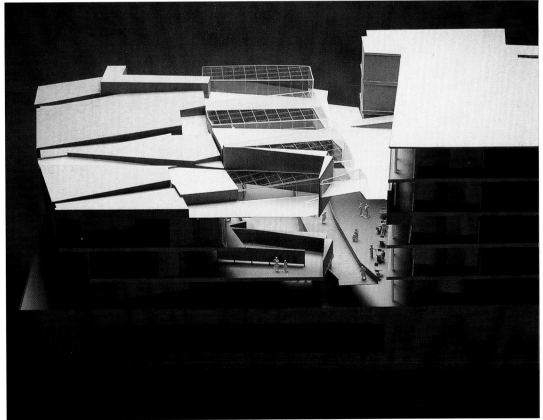

RICHARD MEIER AND THE MODERN TRADITION

Siegfried Giedion subtitled his polemical history of Modern architecture, *Space Time and Architecture* as 'the growth of a new tradition', and he adjusted the fifth edition of 1967 to recent developments, the change to a sculptural freedom. The work of Jørn Utzon, Kenzo Tange and Fumihiko Maki and the Brazilians showed where the 'third generation' of Modernists were going: 'architecture is approaching sculpture and sculpture is approaching architecture'. Or, as he formalised the new-found permissiveness of this generation: 'the right of expression above pure function'.

Since then, of course, we have had the fourth and fifth generation of Modernists – this tradition speeds up its breeding cycles like everything else – and if Giedion were alive today he would, no doubt, include a key chapter in the latest version of the New Testament called 'Richard Meier and the Mastery of Light and Geometry'. Meier fits into the canonic line of Modernist development as smoothly as Bramante continues fifty years of Renaissance practice. In both cases an architect is assuming and extending a well-known language at a very high level of creation and execution and in both cases there is a certain begrudging admiration on the part of contemporaries.

Raphael and Michelangelo were impressed by Bramante's undoubted virtuosity, but they found it a little tiring, the brilliant solution of old problems. The complex situation of a plural architecture today displaces these same feelings to a host of traditions, and many contemporaries are now bored with the Post-Modernism of Michael Graves, the revivalism of Quinlan Terry, the High-Tech of Rogers and the Modernism of Meier. People are simply bored by *any* tradition, even if it's done well and extended.

I mention this pervasive *ennui* because it has coloured the appreciation of Richard Meier's work from the very beginning. When his *Smith House* was first published in the late sixties and *The Five Architects* soon thereafter, several American and European critics reacted against what they took to be a devaluation, distortion or deconstruction of the Modernists' social message: 'Le Corbusier à la Mode, or Revolution for the Sell of It', as Peter Papademetriou wrote in *Architectural Design*. The translation of the white architecture from social housing into private temples for the *nouveaux riches* was considered reactionary, and by some a betrayal.

Such views, while understandable, missed some important qualities of Meier's work as well as a key ambiguity of the Modern Movement. As Adolf Loos proclaimed (and Tom Wolfe was later to argue) Modernism has been built essentially for and by the bourgeoisie, no matter how much its ideology has favoured mass housing and a working class, and machine, aesthetic. Without the *nouveaux riches,* just as without industrialisation, Modernism would be dead. A new class of patrons intent on showing its cultural acumen is essential for its continual well-being and if there is a basic dynamic to Modernism it rests on one fundamental fact: for two hundred years it has been

The Atheneum, New Harmony, Indiana, 1975-9

The High Museum of Art, Atlanta, Georgia, 1980-3

Modernisation, development, a progressive technology and economic growth. Both cultural Modernism and economic Capitalism depend on the dynamic of innovation, the shock of the new, the destruction of the old.

This is what gives Meier's work such poignance and pathos: it is 'new/old' like Bramante's architecture must have seemed in 1500, and also 'capitalist/socialist' in its overtones, like so much current art. Building luxury dream houses with a workers' vernacular may seem a paradox to Tom Wolfe, but to anyone who watches *Dynasty* and *Dallas* it's a normal event. The Modernist aesthetic lends itself to class and probity as readily as did Palladian architecture in the eighteenth century and it is only sentimentality for the twenties, when the Heroic Period and socialist ideology were in their prime, which keeps us from acknowledging this truth.

Meier's architecture, like so much Neo-Modernism, makes an art out of this quandary. It takes readily available industrial materials – particularly the porcelain enamel panel – and turns them into ideal, luxurious tokens fit for a king, or at least a museum committee. The abstraction and geometry appeal to the intellectual – another class of Meier admirers – and of course the professionals (which is one reason he received the Gold Medal in 1988). And there is also the *populi* who are impressed by all the glittering white promise of a shining new instrument (the Atlanta Museum *is* a popular public space), so the work does indeed cut across different groups and tastes by using industrial materials in a fabulously pristine way.

What does it add to Giedion's 'modern tradition'? Among other things a delightful repetition of the grid motif used at different scales and in various materials, an idea of Josef Hoffmann's played at a new tempo; the skew and shifted grids leading to ever more sharp and dissonant angled planes – 45 degrees, 22.5, 12 and finally the 3.5 degrees skew at Frankfurt. These result in exquisite intersections and a spatial dissonance which keeps one moving. Then there's the new version of Baroque light rebounding through – not Le Corbusier's double-height spaces but four-storey sections, and the fragmented piano shapes and broken-up Purist forms: equally indebted to Corb's synthetic Cubism, but more complex, dissonant and picturesque – the reason Meier was termed 'Post-Johnson-Corb' in the sixties.

Such fractures and collisions signify 'imperfect perfection', 'unclear clarity', 'irrational rationality' – the oxymoronic figures and meanings which destabilise the certainty of the Modernist white aesthetic. And here lies the essence of Meier's contribution to the 'new tradition', to Late-Modernism or Neo-Modernism (I would use the terms interchangeably in his case): it is the note of celebration amidst a questioning doubt, an affirmation of the 'Modern project', of reason and the Enlightenment, at the same time as it's a sensuous denial of the dogmatism of that ideology through the play with sculptural form and light. Those who want to find in Meier's work an intellectual ordering – the abstract distinction between public and private, geometry and nature, necessity and freedom – will continue to be transported by this abstract language, because it is played with a brilliance that would have pleased Le Corbusier. It won't please everyone – no architecture does in an age of pluralism and where the limits of abstraction are known. But unlike so much Modernism today, Meier's is kept taut and fresh, reminding us that architectural languages don't die, but rather that certain architects get tired of using them.

Museum for the Decorative Arts, Frankfurt, 1979-85

The High Museum of Art, Atlanta, Georgia, 1980-3

DIALOGUES WITH RICHARD MEIER ON LATE, NEO AND POST-MODERNISM

— *I'd like to raise a general philosophical question and ask whether you accept the term Late-Modernism as a designation and a concept?*

I accept it as a concept and designation if one feels obligated to classify works into categories. I always fight against that as you know from our previous conversations.

— *And yet you accept the term Modern Architecture.*

I think it's one thing to accept something in a historical context and another thing to accept categorisation of our present situation that is always changing. It's really not for either a practitioner or a teacher to question or categorise.

— *Why not? A lot of architects try to shape history.*

Shaping history and categorising history are two different things.

— *Yes but they are logically interdependent; you can't shape something unless you know what it is, you can't know what it is unless you've labelled it and have a concept about it.*

I think that you can have a concept about it and know what it is without necessarily labelling it.

— *A label is a term that classifies and therefore judges; it is an aid to thought.*

The terms Late-Modernism and Post-Modernism have many different meanings. Post-Modernism has a very specific meaning to you; it has a very different meaning to, say, a dozen critics. That is why categories of our present situation are difficult.

— *How would you prefer to be designated?*

I don't think we have to designate my own practice. Some people classify us as Post-Modernists; I don't. How can one be Post-Modernist in one classification, Late-Modernist in another and High-Tech in a third? Categorisation by its very nature tends to be exclusive.

— *It is reductive and exclusive but it still pigeon-holes major philosophical, stylistic and ideological positions.*

In that sense I would have no problem with the Late- or Post-Modern labels, if you look at them in a certain light. It is important to identify what you mean by the terms. I find your charts fascinating in this respect, because they, more than any series of essays, can indicate not only an overlap but also the placement of individuals or groups of individuals in more than one category during one period of time. The problem with so many categories historically is their static exclusivity. They're set, and if you are in one you are not in another. I think that our times are much more complicated and complex and that's why your charts are so much more interesting than a single classification.

— *I would classify you along with Norman Foster, Richard Rogers and Peter Eisenman as the Late-Modern architects, and I don't mean that in a disparaging way. A 'Late' period is perfectly valid: Late-Baroque like Late-Gothic signifies a relationship to what went* before.

Museum for the Decorative Arts, Frankfurt-am-Main, 1979-85, detail. A Late-Corbusian grammar of pure white abstraction gives a timeless, placeless quality to this cross axis leading to the garden.

There are however overtones of Lateness which are critical and, if not derogatory, at least questionable. These have to do with a period of architecture being over-ripe, or decadent; a lot of Late-Gothic is considered decadent because it uses motifs on a purely stylistic or ornamental level.

Would you consider Late-Baroque decadent?

– If I do it's nicely decadent. I'm prepared to admit decadence as a double-edged sword today. I think that your architecture is, in a sense, decadent. Adolf Loos has been discussed as decadent and as a dandy and he was in a sense Early-Modernist. I don't necessarily mean decadent or over-ripe negatively; I would say your coffee set for Alessi is over-ripe.

Coffee *pitcher.*

– Pitcher or picture – it is highly elaborated. It's made up of sectioned mouldings and stepped cylinders and it's a conglomerate composition – almost a collage. And at the same time it's still very abstract. It treats in an almost decorative way a lot of the formal notions that you've developed in architecture. But it treats them like the coffee pot that Aldo van Eyck attacks as a 'contradiction in terms', the coffee pot that's solid all the way through. (Venturi designed one by the way, and I don't know if Van Eyck knows about it). This would be a decadent coffee pot because you can't pour coffee out of it. Yours is decadent because it doesn't immediately relate to its function, although it may work.

It has a bottom, middle and top, a handle and a spout. It holds roughly a quart of coffee.

– But there are a lot of excessive signs, with say, the frontispiece.

It's dealing with the idea of a grid with all sides different. One can think of it as an object which has reasons not to be the same all round.

– Your word 'object' is very important; you have turned it into a monument. Yes, the monumental coffee pot built at thirty storeys, like an Oldenburg statement, is a decadent object which is a comment on our times. I believe that Loos and Corb, the classic Modernists, said 'objects of use should not be made into works of art' and should not be made into monuments. Architecture is reserved for the grave and the monument or else a few public buildings. Now you have turned a useful object into the most excessive monument.

That is the nature of the programme, this very specific programme that Alessi is asking for a run of ten or twelve sets.

– I didn't see it that way, I saw it as the chance to mass-produce something.

I never saw it that way – but rather as a chance to design one-off tea services.

– You saw it as an art object?

Yes, with this international circle of designers . . .

– Your 'object' more than Portoghesi's or Venturi's (which is certainly ornamental and elaborate), Yamashita's – yours and Hollein's are the furthest removed from utility, and are not the object that goes away and sits happily in the background. This is a monument, and I feel it is slightly decadent; you may argue that it is appropriate.

If I were asked to design an ordinary, everyday coffee pot service, I would request an understanding of the process by which it is made. I have no idea what Alessi's capabilities are.

– He didn't take you to the factory?

No.

– We went – Michael Graves, Venturi and the rest.

I had no idea of the process by which they made coffee pots nor their manufacturing

Coffee Pitcher for Alessi, 1979-83. The Cubist pot with its main planes stepping back and forth and its highly reflective surfaces in silver turn this utilitarian object into a monument. The multiple layering and facets are so complex that it is hard to actually understand the literal volumes, as in the paintings of coffee pots by Picasso and Braque.

capabilities. My total involvement was a meeting in my office with two Alessi brothers.

– They gave you the impression that they wanted an art object?

And that's what I did, otherwise I would need to know a lot more about what they wanted.

– So you are admitting it's a decadent commission?

Yes.

– I want to focus on the notion of a 'Late' period, with the very notion of periodisation – Archaic, Early, Classic and so forth. This periodisation often has to do with the internal development of form and semantics. It's caused by discontinuous forces – the logic of form, and also the way people tire of form and need new stimuli, both artists and consumers. For its logical development I feel that some of your work, Eisenman's and Hejduk's is directly Late-Modern as it is an elaboration, a Mannerist and Baroque elaboration of Modernism.

It's making comments on Modernism, but it's also making comments on architecture in general – all very different from other people who are reusing elements, or adding on this detail or that. I see myself as part of the continuation of Modern Architecture, because there are explorations still to be made in its language that are valid for our time.

– I would say you outshoot Modernists like Corb, and are 'better' (and that's another aspect of the Late-period) in certain respects: for instance instead of a mere double-height space the Douglas House goes through five storeys, and even shifts back. And you get the straight line Corb could never get; your Machine works and it doesn't peel after twenty years. Your Bronx Center actually looks the way he describes the Parthenon, as sharp and precise as steel. In that sense you have managed to realise the qualities that Corb hoped for; you and other Late-Modernists are part of his dream. For me that is an interesting aspect of the relationship between 'Early' and 'Late'. Would you agree with that?

I could obviously not create the buildings I do without knowing and loving the work of Corb, and this goes back to the time when I was a student. Corb has been a great influence on my life and my thinking about the making of space.

– He's been the major influence?

As much as Frank Lloyd Wright. One of the first buildings that I had the opportunity to design was a house just before the Smith House in Essex Villas. Coincidentally at the time I was invited to go to Falling Water – a building I'd never seen before. I stayed the whole weekend and just stopped work. It had such an effect on me, more than any other building I've seen.

– Was there any one aspect?

It was the way the trays interrelated to one another and the landscape. The simplicity of that house; in terms of conception there is a simplicity that doesn't exist in a lot of his other work. There is also (when compared to his Prairie Houses which are spread out and horizontal) a vertical organisation of space – more so than any other residence that I can think of. In some ways the vertical penetration of space exists there in a totally different way from all his other houses.

– Has this happened in your work?

What is important to me there, having read, as a student, all Frank Lloyd Wright, and believing there was an extension of interior space into the landscape, to find at Falling Water that it was a *visual* extension into the landscape. Rather than *planes* of space

Bronx Developmental Center, New York, 1970-7. A centre for mentally handicapped children is treated with Corbusian imagery – 'neat, clean and healthy as a ship' – and also like the way he describes the Parthenon, 'like naked, polished steel'.

reaching out as in many Oak Park houses or the Johnson House in Racine, which has the spaces *on* the land which reach out onto the landscape. So when I came back, my problem was one little house where there was no opportunity to get that sort of vertical space within the inside. I believed however that there *was* a way that I could extend the house into the landscape, and so the brick walls that enclose the major living spaces continue out and start to form spaces in the landscape. When I finished the house I had the sudden experience of a difference caused by the transparent plane. Inside the glass wall, as it runs perpendicular to a brick plane, is different from that which is outside, and no matter how you talk about this extension of space the glass wall as a plane existed. Therefore the horizontal extension of space onto the landscape was denied by the glass wall, no matter how thin or transparent you'd like to think it was. As the house aged, the wall on the outside of the same material as the wall on the inside looked different and reacted differently to weather. In time colour, with even the brick facing, would change. That's why I think it's right to use certain bricks — some wear better than other bricks. It was this whole sense of organisation of space that as a student I learnt about and began to love, which works in some instances but not in others. It doesn't work in relating inside to outside.

— I see all your buildings reach out arms into the landscape.

They try to embrace an aspect of the landscape, try to tie themselves to the landscape, and in materials suited to withstand time. For instance this outbreaker at Hartford will always look the same as the building. It is a plane of the building which encloses space, but it is never something that will penetrate a glass plane the way that Wright used it. It is always an extension of an external plane which is opaque and solid and is thus read as a plane; it does not deny the existence of the glass wall. So when I say I learnt a lot from Wright, it's not always in terms that it looks like Frank Lloyd Wright. But rather, there are things you can understand from previous architects and their work that enables you to clarify your own thinking.   (June 1982)

On Neo-Modernism

— A major philosophical question is raised by the phrase 'Neo-Modern Architecture' which you said in an interview in 1987 has replaced Post-Modernism. What is the first use and best use of 'Neo-Modern' as far as you're concerned?

Well I would say that it is something which is an outgrowth of the Modern Movement. It uses the Modern Movement, recognises its existence and says 'yes but', acknowledging that the Modern Movement had its limits. And for me in reading a number of those who criticise the Modern Movement, really what they're criticising is not basic works, they're not criticising Aalto or Loos, or the good architects in Germany in the thirties, or Corb. What they're talking about is the industrialisation, the bastardisation, the commercialisation of the Modern Movement and I think that we do that to some degree too. They are criticising the way in which commerce has taken that and made it an unfortunate situation. For me there is, and was, a whole freedom of volumetric exploration, of spatial exploration, which the Modern Movement allowed and fostered and which seems viable today.

— But Neo-Modern is being used and you've used it, precisely in the polemical way, as a stick to beat Post-Modernism. I am asking you a very specific question: when is the first use

Bronx Developmental Center, New York, 1970-7. Precisionist control of a flat surface – always a hallmark of American corporate architecture as Vincent Scully asserts – is carried out with modular panels and rounded 'bus windows'. Is the aesthetic appropriate for a healing, semi-domestic function?

of the word Neo-Modern as far as you're concerned? When did you pick it up and what is the best use of it? In other words, who else is using it?

That I don't know. I think in that article I was using it to answer what's happening at the end of the eighties and where do I see architecture going.

— No, I know, the word Neo-Modern has been around. I'm asking you when you were aware of picking it up as a concept?

I'm not aware. I was looking for a word to top your words, and it seemed like one that was possible for such a description of the evolution of things.

— Neo-Classicism happened after a relatively long hiatus of Classicism, after the ascendancy of the Baroque and Rococo. Has Modern architecture died for long enough for there to be a revival of Neo-Modernism?

I don't read it as a complete revival, I see it as an outgrowth, and I think that it is prevalent, in various areas.

— I agree it's out there, I'm just disputing the label. Neo-Classicism was a self-conscious revival and a critique of Classicism in the 1800s, and it was a new style and philosophy. Is it true of today that we have a new style and philosophy that warrants the label Neo-Modernism? Is there a critique of Modernism that resulted in a New Modernism?

There is a critique. I think the critique of Modernism has been going on for some time. I would say for the past fifteen years.

— But compared to Post-Modernism?

Well Post-Modernism was one critique of Modernism, certainly. I think at the same time that Post-Modernism existed, just in reviewing our discussion of five years ago, in talking about Hejduk and Eisenman and others, that there certainly has been and continues to be another critique of Modernism. And tomorrow night there's Daniel Libeskind talking at UCLA, again another type of outgrowth that certainly is a critique of Modernism in a different way.

— Well Libeskind I would certainly say is very Late-Modernist, positively late Late-Modernist. So how do you fit it in?

I think it's a different kind of critique from Post-Modernism.

— But is there a new philosophy, and is there anything remotely like Towards a New Architecture? *Is there a statement? Is there a figure? Is there a philosophy out there? If I want to read about the philosophy of Neo-Modernism where do I go? Who do I read? Who do I listen to?*

I think that it is not a philosophy that's been written, but I think that it exists in the work of a number of people and if there is a philosophy, then it is expressed in their work rather than through a pamphlet or a book.

— Well do you really believe that Neo-Modernism has coped with the urbanistic and social failures of Modern architecture?

No, not yet. I don't think so yet. But I think that it has a potential of doing that. I think it has a possibility of it, because unlike Modernism which for the most part really wanted to destroy everything that came before, Neo-Modernism is more accepting of the past, more reflective of the past, and more discriminating, you might say, in terms of the past. That doesn't mean that anything that is old is good, but I think that it is more accommodating of the past than Modernism ever was and therefore has a potential to move ahead in a way that Modernism wasn't able to, because Modernism really

Des Moines Art Center Addition, Des Moines, Iowa, 1982-5. Courtyard pavilion and pool. An addition to IM Pei's and Eliel Saarinen's museum, this is one of the first projects where Meier introduces masonry contrasts to his white aesthetic and sets up stronger oppositions between forms and materials.

Des Moines Art Center Addition. The main gallery addition carries the subtle juxtaposition even further: the grid is played at different scales and the opposition of spatial types is underlined by the change in material.

249

called for, demanded, the destruction of the past in order to proclaim a new goal.

– *The destruction of the City.*

Yes, that's right.

– *I agree that they're more accommodating, because they have to be don't they? Being Neo-Modern they have to admit at least that Modernism was worth reviving and worth looking at and continuing. This is the year of Corbu, 1987, the hundredth year of his birth. What do you think of the social and urban implications of his* Unité d'Habitation *in Marseille and elsewhere? Is there a critique of those from the Neo-Modernist position? What is the Neo-Modernist line . . . ?*

Well I don't think that there's a Neo-Modernist position *per se* to begin with, and if there were one, it certainly wouldn't be to take housing, public housing, mass housing, as a singular part of Corb's work, but to view Corb's work as a whole and what it meant.

– *Mass housing has been the failure, though. Mass housing dragged down Modernism and is the fundamental reason Modernism failed – because of mass housing and the urban approach.*

But go to Frankfurt and see Ernst May's public housing of today and it's damn good, you know.

– *But it isn't Corb's.*

No it isn't Corb's, but Corb did it, and I think it was in the air at the time. Everyone was doing it, doing it much worse by the way. How do you do high rise, high density housing and make it work? And who has done it and made it work? I mean forget Corb as the protagonist, but where has high rise, high density housing been a success?

– *Well I think it's one of the attempts of Post-Modernists.*

High rise, high density housing? No, come on.

– *Not high rise, but high density housing.*

Come on, those semi-attached suburban villas?

No, I don't mean Bob Stern, I mean more in the city. There are a whole lot of people from Bofill to Dixon to IBA. IBA is the Post-Modern city.

It is not high density?

– *Parts of it are. The intention is to have fairly high density, not high rise.*

I'm not implicating high rise, I'm just saying that to attack Corb for the failure of *Unité d'Habitation* in Marseille . . .

– *Not in Marseille so much but in the others.*

But it also has to do with the failure of architecture to change social values.

– *But it is also positively destructive of social values – shopping centres raised seven storeys off the street.*

But we learned that is true.

– *But did we* have *to learn that? Isn't it true that Lewis Mumford and Jane Jacobs and critics of the twenties were saying that these will fail for precisely the reasons that they did fail? We could run those tests in a much less expensive way. You know and I know that they destroyed half of Europe. Leon Krier has a case because half of Europe was destroyed due to the alliance of the Corb dream of Mass Culture and greed. It was a triple alliance of power. That is from where Post-Modernism stems, where Neo-Modernism stems, where all your Modernisms stem.*

My fundamental argument on the philosophical level is this: you've said so far that Neo-

Des Moines Art Center Addition, Des Moines, Iowa, 1982-5. The more public circulation space of the gallery addition is carried through in the Corbusian white grammar to contrast with the more domestic gallery space in granite on the exterior.

Modernism exists in a group of practitioners. Let me ask you one more question. Who are the Neo-Modernists besides you and Daniel Libeskind? Who are your favourites? And why do you like them? Fumihiko Maki?

Well, I like Maki, but I don't think I would put him high on my list. I would start with John Hejduk. John has a certain clarity, yet builds in a most forceful, personal and poetic way. And has a devotion, an intelligence which is to be admired.

– I agree, but what makes him Neo-Modern?

The way in which he has taken Modernism and the very basic principles from his early work. The way in which he has taken Mies and said okay, I'm just going to explore the whole basic ideas of Mies van der Rohe in a different way, as nine square problems. In all of his house projects from the very beginning he has taken a very basic principle of Mies and in a sense out-Miesed Mies.

– Alright, I might grant you one-half Hejduk, but who else?

Peter Eisenman has certainly taken elements of De Stijl, and his own sort of pointed, overlay, gridded, structural, organisational elements clearly are an outgrowth of Modernism. He's collaged them in such a way as to create a subterfuge for making quite interesting buildings. He wouldn't tell you that is what he is doing, he would deny it to the end. But in the end, he is basically using very fundamental Modernist principles to establish a vocabulary and a method of working.

– Who else?

Well there are a lot of younger people. Morphosis for instance I think is very interesting. Perhaps not as clear, but people like Robert Mangurian. And then I think Peter Cook to some degree.

– Zaha Hadid?

Yes, certainly.

– Would you say that she is an archetypal Neo-Modernist?

No. I would say Arata Isozaki in some areas, but then his work is varied and less categorisable.

– What about people like Norman Foster and Richard Rogers? How would you classify them?

I guess I would put them into the Neo-Modernist category. I have not seen Lloyds and I have not seen the Hong Kong Bank. My impression in both cases is that there is a very clear organisational system, but their almost obsession with High-Tech ways of doing things becomes the classifier. A distinct category in a sense. But if there are only two categories in the world, yours and mine, then I would put them into my camp.

– But my category is also Late-Modern. And I am now going to argue that you're really redefining Late-Modernism, because it is an outgrowth of Modernism in its late phase. I am genuinely wondering whether I should change the phrase from Late-Modernism to Neo-Modernism. I'm asking myself is it warranted? But I have seen nothing in what you have said so far to lead me to believe that it doesn't perfectly well describe about thirty categories of things that I have said categorise Late-Modernism. I would change if there were a new philosophy, if there were a Towards a New Architecture, *or if there were a real social and urban critique of the Modernist failure. Or, if like Neo-Classicism, Modernism was being self-consciously revived in a new way. I don't believe we've gotten there, but we may be getting there. I think there's a build-up towards it, but I don't think we're there yet.*

Ackerberg House Extension, Malibu, California, 1984-6. Perhaps the most successful conjunction of site and aesthetic in Meier's oeuvre. Here the sea, sand and Malibu sun, are a perfect foil for the white architecture – a dream of purity and space intelligence as convincing as anything the Greeks and Corbusier attained in the Mediterranean. Here *the* Western aesthetic faces East – the Pacific Rim.

I would say in America, we're certainly not there. My experience in Europe especially in Germany and now in The Hague makes me realise that there is a public attitude toward Neo-Modern (for lack of a better word) which doesn't exist in the United States. The Mayor of Ulm sees the work that we're doing in the Cathedral Square – opposite one of the highest and best Gothic Cathedrals in West Germany – as being politically important as a statement of the best he can get. The best new building, the best personification of a moment in time in which Germany, especially, wiped out an important intellectual part of its population and life and there's an appreciation and a desire to bridge a gap that was artificially –

– *Well you're referring both to the Jewish problem but also to the Weimar Bauhaus and the destruction of Ulm. They may be using you as solving their guilty conscience. Is that coming to terms with it, or is it just paving over the cracks? You see the problem there Richard?*

Yes, but in knowing the people involved, and also the people who say we want a Modern, Neo-Modern building in our town, a building of quality, of significance I would say . . .

– *They want to heal wounds.*

I think it is more than healing wounds. It is political.

– *Yes it is political, especially in Germany.*

Exactly, but my point is it doesn't exist here. It exists in France but in a different way.

– *Well Modernism has always been tied to Socialists and social idealism.*

But this is in answer to your question 'Does it have political significance?' and I say today in Europe it does have some.　　　　　　　　　　　　　　　　　　(*March 1987*)

These two excerpts from very long interviews are published here because they illuminate the concepts of Late- and Neo-Modernism and will not be published in the monograph on Richard Meier to appear shortly.

Frankfurt Museum for the Decorative Arts, Frankfurt-am-Main, 1979-85. Aerial axonometric shows the old, eighteenth-century Villa Metzler used as one-ninth of the Classic 'nine-square problem'. Some of Meier's addition and circulation space are skewed $3\frac{1}{2}$ degrees to this grid to pick up the Main River and adjacent city geometry – a skew which, like *entasis*, needs a second glance to appreciate.

Frankfurt Museum for the Decorative Arts. View from the park with the grid *appliqué* played at different scales and the ever-so-slight reference to the Villa Metzler cornice line in grey granite.

Frankfurt Museum for the Decorative Arts. View of the courtyard showing the skeletal frame and windows as an abstract white grid which sets off trees as much as it does furniture inside. When this grid has no function, as it does in the landscape or garden, it fragments arbitrarily into giant curving frames.

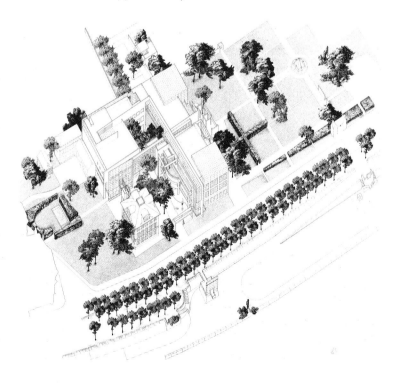

DIALOGUE WITH FUMIHIKO MAKI

The Master of Creative Detailing

If there is an architect, in addition to Peter Eisenman, who epitomises the New Modernism it is Fumihiko Maki. Intelligent, sensitive, charming, full of an explosive laughter that reminds me of a character in a Kurosawa film, he is that rare architect who can thoughtfully detail a building *and* oversee construction in a creative way. In this sense he really is unique and his contribution to Modernism is new.

One of the greatest problems of Modern buildings is their notional quality, their flat abstraction, their lack of material finish. They may have sculptural boldness and conceptual clarity, but all too often – especially when large – they look like illustrations of a thesis. 'Cardboard architecture', 'the built diagram' are two epithets rightfully directed at these impoverished structures. Their lifeless details and dumb surfaces result in part from a contractual situation dominant in the West. After the architect finishes the design and working drawings, creativity must stop to guarantee the budget. It's as if a painter always had to make do with an initial layout and couldn't modify the canvas in response to previous brushstrokes and developing ideas. It's as if there were architectural censorship the second a design is agreed.

This baneful situation does not completely control Japanese building and Maki takes advantage of this as well as the continual existence of a craft tradition. In all of his projects he sets up a field office whose job it is to design creatively right up to the end of construction. For the huge Tokyo Metropolitan Gymnasium his field office had twenty people – an extraordinary number even for a huge project. Their job is not only to administer predetermined designs, but to make inventive decisions especially when it comes to resolving the complex problems of his metal roof forms. Here, and at the Fujisawa Gymnasium, design is returned to the cybernetic art of Antonio Gaudí – the last great structural inventor who worked on the site in a responsive way.

Maki's roof forms, like Gaudí's, call up all sorts of metaphors (Fujisawa is seen as a 'beetle', 'frog', 'knight's helmet' and 'spaceship') which are not necessarily intended by their author, but ones which arise naturally from the method of on-site design. Of course they also come from his airy sketches which are meant to suggest hovering and expressive images – though no particular animal or machine. He, like Eisenman, favours the evocative abstraction which has no direct referent, and thus one that can provoke open and dissimilar interpretations. This can also lead to misunderstanding and it's interesting that the word 'Spiral' has now been physically stuck on his famous Tokyo building and museum to make the underlying idea explicit. Evocative forms need *some* cues if the populace is to understand them.

Maki was born in 1928 and, like Louis Kahn, did not produce his master works until relatively late in his career. Three buildings finished between 1984 and 1986 – the

Spiral Building, Wacoal Arts Centre, Tokyo, 1984-5

Fujisawa Municipal Gymnasium, Spiral Building and Kyoto Museum of Modern Art – are mature works and landmarks of the New Modernism. I can think of no other buildings of this scale which show as much creative control of technology and inventive material finish. They are, if you like, examples of transcendental materialism. The Modern Movement in the twenties was long on the promise of the Machine Aesthetic, but short on delivery. Le Corbusier and Mies van der Rohe showed what advanced technology could do at this time, as long as it was fairly repetitive and unresponsive to artistic will and the moods of the architect.

Now Fumihiko Maki returns Modernism to its roots in the Arts and Crafts tradition, writes history backwards from Walter Gropius to William Morris and shows what he and his field office can do with the small tool revolution, 'just-on-time production' and the will to make architecture a *particular* art, responding to site, the client and images in his mind. These may be a film, *Last Year at Marienbad*, or the Bauhaus, or a Japanese *shoji* (in the case of the Spiral Building), but the images and requirements modify the production – not vice-vérsa.

In this way the Modernism of Maki has given us something that *is* new; it is also different from the mainstream in its emphasis on complex forms taken from the past, the present chaotic state of cities and an old-time Futurism. These mixed images are well-scaled and have that quality which critics have found in his manner: *tansei*, meaning 'decorous', a civil response to each situation. Indeed his buildings and personality have been accused of an 'indefatigable civility'. It's true, and I can think of nothing more New in Modernism than that.

This dialogue took place in Tokyo, October 1988 and was accompanied by continuous laughter – something that may be lost in transcription.

Late or Neo?

– You are one of the few architects who thinks historically so I want to bring up larger philosophical questions such as the relation between Modernism and modernisation – one of the key missing concepts in the discussion of architecture. I'll come back to this later, but in your 1986 paper called 'New Directions in Modernism' you speak about the legitimacy of a New Modernism that 'deals in images' and you say the White architecture of the twenties suggests visions of the future. Is this Neo-Modernism, or rather what I might call Late-Modernism?

When I was born in the 1920s I had a chance to see some of the Modern buildings in Tokyo. There were very few, mostly residential buildings, but they struck me because of their singularity in the Japanese urban complex. I had a *physical* contact with this Modernism. Then I went to architectural school and learnt Modernism – as an intellectual discipline, yet it was also a kind of fusion with myself even very early in my career. When you ask me about the precise definition of Modernism I feel it is different from what I experienced as a child. The article you refer to was probably talking about the *industrialisation* of our society and in many Japanese cities whenever you see high-rise, you find it made of glass, concrete or steel – not much wood. Except for houses. We have here faced this reality and the modernisation of Japanese society accepts materialism as unavoidable in this building-material sense.

Spiral Building, Wacoal Arts Centre, Tokyo, 1984-5, interior

– It is certainly avoidable in some cultures, like Burma, which decide not to modernise, or decide to unmodernise.

But Japan has taken the course to modernise. When I look at it on a material level I see two things: one is its indication of the recent past which is related to what I experienced as a child. The glass and steel, even the whiteness, began to have their romantic associations with the recent past. Still the same material used in a different way expresses a needed present and some hint of the future. So what fascinates me is that these modern materials speak of the *recent* past, the present and the future. This kind of ambiguity concerns me: we express the different times, but the future is left over as the glorious Modernist dream. Everything is there – we can have all together.

– You are saying we could have all together?

We can. But once you use very historical idioms, then you express more about the past than the future. What fascinates me about Modernism is that Modernism itself has a kind of capacity to be able to speak on both planes.

– Well there were architects, such as Otto Wagner and the Pre-Modernists who sought precisely that past, present and future conjunction. Whereas the International Style tradition denies that time-binding quality that you are talking about. This is a long debate, but how would you classify yourself in this historical spectrum? Do you think of yourself as a continuer of the Modern Movement or as a reviver?

As a continuer.

– As a Late-Modernist continuation?

A continuation, but with a new qualification. I still see the Modern as a base we can extend, from which we can develop a new language with new spatial properties. It is not the status quo. But one of the things I learnt from Post-Modernists was that Modernism had shortcomings and was maybe too heavy on morals and doctrines and things such as 'structural honesty'. Yet as a *language* I still stick to it and don't 'twist' the structure too far to become a piece of sculpture.

– Nor do Post-Modernists.

We have to depend on a certain rationality and convenience for users – in this sense I still stick to the morality of Modernism. But such functional diagrams are not the basis for formal expression – so you might call me a 'revisionist'.

– That's the canonic Team Ten position. I remember Siegfried Giedion taking up your cause in the late fifties and early sixties – and seeing you as something like the 'fifth generation' of Modernists.

The generations are moving faster now.

– One of the things Post-Modernism has done is to revitalise a lot of people in the fifth generation, and give those that attack it a second life – the 'Neo-Modernists'. On the other hand, Late-Modernists just continue the old orthodoxy. A Neo-Modernist must, by contrast, take the criticisms of the Post-Modernist seriously – as you have done. You have admitted 'memory', 'symbol' and the 'arbitrariness of your language' – the fact that it could be different. These are your three fundamental reconsiderations of Modernism, so you are indeed a 'Neo'.

Yes.

– But this also puts you in a funny position, because there is a strange nostalgia about 'the future in the past.' You pointed this out by saying the White architecture of the twenties

has a memory for you – whereas for most Westerners it signifies a depthless present tense. And for us Futurism didn't work, Buck Rogers went rusty. Bladerunner, the Post-Modern film, makes a lot of this new attitude to the 'White Hope of the Future'. We know it is tarnished, decomposing, full of pollution and post-Chernobyl. The Neo-Modernists of Los Angeles, Morphosis, make quite a lot of this 'dead-tech' – it's already a style, and romance as you say, willingly adopted. The Modernists wanted you to accept their anti-style as a necessity.

While it could be a romance, people must get more from a building than just looking at it. I question the substance that gives you a certain emotion and again I would say it is the quality of the spaces and the way it is made. What we have forgotten in Modernism is this minute substance – the *details* are very important for me and are the substitute for past ornament. Buildings in the past had a tremendous amount of ornament, supported by craftsmanship. Can we produce the equivalent of this through the use of modern materials? Modern society tried to make a building very efficient without this substance – it got rid of ornament – and made neutral, boring space which Post-Modernists criticised. What I like to see is the *substantiation* of a space – not just the image. I can't just decorate (I have a Late-Modernist hang-up), but I believe in craftsmanship in industrial society. Ando also tries to get this in his concrete.

– You use the grid as an ornament.

Yes, sure, geometrical ornament – if you broaden the definition of ornament to that extent.

– Yes, anything can be an ornament if it is used redundantly as a sign of itself – your grid, or whiteness.

Yes, sure.

The Gymnasium as Beetle

– You've also responded to the Post-Modern use of metaphor – in your Fujisawa gymnasium. You obviously spent a lot of time designing the roof and giving it that substantiality, but it also relates to Expressionism of the twenties and anthropomorphism of today – one of the strongest canons of Post-Modernism.

I don't disagree – that's your freedom to intepret.

– But you mention these images.

When I designed Fujisawa it came through certain intuitions as a particular form, space and structural rationality. However at the end the building evoked certain animal images – a frog or beetle or airship. People have the liberty to interpret, but I never intended to make a building look like one of these things. The internal form of the spaces are the important thing.

– 'From the inside – out'; that's the classic Modernist dictum, just as is 'no conscious literary or visual metaphors, SVP'.

Not exactly. We covered spaces in model form with certain surfaces, moulded them and then began to look at them.

– But it's what you allow to come into your mind, as you design, and become a limitation or direction that counts. Of course you do have some aesthetic preconceptions such as 'roof architecture' – and that's quintessentially Japanese (so you're almost a Post-Modernist) – but your style is mostly restricted to grids, whiteness and Modernist preconceptions. Surely when you saw the end elevation of Fujisawa you must have recognised a beetle or face?

Fujisawa Municipal Gymnasium, Fujisawa, 1984, with east elevation above and west elevation below

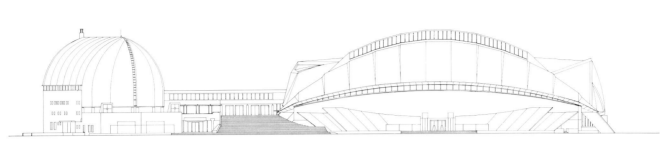

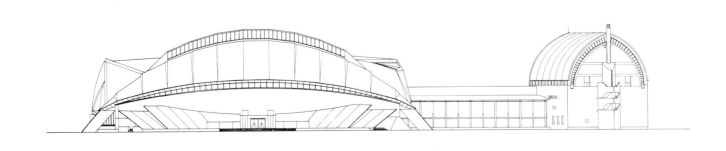

Yes, at the end of design we recognised these images and laughed – but we didn't seek them at the beginning.

– Then I have a criticism. Because architecture is a public art, language and symbolism, the architect must be responsible – at the end of the day – for the formal meanings: not say they are the by-product of a process of structural rationality, 'inside-out', and all the rest of it. An architect must be responsible for his or her symbols – no one else is!

Really? Charles, I must tell you I don't aim for a symbolism. What I described as a process is pretty true. I must admit in some cases using this method we do *not* arrive at symbolic expression, and sometimes we do arrive by accident. Fujisawa is more accidental and we may not repeat it. I don't particularly subscribe to this form although I *like* it very much. I have tremendous emotional attachment to it.

– Intuitive?

Yes, I believe in my eyes. In some cases the result of my method is not as good as I expect, but to me this is the way architecture is made.

– Of course you have history on your side to say architects have the right to design by intuition.

A hundred times.

– That's why I put you in Architecture Today *under a chapter called 'Intuitive Modernism' . . . I find no rule besides your own intuition and sensibility with which you design. Therefore you, Kurokowa and Meier are as good or bad as you are that particular day. The whole point of rules and canons is to have something to measure and agree with the public. So the public can say 'hey, we don't want to use a beetle for a gymnasium'. In traditional societies there were always formal rules, prohibitions and canons of usage to help and hinder the architect. Sumptuary rules for instance.*

But that is gone.

– But they remain in residues – they're never entirely gone.

Intuition and the Spiral Building

I don't think we can re-introduce the kind of style images which could be shared by a community at large, and . . . I don't think we can do it and I wouldn't believe in it. But I think these *intuitions* must be constantly cultivated to reflect the particular time and that is the only basis of my continuing in practice. As soon as I fall into establishing my own canon – even a personal one – then my search would stop. I fear for such a moment of stagnation: I am a very personal artist, or artisan, and believe in continuous training.

– That's another classic Modernist position – the romantic notion of 'make it new', we must have a continued revolution in sensibility . . .

Exactly.

– . . . Must design every building as if it's a unique situation. One of the problems is that then the public can't 'speak architecture' as they can speak a slow-changing language. And you say 'that's too bad, we can't have a public language any more, because it would be stagnating and impossible to lay down'. Post-Modernists and Classicists would dispute this – just as descriptions – because there are conventions today for an office building, museum etc, even if they are very loose. There have to be conventions – and therefore stagnations – for architecture to communicate.

Spiral Building, Wacoal Arts Centre, Tokyo, 1984-5

Yes I can see the need for a typology, or public canon, but still I would criticise some Post-Modernists. While their *images* may be very interesting, quite often I am disappointed once I get inside them. The experience of the total building doesn't correspond to the excitement of the first glance. Here again I go back to the lesson of old buildings. Of course they had both – overall form and interior substance – and that's what I mean by *substantiation*, the everlasting principles of good building.

A metropolis like Tokyo cannot suggest there is one kind of publicness. It's very elusive. For instance it's no longer necessary to be an institutional building any more. Even commercial buildings can be public (such as the Spiral Building). So although I will defend intuition, I don't deny the meaningfulness, or the search for publicness.

– You know my criticism of Mies at ITT, where the observer might confuse the chapel for the boiler house, and the architect's building for a temple to the president. It has the substantiation and the good detailing of your work, but misuses conventions and recognisable elements. The problem with Modernism is that, pace Giedion, a tradition hasn't grown with public roots – but rather professional ones. One of the reasons is that architects have refused to use signs and rhetorical figures in a conventional way – or else restricted them to the crudest of levels.

Publicness could be reached not by establishing formal canons, but by pursuing architecture in a different way.

– I agree you do do some of this through abstraction, but I'm not sure the public understands in the Spiral Building, that the cone refers to the Bauhaus. The collage of different fragments you see as an aspect of Modernism?

I have faith in the capacity of a Modernist language by which we could produce forms responsive to this particular age: we don't have to borrow from the past our languages.

– But you have admitted you do borrow from the 1920s past.

The recent past.

– So you can borrow from the recent past.

Yes, because this is a language I have contact with physically.

– But most of the Japanese haven't! They don't know the cone refers to the Bauhaus. It's a private language.

Yes, when I use it, it is private. But as soon as it is built and seen and appreciated, it becomes gradually part of the public domain.

– You talk about the cone and free-form wall as Modernist icons – so you admit the symbolic content of architectural language and you say the spiral motion is implicit in the facade (which you can see once it is pointed out). But these are professional, semi-public signs.

Maybe my position is élitist, but I believe the élite can bring along the public if a building is well designed and built. It has been so.

– Yes. You have also talked about 'multiple meanings', another phrase of Post-Modernists. One critic has talked about the grids of the Spiral Building as a jumble of shoji, so it has even popular meanings. If I can make you a Post-Modernist for a second – your Steinbergian facade assembles images of the Acropolis at the top, an Indian ruin, Chinese landscape painting and Japanese interiors.

This is Paestum and Katsura palace . . .

– Very PM, very musée imaginaire. You're saying a museum is a collage of disparate cultures –

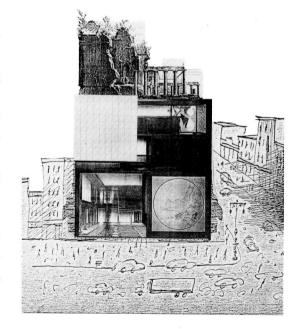

Spiral Building, Wacoal Arts Centre, Tokyo, 1984-5, Steinbergian drawing

Within a modern language –

– *So what happened in the translation from a PM collage into a Late-Modern language? You see the irony. By analogy you are acknowledging plural taste cultures and then you're translating them into abstraction. Pluralism exists by analogy, not in reality!*

Yes, my latest building under construction is like a collage with a top (solar system) a body (a horizontal) and then many requirements from the site. But this building still derives from basic syntactic or compositional principles.

– *Paul Goldberger calls it 'The New-Baroque', but it is closer to the 'New Picturesque' because of the emphasis on movement, asymmetry and the informal. You refer to an indeterminant rather than classical facade, because it expands outside the frame and it's chaotic. A critic compares it to the rollicking townscape of Tokyo, which is close to chaos theory and the idea of Shinohara. This simulates the positive economic growth of the city – its 'messy vitality' and imbalance. We're getting a rule of decomposition here which you share with Eisenman and Tschumi – their canon of L-shapes and fragments and self-similarity.*

What makes me different from the Deconstructionists is that I still believe in achieving the 'difficult whole', not the classical whole.

– *Well that's Post-Modern, that's terrific.*

I believe in the 'difficult whole' with familiar parts, so people can see the familiarity in the parts, but not the entirety.

– *But the suit you are wearing and the YKK Guest House you have designed are partly symmetrical – the latter is even Post-Modern Classical and very well done with Japanese aspects. At times you flirt with Classicism.*

Sure, only with the parts. In collage you have to have your own personal canon against which whatever you are doing must be measured. The yardstick in your head is to achieve this 'difficult whole' – it's always in my mind, but I can't say what it is at the outset.

– *It seems to me not enough to suggest chaos theory and to simulate Tokyo and argue, with Venturi, that 'Main Street is almost all right' – you must also provide alternatives.*

Even with fragments – in the Spiral Building – there is a momentary stability achieved within a difficult whole.

– *The mixing of building type at the Spiral-Wacoal Building is extraordinary – fashion house, women's lingerie company, a bar, museum, auditoria, restaurant, apartment. Extremely incongruous for a Westerner, and ultimately surrealist.*

Just everyday life for us. We cannot depend any more on Classical building types – 'This is a school' etc. Instead we have a multifunctional reality, so building types become obsolete.

– *Don't you, as a Modernist, want to express the incongruity and hybrid quality? A collision of taste-cultures, instead of grids – perhaps the client wouldn't like it?*

No. Some clients in Japan will accept outrageous statements. But some of our *nouveaux riches* clients will say that once you give a commission to a name architect, then anything goes as long as he meets the budget and gets public attention. In the case of the Spiral it is one of the three places in Tokyo which is very fashionable – so they have no complaints, even if there's a collision of irony or chaos.

Tepia Building, Science Pavilion, Tokyo, 1989. .Maki mentions its tripartite composition with solar panels at the top. Also apparent is the De Stijl handling of metal planes which slide past each other or have an exaggerated break to accent a change of material. 'Tepia' is an acronym of 'technology-utopia' and it holds exhibitions on the latest High-Tech machines. The detailing, not visible here, is, as usual, masterful.

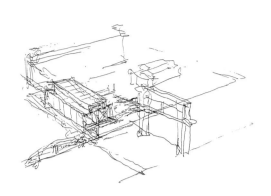

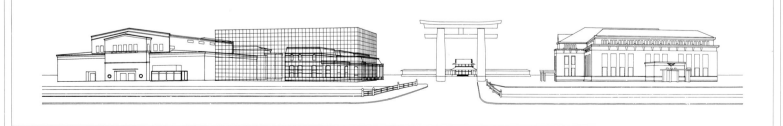

Change and Modernisation

– Who do you admire among recent architects?

Well, in a way, the late work of Eero Saarinen, because it was always unpredictable, because he was always searching for something new, always changing. Some of his buildings, such as the CBS in New York and Dulles in Washington, still have a freshness.

– Lastly, what of the connection of Modernism to modernisation – and the fact that industrialisation has meant westernisation as Theodore von Laue argues.

Well for me modernisation is no longer westernisation, but something more common or shared.

– But you are wearing a western shirt and tie, whereas if Japan had been the first to modernise I would be wearing a Kimono and sandals. You can't say the business suit and reinforced concrete are 'universal', or can you?

The international Modern *has* spread, but we are beginning to have a subtle regionalism based on this international mode. We cannot go back, time is irreversible.

– But in a post-industrial society you can do everything – shoji screens and wood buildings and there's no way you can argue for the necessity of one approach. It becomes a symbolic act, something you approve of – at least part of the time. Today necessity is thrown back onto culture and it becomes relativistic to argue for one language of building rather than another. The profession could go the way of Richard Rogers' Silver Aesthetic, Prince Charles' revivalism, Ricardo Bofill's prefabricated Classicism, or an inventive vernacular and there's no way to argue that one approach is more 'necessary' from a technical viewpoint than another. From now on, in a post-industrial society, culture becomes the leading source for arguments.

Well, for my own work, I like to do new things and not repeat myself. I have my own personal principles, but like Saarinen, I may change in the future; and I don't want to act under the labels or categories you like to put on my building.

– You're not the only one – but categories are as inevitable to thinking as style is to building.

National Museum of Modern Art, Kyoto, 1986, with conceptual sketch above and perspective below

THE RHETORIC
OF NEO-MODERNISM
A Pictorial Essay

The variables that define the New Modern Architecture are given in a chart at the beginning of the book and only some of these are illustrated here. Since this is a pictorial essay I have concentrated on stylistic motifs rather than ideological and design issues, but a few of these are also touched on. The order of the chart is followed treating points numbered 1, 10, 11, 13, 16, 19, 20 and 22 but the other subjects are no less important.

DANIEL LIBESKIND, *Berlin City Edge*, 1987, detail of 'Cloud Prop', Alpha model

Hermetic Coding

If Modernism had a primary place for abstraction, then the new movement emphasises this to such a degree that it often becomes completely hermetic – carried out in a private code. All art languages are in part specific and have to be learned, but Neo-Modernism demands a considerable self-education on the part of the beholder. This, of course, is a problem for architecture which must be a public art; there are many people who simply won't make the effort to learn private, fast-changing languages. For them the new approach will only be another style, a sensual mode to be appropriated and misinterpreted as they see fit.

This aesthetic accommodation to the arcane is quite usual. After all, most people don't know the meaning of a Corinthian capital or the *rocaille* of the Rococo, both of which are conventions which have to be learned to be fully understood. Perhaps the Neo-Modern repertoire of 'cocktail sticks' and 'flying beams' will become equally conventional in the future, but at present these motifs are half-understood and evocative.

No-one is more hermetic than the designer-musician-poet Daniel Libeskind, an architect who has recently won two competitions in that city of the 'degree-zero', Berlin. His 'City Edge' proposal, 1987, is a frenzied cacophony of cocktail sticks holding up a flying beam – all of it covered with newsprint and pages torn from James Joyce, maps, Russian telephone books and Bibles. Here we have in his words 'the substance of a city . . . a realignment of arbitrary points, disconnected lines and names out of place along the axis of Universal Hope'.

Berlin, for Libeskind, is the ultimate Modern city where texts are confused, erased and reasserted in a new way. His 'axis of Universal Hope', the flying beam, would contain, if built, some housing, offices and public administration. It also connects, at the lower end, a memory of Mies van der Rohe, with that of Albert Speer, at the higher end. Universal Hope? Libeskind refused to design the typical IBA project for Berlin and rebuild fragments of the pre-existing city, or adopt the healing form of the perimeter housing block: 'I suggested not rebuilding. I believe the Holocaust is not something you can get away from. The placelessness should not be bemoaned . . . How do you grasp emptiness . . . Architecture is getting more obscure, and like the human quest will get completely lost . . . Don't seek to find your way out, but rather your way in . . . ' In his and Eisenman's work in Berlin the metaphysics of Neo-Modernism are most clearly stated.

Berlin City Edge, 1987, Alpha model

269

Disjunctive Complexity

The Neo-Modernists, like so many others today, try to deal with the complexity and contradiction of daily life. They do not sweep away the mess and banality of the city, nor impose a rational strait-jacket nor a set of formal categories (beyond those motifs mentioned here). Rather, like Frank Gehry, they improvise with existing structures the requirements of a client and industrial materials. They do not seek, as do the Post-Modernists, to make of this complexity 'a difficult whole'; in fact they are suspicious of overall unities beyond the most pragmatic – those of colour and material. Thus their work is anti-classical in the strict sense.

Gehry's conversion of Edgemar Farms, Santa Monica, into offices, retail and a small gallery is typical. A silver-grey tonality dominates these buildings and the piazzetta. Concrete, sheet-steel, aluminium and chain-link fence are naturally grey. The commercial street vernacular is absorbed behind green tile. Everywhere forms jut about in awkward dissonance. A diagonal stairway takes on huge, bloated proportions – at once an Egyptian gangway and menacing industrial object, becoming an icon of entrance.

Truncated towers rise above the central square, almost useless spaces which are sometimes splayed and shifted. These could be reminiscent of San Gimigniano except they have no defensive function and are excessively rhetorical about their lack of use. Also with their neutral industrial look they remind one more of airplane hangars than palaces. The most extraordinary and refreshing view is from within the chain-link cage: from here the moiré patterns and interfering metal wires shimmer and further distort one's perception, making this group into an evocative industrial landscape, a place where anything might happen.

FRANK GEHRY, *Edgemar Farms Conversion*, Santa Monica, 1987-9, rehabilitation for shops, a museum and offices.

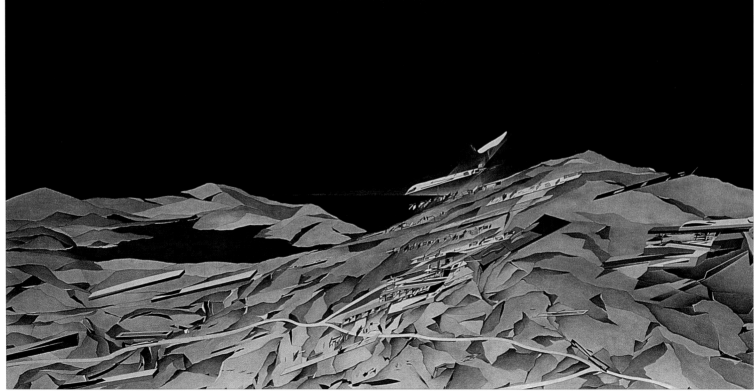

Explosive Space

Cubist space as translated into architecture during the twenties was layered, fractured and a continuous sequence of interpenetrating planes. Transparency and overlap were two of its salient features. With the constructions of Tatlin and the tektonics of Malevich it took on a more dynamic quality and now with the 'anti-gravitational' architecture of Zaha Hadid and Rem Koolhaas it becomes even more explosive. Rectilinear flying beams skew and bend away from the cartesian co-ordinates. Floors tilt, facades peel back and hard-edge coloured planes ram through each other. The implications are violent: architecture has suffered an earthquake.

One of the first projects to convey this dynamic space was Zaha Hadid's winning competition for the Peak Club in Hong Kong, 1983. In one of her 'exploded isometric' paintings she shows architecture flying apart over the stylised mountains of this coastal city. Building elements and rock outcrops, which are polished grey, are equated. All of this is made more explosive by an oblique viewpoint – anamorphic projection – which gives a distorted picture except from one point of vision. The fractal geometry of nature is represented here and closely linked with Hadid's 'planetary architecture'. The paintings are impossible to decipher as functional diagrams, but the Club was to have three superimposed layers: a beam of fifteen double-height studios dug into the hillside surmounted by a beam of twenty hotel apartments, then a void and finally a topmost beam given over to a penthouse. Many of the open-air facilities were meant to 'hover like spaceships' on the top of the Peak, an imaginative response to an extraordinary site and hedonistic programme. Unfortunately the Club was not built.

Equally brilliant was Hadid's project for the Kurfurstendamm office building, Berlin, 1985. Here on a very tight corner site she has placed most of the functional and structural requirements on the interior blank side while opening out the free side in a gently bowed curve. The transparent curtain wall tilts out as it rises thus allowing more space on each successive floor and a welcoming gesture on the roof. All the visual forces lean up towards this point and culminate in an outdoor room, open to the sky – the deck of an ocean liner. The warped prow, streamlined balconies and sleek detailing make this a battleship crossed with a hand-glider. Boomerang walls and leaning piers punctuate the inside, while the outside – represented in a series of rotated views as the spectator walks along – is seen as grey blades cutting through the sky. The control of these paintings underscores the refinement. Each knife-cut and slice, each peel and incision, is carefully balanced in colour and tone. The dumb slab of Modernism has finally achieved a welcome and unlikely aristocratic elegance.

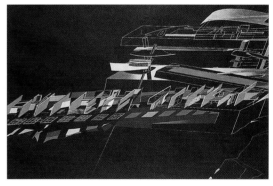

ZAHA HADID, *The Peak Club*, Hong Kong, 1983, *Studio Apartments and Void*

Kurfurstendamm 70, Berlin, 1985, *Rotation*

Kurfurstendamm 70, Section and Firewall Elevations

The Peak Club, Exploded Isometric

Rem Koolhaas' National Dance Theatre in the Hague, 1984-7, is a modest realisation of the new explosive space made within a restricted budget. Here architecture finds its equivalent as frozen dance. Leaning piers (fat 'cocktail sticks') march on the outside towards an inverted cone in gold leaf which does a pirouette at the entrance. This holds a restaurant. On the inside foyer an ovoid satellite (champagne bar) is suspended overhead by cables and a blood-red I-beam. A black stairway rushes up a wall, a grey balcony zooms by and multi-coloured columns stand to attention. They also skewer a tilted ceiling plane that slopes down into the floor.

Curved walls add to the feeling that this is an anamorphic projection, an impossible space where parallel lines have given up their rationality and miraculously converge. Scale is further distorted by an infinity of randomised dots. Pools of light, reflective surfaces and contrasting colours add to the dislocation and movement. Koolhaas has here combined the symbolic architecture of Leonidov – and its 'tensions in space' – with the sleek forms of Niemeyer and Wallace Harrison. The twenties and fifties re-emerge in this new architecture of hedonism, where the play is deeply serious.

REM KOOLHAAS, *National Dance Theatre*, The Hague, 1984-7

Frenzied Cacophony

The ultimate stylists of the New Modernism are the group Coop Himmelblau – Wolfgang Prix and Helmut Swiczinsky from Vienna. Using lightweight tensile elements in juxtaposition, they have created that airy, scratchy filigree of complex lines and angles which architects as diverse as Peter Cook and Daniel Libeskind have projected in drawings. Thin white lines of steel jump about and cross in contradiction. Leaning or tilted structures play off each other achieving a dynamic balance. I-beams and diagonal cross-braces collide at a dissonant angle. These creations have an affinity with the 'tensegrity' structures of Buckminster Fuller playing compression versus tension, but they are rhetorically complex and redundant, not efficient.

Coop Himmelblau's Funder factory shows the frenzied cacophony of their method. A long low production hall – basically a shed – erupts at certain points with cantilevered canopies punctuating its flat surfaces. The most dramatic eruptions are the front door marked by a zig-zag awning in blood-red (favourite colour of the Neo-Mods) and a volume in glass and steel – the main office area which faces south. Here trusses penetrate the skin, the roof tilts up and turns into a trellis and diagonal beams splay into the leaning glass wall. This is the 'violated perfection' of the Deconstructionists: the perfect white cube suddenly smashed, skewed and skewered into a frenzy of oppositional forms. Another such crescendo occurs in the adjacent power house where the chimneys suddenly tilt off the right angle. In both cases a rational predictable solution is partly violated by an expressive outburst – and the balance of one and the other is mutually heightening.

This is not true of their attic conversion in Vienna, a riotous mélange of twisted and warped shapes which resembles a dead pterodactyl that has crash-landed on the roof. There is no calm and perfection to set off the cacophony, unless it is the classical architecture below. Nonetheless the thin steel lines, which slightly bow and stretch, have a taut beauty. Their counterpoint is so tense that it seems the architecture would explode into life if one tendon were cut. Perhaps it would. In any case this is the image of dynamic, moving, balancing forces frozen into architecture.

COOP HIMMELBLAU, *Funder Factory 3*, Carinthia, Austria, 1988-9, isometric

Rooftop Conversion, Vienna, 1986-8, section and design sketch

Thematised Ornament

While Neo-Modern architecture is usually abstract it is also, in the hands of Peter Eisenman, an abstraction given a representational role. Eisenman will invariably adopt two different kinds of themes to represent those coming from his preoccupations such as fractals, self-similarity and catachresis and those coming from the specific job at hand. For the Bio-Centrum project in Frankfurt he represented fractal geometry and the process which DNA undergoes. Characteristically this representation is so complex that it defies easy comprehension – even by Eisenman himself.

For the Wexner Arts Center in Columbus, Ohio, the themes are a little more accessible, but no less complex, and they are turned into a giant ornament. The main themes are the shifted grid and the resurrection of a nineteenth-century armoury that was demolished.

With the new grid representing that of Columbus, Eisenman 'blasts through' the old grid of the Ohio State campus, thus setting up a series of oppositions at twelve and a half degrees. This intrusive, angled line – emphasised by white scaffolding – also tilts upwards and 'plunges like a north arrow' at the parking lot. In its aggressive march, it slices into a hall and auditorium on either side connecting them to a larger arts complex. The motives are functional and philosophical: to provide a new pedestrian path – reinforced by a grove of trees – and to challenge the customary way of presenting art. The client asked for a new way of displaying vanguard art and hence Eisenman has provided walls of glass – where paintings cannot be hung – and broken down the idea of the building as a frame, or pedestal, or contained edge. It has no clear beginning or end: it is all middle and process. In effect the building/landscape is itself an analogue to the performance and computer art it is meant to not-shelter.

As one looks through one grid of scaffolding – sign of the twenty-first century – one sees another grid shifted to it, and then another at a different scale. This self-similarity and scaling of the same form is an ordering device of fractal geometry which Eisenman exploits because it is both Platonic *and* natural – that is an ambiguous, in-between formal device.

The fragment of the former Armoury is built of a new 'non-brick' material to at once recall the past shape and signal its artificial difference. It contains offices, marks an entrance and is sliced and layered to avoid any interpretation as a nostalgic reconstruction. No-one could possibly mistake it for the towers of the old Armoury and in this way its 'anti-memory' both recollects the past and denies its continuity into the future.

With all its skews, collisions and thematised ornaments the Wexner Center is still an amusing and highly sensual work of architecture and landscape. As usual Eisenman shows – in the words of Raquel Welsh – 'that the sexiest organ of the human body is the brain'.

PETER EISENMAN, *Wexner Center for the Visual Arts*, Ohio, 1985-9, model

Wexner Center for the Visual Arts, view of tower

Wexner Center for the Visual Arts in construction

Traces of Memory

The preoccupation with the past has been a keynote of Post-Modernists, but it has also inspired Neo-Modernists such as Peter Eisenman and Emilio Ambasz, who invariably use the figure of excavation to represent history. To dig down into the earth is to excavate the subconscious and collective memory. To build above the earth plane is to construct for the future. So excavation represents the past, the ground plane signifies the present and a new structure represents the future. This natural symbolism is adopted by Eisenman and given further twists. For one thing 'false memories' or non-existing but conceptual landmarks are excavated (buildings which should have been there); for another, the language in which they are represented – the grid and fragmented 'ghost' building – is often so abstract as to be unrecognisable. However, once one knows the private Eisenman code, these memories become clear and pertinent.

A case in point is his Social Housing in Berlin, 1982-7. The original plan for this area consisted of a museum, walkways and an 'artificial excavation' down to eighteenth-century foundations. In the event only a corner of the block – and thirty-seven apartments – were built. In Eisenman's private code the light green wall with a white grid *appliqué* represents the existing buildings on the site, while another grid – shifted by 3.3 degrees – represents the eighteenth-century foundations, and also the Mercator Grid of the world *and* the Berlin Wall. In other words this dialectic of grids locates the scheme in cultural space and time. It ties in with those buildings which remain and the Wall that traumatises the present. It also provides a very effective ornamental counterpoint and scale. The self-similar rhythms are a hallmark of fractal geometry and something which breaks down the large mass. The only problem is that these codes are abstract and no-one would understand their referents until after reading an explanation. No supplementary, conventional codes are used.

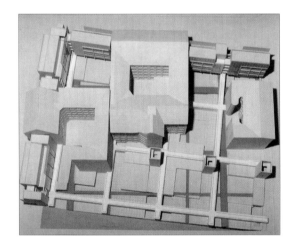

PETER EISENMAN, *Social Housing, IBA*, Berlin, 1982-7, plan

The same is true of other Eisenman schemes. His Cannaregio project for Venice, 1978, is a series of excavations and superimpositions on a site which recall previous buildings such as an abattoir and a design of Le Corbusier for a hospital here. The 'point grid' of the French-Swiss designer is indicated by voids cut in the surface, while Eisenman's new buildings – in the form of L-shaped blocks – are set on a shifted grid at different scales. The L-shapes and different size red blocks are meant to destabilise memory at the same moment as they affirm it.

Ten years later, for the 'park of the twenty-first century' in Paris, Eisenman was asked by the French-Swiss designer Bernard Tschumi to design a garden with Jacques Derrida. At the Parc de la Villette he, along with Derrida, had proposed a recollection of both the Cannaregio design and previous buildings on the Paris site. Again the 'point-grid' is recalled in plan with incisions – but now Tschumi's as well as Le Corbusier's. An abattoir is also indicated with gold forms, but now a Parisian as well as Venetian one. The process of subtracting from the earth while adding buildings to it – 'quarrying and palimpsest' – leaves 'traces' which Eisenman represents. A nearby canal and grid and swirling paths of Tschumi (called the 'cinematic promenade') are also miniaturised. The ground plane – made in Corten steel to age with a permanent rust colour, thus stopping time in the present – is tilted at an angle. This perhaps indicates the present as an unstable rush from past to future. Virtually the only signs which are accessible

Social Housing, IBA, exterior view

are the stylised zig-zags and indentations in gold, a clear reminder of the ramparts of Paris which were here.

The garden design of Eisenman and Derrida is thus an esoteric palimpsest and excavation of things which are present (Tschumi) and absent (the past), coincidental (French-Swiss designers) and determinant (point-grids). They ultimately represent for the designers that ambiguous flux between life and death, the 'chora' of making and unmaking at the same time. And they also provide a very enjoyable pastime of 'hunt the symbol' – with the Eisenman text in your hand.

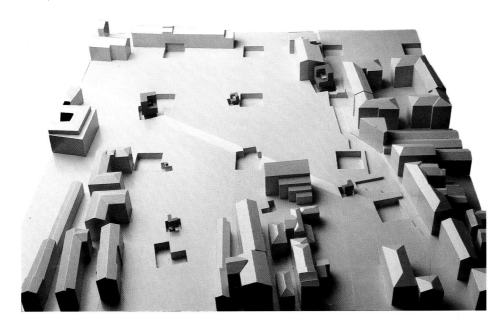

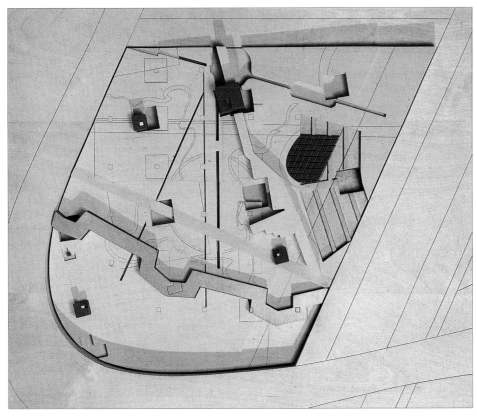

Cannaregio, Venice, 1978, gold model

Parc de la Villette, Paris, 1988, view of garden model

Comic Destructive

The Modern world has triumphed through analysis and decomposition. It has reduced biology to chemistry, chemistry to physics and physics to a search for 'ultimate particles'. However much this reductionism is crazy ('we murder to dissect' as William Blake wrote) it has produced powerful results and a fragmented environment of extreme contrasts. When not tragic, this decomposition can be amusing and fascinating as any child knows who has pulled apart a radio to see how it works. The urge to dissect is spontaneous, a natural result of curiosity. And when confronted by an array of parts, their juxtaposition can be funny. The Comic Scene, as represented by Serlio and other architects, shows an environment in disarray – decomposing with age, gone to seed, full of Gothic, Classical and vernacular bits strewn around. Their conjunction makes no sense, except that of the joke – the fortuitous encounter of opposite systems which may have a serendipitous element in common. Any old urban environment is a tissue of *non-sequiturs* and some Neo-Modern architects – Frank Gehry, Kazuo Shinohara, Fumihiko Maki and the group SITE – have sought to make an art from this truth.

For a Museum of Modern Art in Frankfurt, SITE proposed a rectilinear, masonry building sliced away by a triangular glass cage – the representation of the triangular site. The intersection of the two geometries and two material systems dramatises a set of contradictions – nature/culture, contingent/ideal – and this drama is heightened by the crumbling walls and the architectural convention of the 'cutaway section'. SITE has continuously made a comic 'de-architecture' from such deadpan collisions and the opposition between new and old. But where Eisenman will be oblique, abstract and hermetic with his 'ghost' buildings, this group will be explicit and conventional in the attempt to reach a wider audience.

Frank Gehry, at the Winton Guest House, has pushed the *non-sequitur* in hermetic directions while exaggerating the oppositions in material. Thus stone, polished aluminium, black metal and brick accentuate different volumes while some of the truncated shapes almost refer to a 'fish', 'potting shed', 'turret' and 'obelisk'. But not quite, because these conventional shapes are so distorted. The heterogeneous referents have nothing to do with each other and in this sense are part of the developing genre – comic destructive'.

Jean Nouvel does not decompose, as do these other architects, but he does use extraneous images in his mechanistic inventions. Thus his Social Housing in Nîmes is at once train, bus, and ocean liner in its material and overall shape. But with its punched aluminium balconies that flare out and cornice of metal trellis it is also a reminder of classical precedents for mass housing. There is no attempt to unify time and culture as in the old Modernism. Heterogeneity and divergent meaning are accepted as the conditions for present architecture and in this way Nouvel is perhaps more open and inclusive than other Neo-Modernists. His work always shows a fresh response to particular situations.

SITE, *Frankfurt Museum of Modern Art*, Frankfurt, 1983, model

JEAN NOUVEL, *Social Housing*, Nîmes, 1986-7

FRANK GEHRY, *Winton Guest House*, Wayzata, Minnesota, 1983-6

Non-Place Sprawl

Virtually everybody hates suburban sprawl, even those who choose to live there to escape the ills of the city. Chaotic, for the most part unplanned, ugly, non-centred, away from the action, provincial, boring – you make the list, it is in everybody's *enfer imaginaire.* The only thing to be said for exurbia is its occasional peace, its fleeting moments of freedom, greenery and safety. But in a way it is our characteristic environment, whether on the outskirts of Moscow, New Delhi or New York. The whole world is sprawling and it has taken two different kinds of architect to recognise this fact: the Post-Modernist Robert Venturi, who teaches us the 'lessons' of Levittown and Las Vegas, and the Deconstructionist Bernard Tschumi who has largely built a 'park of the twenty-first century' to its reality; I won't say its virtues, because Tschumi is not defending or celebrating this non-place sprawl: just essentialising its qualities.

In the Parc de la Villette, a commission he won in competition narrowly beating Rem Koolhaas, he has like Koolhaas superimposed a set of different organising principles: *lines* of circulation such as the covered walkways and curvilinear 'cinematic promenades'; *surfaces* of grass, garden, canal and places for mass entertainment; and above all the *point grid,* thirty or so red *folies,* or pavilions, located about every hundred and twenty metres on a square grid. In effect three fire-engine red machines constitute a single building that is dispersed, destabilised, disjoined, displaced, dislocated – or all the *de's* and *dis's* Derrida talks about in Tschumi's Deconstruction. The ultimate dissociations are between form and content, signifier and signified, because no-one really knew which functions would be poured into the *folies* except notionally: cinema facilities, restaurants, health clubs, childrens' school, science centre etc.

Each pavilion is, in effect, an abstract cube responding to both Tschumi's and the Neo-Constructivists' rules of decomposition. Where Eisenman adopted his dislocated L-shapes for a similar point-grid, Tschumi adopts Iakov Chernikhov's 1930s language. He enamels this syntax a dark blood-red (for Tschumi this is a non-colour!) and has a lot of fun breaking it up into giant wheels, useless trusses and spider's legs.

BERNARD TSCHUMI, *Parc de la Villette,* Paris, 1986-7, folie

Parc de la Villette, folie

Parc de la Villette, walkway

I underline the fun since it is precisely what a Deconstructionist sublimates with all his high-minded metaphysical rationalisation about the end of the author, the death of subjectivity, romance, the city and so forth. And it makes this non-place sprawl, and sometimes pretentious jargon, a delight. Anyone who goes to the Parc de la Villette will be enchanted by these elegant machines, the metal stools that whirl about, the gardens which are excavated and tilted, and the light springing walkways (engineered by Peter Rice). If Neo-Modernism has created a magnificent urban *topos*, it is surely this 'non-place'.

Tschumi's *lines* of movement are partly sheltered from the sun and rain by an undulating canopy suspended from a Decon structure that is an asymmetrical mixture of metal cables and columns. These dramatise the opposition between tension and compression – the tendons and bones of a living body. Sometimes, by the canal, these also become bridges of movement that fly through a cantilevered pavilion. At other times similar aluminium bridges leap across a garden excavated on the site.

Tschumi says the Park is 'not a plenitude, but instead "empty" form: *les cases sont vides*. La Villette, then, aims at an architecture that *means nothing*' (his emphasis). Thus one of the fascinating games to play in this meaningless architecture is to guess the function of each pavilion (if it has yet been determined). The most extravagant display of red enamelled metal, with open caged space and giant water wheels, serves one day per week as a red-cross station – for giving blood! The pavilion with spider-leg-outriggers is a nursery station where children make their own wild constructions. The first to open were a cafe and a display for plants.

The idea that architecture should be autonomous, while functions change, was of course a key notion of Mies van der Rohe; but even the classical agora adopted this notion of indeterminant function sublimated by autonomous form. However much it may be possible, and even necessary, it reduces architecture in meaning and depth. For garden pavilions this may be desirable.

Parc de la Villette, folie

Parc de la Villette, Programmatic Deconstruction, 1983

Parc de la Villette, view of canal and folies

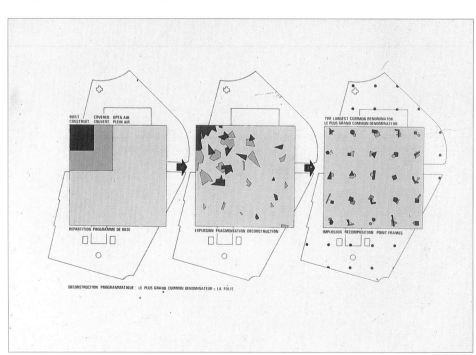

NOTES

SECTION I
CHAPTER I
The New Moderns

1 For a mention of Lublinksi and another of his books, *The Balance Sheet of the Modern,* see the very thorough discussion *Modernism 1890-1930,* edited by Malcom Bradbury and James McFarlane, Penguin Books, Harmondsworth, 1976, pp 39, 78.

2 *Ibid,* p 33.

3 Peter Eisenman, 'Post-Functionalism', editorial in *Oppositions 6,* Autumn 1976, but published in Spring 1977.

4 Douglas Davis, 'Elegant New Geometry', *Newsweek,* June 27, 1983, pp 46-8. Davis also mounted an exhibition at New York University which put forward several of the ideas of Neo-Modernism: 'Modern redux: Critical Alternatives for Architecture in the Next Decade', March 4 to April 19, 1986. The catalogue does not make clear distinctions between Neo-, Late- and Post-Modernism.

5 Paul Goldberger, 'Modernism Reaffirms Its Power', *New York Times,* November 24, 1986, Section 2, pp 1-2.

6 E H Gombrich, 'Classification and Its Discontents', *Norm and Form,* Studies in the Art of the Renaissance, Phaidon Press, London, 1966, pp 81-98.

7 George Kubler, *The Shape of Time,* Yale, New Haven, 1962.

8 Anthony Blunt, *Some Uses and Misuses of the terms Baroque and Rococo as applied to Architecture,* Oxford, 1973.

9 Kazuo Shinohara, 'Chaos and Machine', *The Japan Architect,* May 1988.

10 *Ibid,* p 28.

11 *Ibid,* p 19.

12 *Ibid,* pp 30-31.

13 *Ibid,* p 31.

14 The exhibition *Deconstructivist Architecture* at the Museum of Modern Art, July-August 1988 was first mooted several years before by Peter Eisenman, Aaron Betsky, Paul Florian and Stephen Wierzbowski as an exhibition called 'Violated Perfection'. In the event Philip Johnson took over this show and steered it in a more Neo-Constructivist direction giving it a home in the Vatican of Modernism.

15 Marshall Berman, *All That is Solid Melts Into Air,* The Experience of Modernity, Simon and Schuster, New York, 1982, Verso Books, London, 1983. Although Berman's book can be read as an attack on Modernism, which he shows to be repeatedly nihilistic and destructive, he draws different conclusions in the last chapter. Both Leon Krier and I think he misunderstands his own brilliant creation, an idea I pointed out to him at a conference on Modernism in Amsterdam, 1987, but obviously he is in a privileged position with respect to his own intentions.

16 Marx quoted in Berman, *ibid,* p 95.

17 *Ibid,* p 100.

18 Friedrich Nietzsche, *Thus Spake Zarathustra* (1883) quoted from Will Durant, *The Story of Philosophy,* Washington Square Press, New York, 1961, p 417.

19 Le Corbusier's reading of Nietzsche and his adoption of the superman's role is explored in my *Le Corbusier and the Tragic view of Architecture,* Penguin Books, Harmondsworth, 1973, second edition 1987; see new introduction. His phrase 'love what you burn and burn what you love' apparently extended to his fellow draughtsmen who he would periodically fire – every seven years or so.

20 Adolf Loos, *Architecture,* 1910, quoted from *Form and Function,* ed Sharp and Bentons, Granada, London, 1977, p 42.

21 Tom Wolfe, *From Bauhaus to Our House,* Pocket Books, Simon and Schuster, New York, 1981.

22 *Ibid,* p 17.

23 Kenneth Frampton, *Tadao Ando, Buildings Projects, Writings,* Rizzoli, New York, 1984, pp 6-8.

CHAPTER II
Late-Modernism and Post-Modernism

1 A general point about historical periodisation. The length of a creative movement is often not more than twenty years. The High Renaissance or High Baroque only lasted about this length, so by comparison High Modernism, if we want to call it that, was longer lived – roughly from 1920 to 1960. The second general point concerning historical periodisation is its discontinuity and the excellence of individual architects. By and large the best architects work when a movement is young, or has just started, but there are exceptions to this rule. Thus good High Renaissance buildings were produced in provincial centres right up until 1620. Indeed English architects such as Inigo Jones practised it *after* the country had gone through a 'kind of' Mannerism. High Baroque flourished in parts of Spain, Northern Italy and Bohemia long after it had died in Rome. Today of course movements travel around the globe with the speed of an issue of *A + U,* so time disjunctions tend to disappear, but they are replaced by the plurality of styles and approaches. The previous historical discontinuity and the present pluralism should warn us that good architecture, formally creative, can be found even after a period has 'died'. This leads us to the conclusion that some form of Modernism, or rather the International Style minus its Utopian and social ideology, will be practised into the twenty-first century. It needs to be called Late-Modernism to distinguish it from the

previous mode and ideology of the Pioneers.

The last general point concerns the classification of schools, movements and entire periods. How do historians ever come to agree that any period as diverse as the Renaissance should be fixed by one, or at least a very few labels? First of all the classifying process is a long and cumulative one created by a few individual historians – Vasari, Wölfflin come to mind – and then spelled out and modified by much subsequent research, which shows, for instance, the exceptions to straight-line development. The general categories or periods may remain, but are modified in shape. Thus the Mannerist period is shown to have mini-Classicist revivals, the Baroque is seen to be distorted by the influence of Gothic and exotic sources. The general rule is, I believe, that in any one cohesive movement there are many lesser trends as well as conflicts within the reigning approach. We can never find complete agreement or unity and thus we classify on the basis of a constellation of related motifs and ideas rather than a completely integrated system. Out of ten or so aspects of the Renaissance, only seven or eight are shared by diverse architects such as Alberti, Palladio and Inigo Jones. Classification into groups is thus a matter of statistical degree, of loose overlap, rather than exact correspondence between architects.

2 Portoghesi explained these meanings in a lecture at the Architectural Association, October 1978. Further interpretation, especially concerned with his notion of 'place', can be found in Christian Norberg-Schultz, *On the Search for Lost Architecture*, The works of Paolo Portoghesi, Vittorio Gigliotti, 1959-1975, Officina Edizioni, Rome, 1976, pp 55-64.

3 In Italy his battles with Bruno Zevi and Marxist critics are well known. Outside of Italy his work is not very well known.

4 The Crooks House, 1977, is the first key building where Classicist historicism becomes apparent. How much this is due to other Post-Modernists, including myself, is hard to say, but Michael and I had many discussions on implicit versus explicit metaphor in London and Los Angeles over a period of two

years. No doubt since his two year stay in Rome years ago he has always been aware of this bank of historical reference. The influence of Robert Stern and the exhibition on the Beaux-Arts should not be discounted.

5 Conversation, April 1978, looking at his drawings. My analysis here is partly based on the references he mentioned and those which are implicitly coded.

6 For the idea of suggested metaphor and the 'penumbra effect' see *The Language of Post-Modern Architecture,* Academy, London, 1978, pp 48, 117.

7 In *The Language of Post-Modern Architecture* I gave several historical examples including the classical temple pediment which mixed representational and abstract codes. Dual-coding and a desire to communicate, rather than stylistic qualities, distinguish Post-Modernists as a school.

8 See the *New York Times,* March 31, 1978, p B4. This project was also featured on the front page of the *New York Times* that day; in its *Sunday Color Magazine,* May 14, 1978, and on the front page of *The Times,* London, May 13, 1978. Its 'news' value as the first historicist skyscraper was obvious.

9 From their descriptive brochure, *Pavillon Soixante-Dix,* 1978.

10 Yasufumi Kijima 'Making an Image Sketch After the Building is Finished' from *The Japan Architect,* Oct/Nov 1977, p 48. The issue is, incidentally, on 'Post-Metabolism'.

11 Letter to the author, March 12, 1978, after our discussion on the Long House.

CHAPTER IV
The High-Tech Maniera

1 Jürgen Kunz, 'Architect's Statement', *A+U,* 86:03, p 63.

2 'Paternoster developer hits back at Prince of Wales', *Building Design,* 18 December, 1987, p 1.

3 Michael Hopkins, 'Architect's Statement', *A+U,* 86:09, p 22.

4 Chris Abel, 'A Building for the Pacific Century', *The Architectural Review,* April 1986, pp 55-61.

5 It is of interest that Foster and Rogers first achieved professional recognition with their Reliance Controls Electronic Factory of 1967

which won *The Financial Times* Award as the most outstanding building for the two years 1966-67. Since then Rogers has designed several notable industrial buildings, such as PA Technology, 1975, UK, 1982, USA; Fleetguard 1979-81; Inmos, 1982; Foster has designed the Renault Centre, 1982-83, an athletics hall for Frankfurt, 1982; the Médiathèque for Nîmes, 1985-; the BBC Headquarters, 1985; Stansted Airport, 1986; and a communications centre for Mexico 1986. The Nîmes building and BBC are, however, only quasi-industrial building tasks.

SECTION II
CHAPTER I
Irrational Rationalism – The Rats Since 1960

1 See Karl Popper, *Conjectures and Refutations, The Growth of Scientific Knowledge,* London, 1963, partly the entries under 'Intellectualism' which correspond to Rationalism. Popper's *Critical* Rationalism should not be confused with this intellectualism, because it is rooted in refutation and criticism.

2 See Giulia Veronesi, *Difficoltà Politiche dell'Architettura in Italia, 1920-1940,* Milan, 1953. Leonardo Benevolo, *History of Modern Architecture,* Volume 2, London 1971, pp 561-76.

3 See *Architettura Razionale,* 'XV Triennale di Milano', by Aldo Rossi, Franco Raggi, Massimo Scolari, Rosaldo Boncalzi, Gianni Braghieri and Daniele Vitale, Franco Angeli Editore, Milan, 1973.

4 Colin Rowe, 'Collage City', *The Architectural Review,* August 1975 and following letters. The book is published by the MIT Press, 1979.

5 The main criticisms in English are: Alan Colquhoun, 'Rational Architecture', *AD,* June 1975, pp 365-6; Manfredo Tafuri, 'L'Architecture dans le Boudoir', *Oppositions 3,* May 1974, pp 42-8; Vittorio Savi, 'Aldo Rossi', *Lotus 11,* 1976, pp 42-52; Vittorio Savi, David Stewart in *A+U* no 5, 1976, issue devoted to Rossi with bibliography.

6 Aldo Rossi, *A+U, op cit,* p 74.

7 Manfredo Tafuri, *Oppositions 3, op cit,* p 45. See also his *Architecture and Utopia, Design and Capitalist Development,* MIT Press, 1976,

pp 170-82.

8 Massimo Scolari, 'Avanguardia Nuova l'architettura' in *Architettura Razionale*, quoted from Alan Colquhoun's translation, *op cit*, p 366.

9 Leon Krier, 'Projects in the City', in *Lotus, op cit*, p 73.

10 Richard Meier, 'My Statement' is an issue devoted to his work of *A+U*, no 4, 1976, p 76.

11 Susan Whittig pointed out the 'foregrounding' of certain themes in Eisenman, Graves and Venturi in her paper 'Architecture about Architecture' delivered at the Semiotics Conference in Milan, June 1974.

12 Colin Rowe and Robert Slutzky, 'Transparency: Literal and Phenomenal', *Perspecta*, no 8, New Haven, 1963, pp 45-6.

13 I have written on the 'Los Angeles Silvers', *Progressive Architecture*, December 1976; *A+U*, October 1976.

14 My own guess is that the movement will split evenly in two directions.

15 These quotes from John Hejduk actually refer to a discussion of Mondrian, Van Doesburg, Le Corbusier's Carpenter Centre and the paintings of Juan Gris, but they apply equally to his Diamond series. See his 'Out of Time and Into Space' in an issue of *A+U* devoted to his work, 1975, no 5, pp 3-24.

16 Ken Frampton, 'Frontality vs Rotation', *Five Architects*, New York 1972, 1975, pp 9-13. See also his 'John Hejduk and the Cult of Humanism' in the *A+U* cited, note 15. Frampton isn't altogether supportive of the Five and Hejduk, but he confines his analysis to formal concerns and then jumps a mile to pure iconological interpretation.

17 The Hejduk quote from *A+U*, p 4; the Frampton one from *Five Architects, op cit*, p 10.

18 This chronology Hejduk outlined in a lecture at UCLA in April 1976.

19 Robert Frost, in 'Mending Wall': 'Something is there that doesn't love a wall. That wants it down'. Of course, as Hejduk shows, walls unite neighbours on a line and are therefore basically ambiguous, half bringing together, half dividing.

20 Rem Koolhaas formed OMA, The Office for Metropolitan Architecture, on January 1, 1975. This office includes his wife Madelon Vriesendorp, and Elia and Zoe Zenghelis and sometimes O M Ungers: two Dutch, two Greeks and an occasional German. Their work has been published in *Lotus, 11 op cit*, and Koolhaas has published *Delirious New York*, New York and London, 1978.

21 Rem Koolhaas, *Lotus 11, op cit*, p 36.

22 *Ibid*, p 34.

23 Elia Zenghelis, *Lotus 11*, p 36.

CHAPTER IV
Wolf Bites Wolfe

1 Tom Wolfe, *The Painted Word*, Farrar, Straus Giroux, New York, 1975, p 7.

2 Tom Wolfe, *The New Journalism*, Pan Books, Picador, London, 1975, p 44.

3 *Skyline*, New York, October 1981, pp 12-3.

4 *Ibid*, November 1981, p 3.

5 *Ibid*,

6 Tom Wolfe, *From Bauhaus to our House*, Farrar, Straus Giroux, New York and Jonathan Cape, London, 1981, p 7.

7 *Ibid*, p 107.

8 *Ibid*, pp 108-15.

9 *Ibid*, p 9.

10 *Ibid*, p 10.

11 *Ibid*, p 42.

12 *Ibid*, pp 45-6.

13 *Ibid*, p 68.

14 *Ibid*, p 143.

15 *The New Journalism*, op cit p 28.

BIBLIOGRAPHY
CHARLES JENCKS 1963-1989

1963 November The magazine *Connection, The Visual Arts at Harvard,* was founded by myself and Gordon Milde. The idea was to 'connect' the different areas of specialisation concerned with the visual arts at Harvard. Among our contributors were Edouard Sekler, Stanford Anderson, Walter Gropius, James Ackerman, Jerzy Soltan, Daniel Moynihan and James O'Gorman.

November 26 'Specialization and Dyspepsia', an editorial attack.

'The Architect in an Overpopulated World', review of Chermeyeff and Alexander's *Community and Privacy,* pp 21-5.

December 18 'GSD. Juries Judged', another editorial attack, pp 1-2.

'The Architect in an Over-populated World II', review of C Doxiadis, *Architecture in Transition,* pp 13-6.

1964 January 28 'Esprit Nouveau est mort à New Haven', an intemperate attack on the Arts and Architecture building designed by Paul Rudolph.

February 28 'Vacuum at the Top', an editorial attack on the lack of leadership in American architecture.

'The Architect in an Overpopulated World III', review of Konrad Wachsmann's *The Turning Point of Building,* pp 14-18.

March 27 'Exhortation to the Unreasonable Planner', an editorial of quotes from Shaw, Nietzsche etc.

'Mr Mumford and Mr Eliot', a review of two books, pp 27-30.

May 4 'Variety and Architecture', concerned with Van Eyck, Bakema, Le Corbusier, etc, pp 22-30.

May 25 'Polar Attitudes in Architecture', pp 5-12

December 'Harvard Architecture', pp 39-43.

1965 April 'No Revolutions, Please', pp 20-6.

June 'Procrustes on the Wilbur Cross', p 62.

After coming to England and the Architectural Association, I started writing for *Arena,* the AA magazine, a series of articles on the major Modern architects which were later collected and revised as parts of *Modern Movements in Architecture* (1973).

1965/7 Articles which were never published because they led to ideas in my PhD thesis: 'The Function of Criticism and Architecture' based on theories of M Weitz and T S Eliot; 'Multivalent Architecture'; 'A Picture of the Tradition'; 'The Modern Sensibility'.
'Safety First, Then Crisis', a review of John Jacobus' *Twentieth Century Architecture, The Middle Years 1940-65.*
'Dr Pevsner's Interludes', a review of his 'Architecture in Our Time – The Anti-Pioneers'.

1966 May 'The Problem of Mies', *Arena,* pp 301-4.

June/July 'Gropius, Wright and the Intentional Fallacy', *Arena,* pp 14-20.

1967 May 'Charles Jeanneret – Le Corbusier', *Arena,* pp 299-306.

June 'Meaning in Architecture', issue with George Baird. 'Complexity and Contradiction in Architecture', review of the book of Robert Venturi, in *Arena,* pp 4-5. This review supported Venturi's ideas, but criticised the lack of a psychological argument which could justify complexity.

November 'Alvar Aalto and Some Concepts of Value', *Arena/Interbuild,* pp 29-45.

1968 Winter 'Pop-Non Pop' *AAQ,* Vol 1, no 1, pp 48-64; Part II, April 1969, Vol 2, no 2, pp 56-74.

January 'Wading Through the Oleaginous Lagoon of Gooey Platitudes', a review of *The Architecture of America,* by J E Burchard and A Bush Brown, *Arena/Interbuild,* p 47.

July 'Adhocism on the South Bank', review of the Hayward Gallery and initial conception of adhocism, *The Architectural Review,* pp 27-30.

1969 Spring 'The Silent Zone', review of Barbara Miller Lane, *Architecture and Politics in Germany, 1918-1945, AAQ,* pp 80-1. Discusses the political compromise of Bauhaus members, Mies, Gropius etc, with the Nazis, a compromise that had been passed over in silence.

June 'Architecturology the Ultraquistic Subterfuge', review of IM Goodovitch, *Architecturology,* in *The Architectural Review.*

October 'The Religious Con-Version of Herman Kahn', a review of Kahn's address to British businessmen, written in the Neo-Hysterical Style, *AAQ,* Vol 1, no 4, pp 62-69.

November 'Pigeon-holing made difficult', on the use of numerical taxonomy as a more delicate way of classifying architects. *Architectural*

Design, p 582.

December 'Points of View', on Venturi and Scott-Brown's visit to the AA, in *Architectural Design*.

December 'After Functionalism, What?', review of Frei Otto, *Tensile Structures* (Vol 2), *The Architectural Review*.

Meaning in Architecture, a collection of essays edited by George Baird and myself, Barrie & Rockliffe, London; George Braziller, New York. Includes 'Semiology and Architecture', pp 9-25 and 'History as Myth', an analysis of recent historians, pp 245-65.

1970 'Modern Architecture – The Tradition since 1945' a thesis under Reyner Banham submitted to the University of London which was revised as *Modern Movements in Architecture*, minus the chapter 'A Theory of Value'. This chapter was the interpretive position behind the book and it was based on the ideas of imagination and multivalence developed by S T Coleridge and I A Richards.

April 'Does American Architecture Really Exist?', a review of Vincent Scully's *American Architecture and Urbanism* which raises the difficulty of defining a plural American architecture, and discusses Scully's interesting use of metaphorical description, *AAQ*, Vol 2, no 2, pp 62-4.

'Architecture Becomes Political', in *The Year's Art, 1969-70* edited by Michael Dempsey, Hutchinson, pp 87-97. Review of the plural trends, the six traditions, later incorporated into *Modern Movements*.

'Le Diable est dans les détails', review of the heavy, later works of Marcel Breuer, *New Buildings and Projects, 1960-70, Architectural Review*.

September 'The Modern Fragmentation', review of several books and a discussion of the break up of the Modern Movement. *Encounter*, pp 73-8.

'Student Dorms on a Scottish Coast', a discus-

sion of James Stirling's buildings at St Andrews, a semiotic analysis where the role of metaphor is seen as a primary agent in communication, *Architectural Forum*, pp 50-57.

October 'The Evolutionary Tree', first approximation at classifying the six traditions of Modernism, *Architectural Design*, p 527.

1971 April 'Revolution in the Art in Revolution', a review, (in French, of the show on Constructivism at the Hayward) discussing the irony of reactions and attitudes, *L'œil*, pp 20-25.

Spring 'The Missing Link', review of *Programmes and Manifestos of 20th-Century Architecture*, edited by Ulrich Conrads. Discusses two aspects of the Modern Movement which have been overlooked: creativity and politics. *AAQ*, Vol 3, no 2, pp 54-58.

Architecture 2000, Predictions and Methods, Studio Vista, London; Praeger, New York.

April 'Towards the Year 2000', a satirical profile of coming events based on my book, *Landscape Architecture*, pp 207-15, also *AAQ*, Winter, Vol 3, no 1, pp 56-60.

May 5 'E Pur si Muove', review of *Kinetic Architecture*, by William Zuk and Roger H Clark, for the *Architects' Journal*.

June 'The Supersensualists, Part I', a discussion of Superstudio, the Italian *Domus* scene and Pasolini, *Architectural Design*, pp 345-7.

September 'Libertarian and Authoritarian Views of Revolution', a discussion of Constructivism and the two opposed left-wing traditions, *RIBA Journal*, pp 389-91.

'Heutige Architektur und Zeitgeist', the perpetual treason of the clerks, part of *Architecture 2000* with additions on political fatalism, in *Archithèse* 2, pp 25-40.

1972 Winter 'Giedion's Last Bible', review of Siegfried Giedion's *Architecture and the Phe-*

nomenon of Transition, *AAQ*, Vol 4, no 1, p 67.

January 'The Supersensualists, Part II', a discussion of Archizoom and death, Hollein, Sottsass, *Architectural Design*, pp 18-21.

'GRRRRRR', review of Peter Collins, *Architectural Judgement*, *The Architectural Review*.

'Life and Architecture', a review of Phillipe Boudon's *Lived-in Architecture*, *Times Educational Supplement*.

April 13 'Kitsch Hikers', review of Justus Dahinden, *Urban Structures for the Future*, *New Society*, p 76.

Summer 'Rhetoric and Architecture', first general statement on semiotics and architecture, address in Barcelona at Semiotics Conference, *AAQ*, Vol 4, no 3, pp 4-17.

Adhocism, the Case for Improvisation, with Nathan Silver, Secker and Warburg, London; Doubleday, New York.

October 'The Case for Improvisation', with Nathan Silver, but 90% my own serious joke about adhocism, *Architectural Design*, pp 604-7.

Autumn-Spring 1973 Letters between Stirling and Jencks on metaphor and Art Nouveau, *AAQ*, Vol 5, no 1, p 64.

1973 January 'Mainstream Modernism', review of Dennis Sharp, *A Visual History of 20th-Century Architecture*, *Times Educational Supplement*.

Summer 'The Triumph of the Muddle Class', review of Robert Maxwell, *New British Architecture* and Philip Drew, *The Third Generation, The Changing Meaning of Architecture*, discusses spelling mistakes and boring Modernism, *AAQ*, pp 59-62.

August 'Mutations in the Avant-Garde', review of *Archigram*, edited by Peter Cook, and Barbara Plumb, *Young Designs in Colour*, *The Architectural Review*, p 129.

'The Urge to Destroy', review of *Vandalism* edited by Colin Ward, and *Defensible Space*, by Oscar Newman, *Times Educational Supplement*, p 14.

September 'Ersatz in LA', the first statement of four kinds of phoney but funny Los Angeles types, *Architectural Design*, pp 596-601.

Winter 'The Candid King Midas of New York Camp', a Neo-Hysterical account of the life and work of Philip Johnson, *AAQ*, Vol 5, no 4, pp 27-42.

Le Corbusier and the Tragic View of Architecture, Allen Lane, Penguin Books, Harmondsworth; Harvard University Press, Cambridge.

Modern Movements in Architecture, Penguin Books, Harmondsworth; Doubleday, New York, (finished in 1971 as revised PhD thesis.)

1974 March/April 'James Stirling's Corporate Culture Machine', *Architecture Plus*, pp 96-103.

'A Semantic Analysis of Stirling's Olivetti Centre Wing', an analysis of metaphorical reactions, *AAQ*, Vol 6, no 2, pp 13-15. Also to be reprinted in *Signs, Symbols and Architecture*, edited by Geoffrey Broadbent, Richard Bunt and myself, John Wiley and Sons, London and New York, 1979.

May 'Adhocism Misunderstood', reply to Ken Frampton's review, *Oppositions* 3, pp 106-7, and 'Meaning in Architecture Misunderstood', reply to Mario Gandelsonas and Diana Agrest, *Oppositions* 3, pp 110-1.

June 'A Detonation in Glass and Brick', review of James Stirling drawing-show analysing the 'controversy', *Times Educational Supplement*, p 21.

September 8 'Cracking the Codes', review of the First International Congress of Semiotics held in Milan, *Times Educational Supplement*.

September 27 'Modern Architecture Collapses', review of Malcolm MacEwen, *Crisis in Architecture, Building Design*, pp 26-7. Also published in *AAQ*.

October 'Architecture that Speaks', an early version of *The Language of Post-Modern Architecture*, given at the Melbourne Oration, Melbourne.

October 12-19 'A Trip to the Antipodes', diary, unpublished, of the trip to Australia.

1975 February 'An Interview', concerned with Oration and current views, in *Architecture in Australia*, pp 50-57.

May 16. 'In Undisguised Taste', interview with Reyner Banham about his *The Age of the Masters*, showing his bias and bringing up taste as the great undiscussable, *Building Design*, pp 12-13.

June 'The Language of Architecture', *Sunday Times*, pp 24-5.

June 6 'Sex and Communication', a Neo-Hysterical take-off of sexologists and their baneful influence, *Ghost-Dance Times*, pp 1 and 4 (written Feb 1970).

July 'The Rise of Post-Modern Architecture', an initial formulation of the new tradition, *Architecture Inner-Town Government*, Eindhoven, pp 78-103, reprinted in *AAQ*, issue partially devoted to the subject, Vol 7, no 4.

'James Stirling versus the Komfy Style', commissioned for the *Sunday Times*, not published; ditto 'Norman Foster'.

September 'Trompe L'Œil Counterfeit', *Studio International*, pp 109-13. (Part of *Ersatz*).

'Reflections on Mirrors', concerning Norman Foster's work and the qualities of mirrors, *A+U*, pp 58-60.

'125 Years of Quasi Democracy', a discussion of AA politics in *A Continuing Experiment, Learning and Teaching at the AA*, edited by James Gowan, The Architectural Press, London, pp 149-59.

1976 February 'The Pleasure House of the Rising Sun', on the Japanese Love Hotels, *Sunday Times*.

March 'The Enigma of Kurokawa', *The Architectural Review*, pp 142-53, also in *Kisho Kurokawa* as introduction, published by Studio Vista.

'Isozaki's Paradoxical Cube', *The Japan Architect*, pp 46-50.

June 'ArchiteXt and the Problem of Symbolism', *The Japan Architect*, pp 21-8.

July 5 'Bricolage', an answer to Reyner Banham on Adhocism, *New Society*.

'The Revisionists of Modern Architecture', on the English Post-Modernists, RIBA conference, July 14-16, published in *Architecture: Opportunities, Achievements*, RIBA publications edited by Barbara Goldstein, pp 55-63.

'Fetishism and Architecture', a discussion of the erogenous zones, parts reprinted in *Daydream Houses of Los Angeles, Architectural Design* 8, pp 492-5.

October 'Review' of Juan Pablo Bonta's *An Anatomy of Architectural Interpretation. A Semiotic Review of the Criticism of Mies van der Rohe's Barcelona Pavilion*, *JSAH*, pp 226-7.

November 'The Los Angeles Silvers', Pelli, Lumsden, Kupper etc, *A+U*, pp 13-14.

December 'Fear, Asceticism and Suicide of the Avant-Garde', paper to Art Net.

'The Pluralism of Japanese Architecture', in French and Japanese versions of *Modern Movements*.

1977 January 'Isozaki and Radical Eclecticism', *Architectural Design*, pp 42-48.

March 'MBM and the Barcelona School', *The Architectural Review*, pp 159-65.

May 'Geneaology of Post-Modernism', an early evolutionary tree, *Architectural Design*, pp 269-71.

May 27 'More Modern than Modern', on Post-Modern architecture and exhibition at Art Net, *Sunday Times,* pp 30-31.

The Language of Post-Modern Architecture, Academy Editions, London; Rizzoli, New York.

'History as Myth II', address to Delft Symposium.

'Irrational Rationalism –The Rats since 1960', *A+U,* 77, 4 & 5, reprinted in Dennis Sharp, *The Rationalists,* London, 1979.

'Venturi et al are almost all right', *Architectural Design,* 7/8, pp 468-9.

'Le Corbusier on the Tight-Rope of Functionalism', a speculative soliloquy on Le Corbusier's defense of architecture, in *The Open Hand, Essays on Le Corbusier,* edited by Russell Waldon, MIT Press, pp 187-214.

1978 January 'Typology, Context and Post-Modernism', an answer to S Cantucazino, *The Architectural Review.*

January 'The Language of Post-Modern Architecture', *Architectural Design,* incorporated as new last chapter to the revised edition.

February 'The Tory Interpretation of History', on D Watkins' *Morality and Architecture, The Architectural Review.*

March 'On Fame as the Engine of Architects and Architecture', unpublished paper delivered to seminar at Yale University.

April 'What is Post-Modern Architecture?', an answer to S Stephens' review, *Progressive Architecture.*

April, May, June 'The Architectural Sign', general considerations on semiotics and architecture, *A+U,* republished in *Signs, Symbols and Architecture, op cit,* 1979.

June 'Architecture as a Peculiar Language', un-

published lecture at Darmstadt.

July *The Language of Post-Modern Architecture,* revised and enlarged edition, with new introduction and last chapter, Academy and Rizzoli.

'The Return of the Missing Body', a review of Kent Bloomer, Charles Moore and Robert Yudell, *Body, Memory and Architecture, The Architectural Review,* and also another review of this same book and *Dimensions* by Charles Moore and Gerald Allen, for *JSAH,* March 1979.

October *Daydream Houses of Los Angeles,* the erotic, largely self-built houses of various districts in Los Angeles, Academy Editions, London; Rizzoli, New York.

October 'Bruce Goff – The Michelangelo of Kitsch', *Architectural Design,* pp 10-14, and a reworked version for the *Sunday Times Colour Magazine.*

December 'Late-Modern and Post-Modern Architecture', a set of distinctions, *Architectural Design,* pp 592-609.

Contributions and conclusion to *The Chinese Garden* by Maggie Keswick, Academy Editions, London; Rizzoli, New York.

1979 March 'The Return of the Missing Body' (a review of *Body, Memory and Architecture,* by Kent Bloomer, Charles Moore and Robert Yudell) *Journal of the Society of Architectural Historians.*

April *Bizarre Architecture,* Rizzoli, New York and Academy Editions, London. Also translated into French and German.

November 'Lord Bossom Lectures on Current Architecture'. May 14, 21, 18. Three lectures on Post-Modern Architecture at the Royal Society of the Arts, later printed in *The Journal of the Royal Society of Arts,* London, pp 742-783. 'The Pluralism of Recent Japanese Architecture'; 'America's New Architecture Culture'; 'European Urbanism and Historicism'.

1980 *Late-Modern Achitecture,* Rizzoli, New York; Academy Editions, London. Also translated into German and Spanish.

Post-Modern Classicism, Rizzoli, New York, Architectural Design Monograph, London. Also translated into French.

Signs, Symbols and Architecture, edited with Richard Bunt and Geoffrey Broadbent, John Wiley, New York and London. Contains 'The Architectural Sign' and 'A Semantic Analysis of James Stirling's Olivetti Wing'.

May-June 'Post-Modern Classicism – The New Synthesis' *Architectural Design,* pp 5-17.

September-October 'Post-Modern Classicism' – paper delivered at the Venice Biennale and in Japan, at two universities, printed in *A+U* (in Japanese), February 1981, pp 3-12.

December 'On Fame as the Engine of Architects and Architecture' (Paper delivered to the Yale University symposium on architecture and later published in Japanese, *A+U,* and in a collection of essays from Yale.)

1981 January 'The Counter Reformation in Architecture', Reflections on the 1980 Venice Biennale, *AD News Supplement,* p 1.

July 'The Battle of the Labels – Late Modernism vs Post-Modernism', *AD News Supplement,* 7, 1981, pp 2-4. 'Stern and Post-Modern Space', *ibid,* pp 6-7. 'Late Modernism and Post-Modernism', *ibid,* pp 8-9.

1982 January *Free Style Classicism,* Issue of *Architectural Design,* Guest Editor, with four articles written.

'Wolf Bites Wolfe', review of Tom Wolfe's *From Bauhaus to Our House, AD News Supplement,* 1, 1982, pp 1-5.

'Eclecticism versus Revivalism'. Review of Edwin Lutyens' Show and design by Piers Gough, *ibid,* pp 22-23.

'William Burges – Symbolic Architect'. Review of the exhibit *The Strange Genius of William Burges, ibid,* p 28.

'Architectures New Ism's, *Sunday Times,* London, January 10, pp 28-33.

October *Architecture Today,* Abrams, New York; *Current Architecture,* Academy Editions, London.

December 'Notes on an Architectural Culture', *British Architecture,* Academy Editions, London, p 12 'Farrell Moves Towards Symbolism', *ibid,* pp 194-5. 'LA Style/LA School', *AA Files 5,* p 90.

1983 'Post-Modern Architecture, the True Inheritor of Modernism', (delivered as the opening paper in a series, 'The Great Debate, Modernism versus the Rest', Royal Institute of British Architects, 1982-3). Published in *Transactions III,* RIBA Publications, London, pp 26-41.

March 'Garagia Rotunda', *Interiors,* pp 84-92, 191.

July *Abstract Representation,* St Martin's Press, New York, Architectural Design Monograph, Academy Editions, London.

September 'Mario Botta and the New Tuscanism', *Architectural Design,* 9/10 pp 82-5.

October *Kings of Infinite Space,* St Martin's Press, New York; Academy Editions, London, based on the BBC TV 65 minute film on Frank Lloyd Wright and Michael Graves.

November 'The Elemental House', *Architectural Digest,* pp 106-113, 202.

1984 March 'The Casual, The Shocking and The Well Ordered Acropolis' (a review of James Stirling's New Staatsgalerie, Stuttgart) *Architectural Design,* 3/4, pp 48-55.

April 'Mario Botta, The Spartan Classicist', *Connoisseur,* pp 134-139.

June 'In Search of a Valid Double Standard: Unifying Dualism', a response to Judy Brine's paper AA Graduate School, June 5.

'House of Elements in Rustic Canyon', *The Architectural Review,* pp 62-69.

August 'The Building as Scenario', *Architectural Record,* pp 118-125.

September 'Bombing Post-Modern Classicism', answer to William Curtis' attack, *Architectural Review,* letters.

October 'Modernism and Post-Modernism' (Paper delivered at the *Inter-Design Conference,* Sapporo, Japan, October 1984).

1985 *Towards A Symbolic Architecture,* Rizzoli, New York; Academy Editions, London.

January 'America the Dynamic', *Architectural Design,* Vol 55, 1/2, pp 7-9.

February 'A Visit to the Mirror' (Description of the Inter-Design Conference in Japan) *Art and Design,* pp 11-13.

March 'In the Steps of Vasari', Interview with Heinrich Klotz, *Architectural Design,* Vol 55, 3/4, pp 9-16.

'Beyond Post-Modernism', interview by Yasumitsu Matsunaga, *Japan Architect,* March, pp 10-15.

May 'Frank Gehry – the First Deconstructionist', *Art and Design,* 1/4, pp 14-19.

August 'The Critical Crisis', a review of Kenneth Frampton's *Modern Architecture, A Critical History, Art and Design,* p 21.

September 'Designing a House', *Architectural Design,* Vol 55, 9/10, pp 1-32.

'Symbolism and Blasphemesis', Review of I M Pei's addition to the Louvre, *Art and Design,* pp 42-4.

October *Towards a Symbolic Architecture,* Academy Editions, London; Rizzoli, New York, 1985.

'Symbolic or Signolic Architecture?', *Art and Design,* pp 14-17, 48.

November 'Symbolic Furniture', *Art and Design,* pp 91-16.

'Symbolic Architecture', TV presentation on BBC2, *Saturday Night Review,* Nov 15

'Translating Past into Present – Post-Modern Art and Architecture', *Country Life,* Nov 21, pp 1620-3.

December 'Ben Johnson and Transcendental Materialism', *Art and Design,* pp 10-13.

1986 *What is Post-Modernism?* St Martin's Press, New York; Academy Editions, London.

Interviewed on two TV programmes on Skyscrapers, East Anglia, BBC TV

January *Charles Jencks,* Extra Edition of *A+U,* no 1. Includes Architectural work, and articles, 'Architect vs Critic' and 'The Battle of the Labels' (version II).

Review of *Josef Hoffman: The Architectural Work,* by Eduard Sekler, *TLS,* January 17, p 54.

March 'Aphorisms on the Garden of an Aphorist', Review of Yves Abrioux's book on Ian Hamilton Finlay, *Art and Design,* pp 18-24.

July *What is Post-Modernism?,* Academy Editions, London and St Martin's Press, New York. (Booklet based on lectures given in Chicago and Hanover, October 1985).

November 'PM at the End of its Tether' answer to *MODO,* no 94.

1987 *Post-Modernism, The New Classicism in Art and Architecture,* Rizzoli, New York; Academy Editions, London.

January 'Post-Modernism and Discontinuity',

article and issue concept, *Architectural Design*, Vol. 57 1/2, pp 5-8, 25.

'Cathay in the West – Pavilions and a Chinese Garden in Bel Air California', Design and article with Maggie Keswick, *ibid*, pp 61-7.

April 'Symbolic Objects', *Art and Design*, pp 63-7.

'Charles Jencks Interviews James Stirling', *The Clore Gallery*, The Tate Gallery, London, pp 45-59. Also published in *A+U*, and *The Architectural Review*, June 1987, pp 47-50.

May 'The Architecture of Suggestion', Review of Michael Graves' Plocek House, *Architectural Digest*, May, pp 141-3, ff.

'Le Corbusier as a Pre-Modern Post-Modernist, or History Written Backwards', lecture at the Hayward Gallery.

June 'Charles Vandenhove – The Missing Link', *House and Garden*.

'The Spiritual in Art – Interview with Maurice Tuchman', *Art and Design*, 5/6, pp 17-24.

August 'The Post-Modernism – an Overview', opening lecture at the Tate Gallery Symposium on Post-Modernism, October 17.

November 'The Aesthetics of Engineering – CJ Interviews Jack Zunz', *Architectural Design*, Vol 57, no 11/12, pp 37-48.

December *The Language of Post-Modern Architecture*, Fifth Edition, includes 20 new pages at the end.

Interviewed in 'The Battle of Paternoster Square', BBC Omnibus, directed by Christopher Martin.

1988 March 'Deconstruction – The Sound of One Mind Laughing (or the Solipsist's Delight)', Paper given at the Deconstruction Conference, March 22. Tate Gallery.

'Deconstruction: The Pleasures of Absence',

Architectural Design, Vol 58, 3/4, pp 17-31.

'Peter Eisenman – An Interview by Charles Jencks', *ibid*, pp 49-61.

April 'The Moral in Art – Reflections on the Finlays' Wars', Paper given at the Talbot-Rice Art Centre, University of Edinburgh, April 21 (to be published).

June 'Prince Charles joins the Architectural Debate', paper given at a symposium at the Tate Gallery, June 15.

The Prince, the Architects and New Wave Monarchy, Academy Editions, London; Rizzoli New York. Excerpts printed in the *Observer*, June 12 and 19.

October 3 'The Octopus versus the Whale or the Battle for Pluralism', paper delivered at the International Architectural Symposium, German Architectural Museum, Frankfurt (to be published).

November *Architecture Today*, Second Edition, with a new introduction and seven new chapters on 'Architecture Since 1980'.

'Richard Meier and the Modern Tradition', *Architectural Design*, front section.

'Royal Advantage', *Observer*, Nov 13.

'Cathedrals of Commerce', *Observer*, Nov 27.

'The Bank as Cathedral and Village', *Die Welt*, and *Architectural Design*, Vol 58, No 11/12, pp 77-79; *A+U*, 89:06, pp 18-23.

December 'Anthropomorphic Machines' Review of Shin Takamatsu AA Exhibit, *AA Files*.

'Ethics and Prince Charles', paper delivered at the Ethics and Architecture Conference, SOM Foundation, Chicago, Dec 10th.

1989 January 'High Tech – The Cryptic Religion', review of *High Tech Architecture* by Colin Davies, *Architectural Design*, Vol 58, 1/2, pp VI-VII.

February 'The City in the City', article on Broadgate for the *Observer*, to be published.

March 'Cutting the South Bank Down to Size', article on Farrell's proposal, *Observer*, March 12, Arts Section.

Interview with Hans Hollein, *Architectural Digest*

April Interview by Kurt Andersen, to be published in *Architectural Digest*

'Hiroshima Acropolis', review of Kurokawa's Museum, *Space Design*, also to be published in *Architectural Design*.

June 'Prince Charles, Lloyd's and Other Tastes', speech given for Jackson-Stops & *Sunday Times*' Country House Awards, June 6.

July Article on Kurokawa's Hiroshima Museum, *The Observer*, July 16.

September Interviewed in BBC Omnibus film, 'Second Chance' in *Prince Charles' Vision of Britain*, September 8.

Interviewed on BBC World Service programme *In a Nutshell*, on 'Postmodernism'.

October 'Ten Aspects of Post-Modernism', paper given at *The Symposium on the Bicentennial of the French Revolution*, Tokyo, October 21. (To be published, but partly presented in Japanese newspapers and television.)

November Chairman of the official debate on the Prince of Wales' 'Vision of Britain' Exhibition: paper delivered 'The Battle of the Poles', Victoria and Albert Museum, November 2.

'Public Opinion and Princely Intervention', article called 'Principles for the Prince', *The Independent*, November 22, p 21.

December 'Fumihiko Maki, Neo-Modern Master', *The Independent*.

'Eisenman's White Holes', *Architectural Design*, 11/12-89.

ACKNOWLEDGEMENTS

I am grateful to my publisher Andreas Papadakis for his encouragement and support throughout this project. I should also like to thank the staff at Academy Editions, in particular my editor Vivian Constantinopoulos, and both Andrea Bettella and Annie Cheatle for the design and typesetting of this volume. Finally, I wish to express my gratitude to Maggie Keswick and Joan Lee for their sharp editorial eye.

The majority of the photographs have been taken by myself, while paintings and drawings have been provided by individual architects and artists. Photographs and illustrations from other sources are as follows:
Jeff Goldberg/ESTO, Jacket front; 223; Richard Davies, 2, 29, 92, 99, 102; Robert Oerleman, 4, 274, 275; Itsuko Hasegawa, 5; ESTO, 8, 42,125, 144, 145, 150, 151, 239, 240, 241, 242, 245, 247, 248, 251, 252, 255 top; Peter Eisenman, 14, 212, 232 top, 233, 278 top; The Saatchi Collection, 15; Charles Gwathmey, 16; Tadao Ando, 39; DG Olshavsky/ARTOG, 1, 40, 226 bottom, 227, 278 bottom; Herman Hertzberger, 44; Kevin Roche, 48 top; Anthony Lumsden, 48 bottom, 49, 85; Oscar Savio, 50; Studio di Porta Pinciana, 53 bottom; Hans Hollein, 56 top, 66; Jerzy Surwillo, 57; Chai French, 58; Brecht-Einzig, 68, 80 top; John Portman, 74 left; Helmut Jahn and CF Murphy Associates 74 right, 81 top; SAUP Slide Library, UCLA, 76; Kisho Kurokawa, 78 right, 79; Ruth Rogers, 80 bottom; YRM with SOM, 81 bottom; Philip Johnson and John Burgee, 83, 87; Cesar Pelli, 84 top and centre, 129; Tim Street Porter, 84 bottom; Denys Lasdun, 89 top; Weber, Brand and Partners, 95 top; Ken Kirkwood, 95 bottom; Ian Lambot, 97 bottom, 101, 103; Shin Takamatsu, 98; Dave Bower, 100; Royal Commission on the Historical Monuments of England, 116 top; Guiliano Gameliel, 118; Ricardo Bofill, 123; John Donat, 128; John Hejduk, 130; Richard Payne, 152, 156; Nathaniel Lieberman, 158; Fiona Spalding-Smith, 167, 168 bottom; John Burgee, 168 top; Venturi and Rauch, 176 top; Moore, Ruble and Yudell, 176 bottom; Le Louvre, 182; Alfred Wolf, 186, 188 top; Le Canard Enchainé, 189 top; Michael Moran, 192, 196, 197, 199; Larry Harris, 195; Edward Woodman, 205, 272, 273; John Johansen, 207 top; Hiromi Fujii, 207 bottom; Dick Frank, 208, 209, 210, 211, 213, 214 top, 215, 231 top; 232 bottom, 237 bottom, 281; Richard Meier, 244; Fumihiko Maki, 256, 265; Taisuke Ogawa/Shinkenchiku, 261, 266; Hélène Binet, 31, 268; Uwe Rau, 269; Gerald Zugmann, 276, 277; James Friedman, 279; SITE, 282; Frank Gehry, 283 bottom; Jean-Marie Monthiers, 287.

I have attempted to identify and credit individually each photographer and, wherever possible, contacted him for authorisation. The majority of the articles have appeared in periodicals over a number of years and indeed a few have been published in my earlier book entitled *Late Modern Architecture*. If I have misattributed I would be grateful to amend the acknowledgements in future editions.